A Great Leap Forward

A Great Leap Forward

Heterodox Economic Policy for the 21st Century

Randall Wray

Professor of Economics
Bard College, and Senior Scholar
Levy Economics Institute
NY, United States

ELSEVIER

ACADEMIC PRESS
An imprint of Elsevier

Academic Press is an imprint of Elsevier
125 London Wall, London EC2Y 5AS, United Kingdom
525 B Street, Suite 1650, San Diego, CA 92101, United States
50 Hampshire Street, 5th Floor, Cambridge, MA 02139, United States
The Boulevard, Langford Lane, Kidlington, Oxford OX5 1GB, United Kingdom

Notices
Knowledge and best practice in this field are constantly changing. As new research and experience broaden our understanding, changes in research methods, professional practices, or medical treatment may become necessary.

Practitioners and researchers must always rely on their own experience and knowledge in evaluating and using any information, methods, compounds, or experiments described herein. In using such information or methods they should be mindful of their own safety and the safety of others, including parties for whom they have a professional responsibility.

To the fullest extent of the law, neither the Publisher nor the authors, contributors, or editors, assume any liability for any injury and/or damage to persons or property as a matter of products liability, negligence or otherwise, or from any use or operation of any methods, products, instructions, or ideas contained in the material herein.

Library of Congress Cataloging-in-Publication Data
A catalog record for this book is available from the Library of Congress

British Library Cataloguing-in-Publication Data
A catalogue record for this book is available from the British Library

ISBN: 978-0-12-819380-8

For information on all Academic Press publications visit our website at
https://www.elsevier.com/books-and-journals

Publisher: Brian Romer
Acquisition Editor: Brian Romer
Editorial Project Manager: Andrea Dulberger
Production Project Manager: Poulouse Joseph
Cover Designer: Alan Studholme

Typeset by TNQ Technologies

Working together
to grow libraries in
developing countries

www.elsevier.com • www.bookaid.org

Contents

Acknowledgment

I would like to thank Chiara Zoccarato for her essential contributions in bringing this project to completion. It is no exaggeration to say that this book would never have seen the light of day without her help. Chiara selected the topics, helped to arrange the sequencing, and provided invaluable advice on the structure of the arguments made. She edited all the drafts as well as the final proofs and put together the references. Her uncompromising passion for the issues raised in this book was an inspiration.

Introduction

As an undergraduate I studied psychology and social sciences—but no economics, which probably gave me an advantage when I finally did come to economics. I began my economics career in my late 20s studying mostly Institutionalist and Marxist approaches while working for the local and state governments in Sacramento. However, I did carefully read Keynes's *General Theory* at Sacramento State and one of my professors—John Henry—pushed me to go to St. Louis to study with Hyman Minsky, the greatest Post-Keynesian economist. As I pursued my PhD, I focused on Post-Keynesian economics, integrating this with the Institutionalist and Marxist approaches I had studied earlier.

I wrote my dissertation in Bologna under Minsky's direction (but also benefitting from working closely with Jan Kregel), focusing on private banking and the rise of what we called "nonbank banks" and "off-balance sheet operations" (now called shadow banking). While in Bologna, I met Otto Steiger—who had an alternative to the barter story of money that was based on his theory of property. I found it intriguing because it was consistent with some of Keynes's *Treatise on Money* that I was reading at the time. Also, I had found Knapp's *State Theory of Money*—cited in both Steiger and Keynes—so I speculated on money's origins (in spite of Minsky's warning that he did not want me to write *Genesis*) and the role of the state in my dissertation that became a book in 1990—*Money and Credit in Capitalist Economies*—that helped to develop what is known as the Post-Keynesian endogenous money approach.

What was lacking in that literature was an adequate treatment of the role of the state in our monetary system—which only played a passive role, supplying reserves as demanded by private bankers. That is what became the Post-Keynesian accommodationist or Horizontalist approach to money. There was no discussion of the relation of money to fiscal policy at that time. As I continued to read about the history of money, I became more convinced that we need to put the state at the center.

Fortunately, I ran into two people in the early 1990s that helped me to see how to do it.

First there was Warren Mosler, a bond market trader, whom I met online in the PKT discussion group—one of the earliest online discussion groups. He insisted on viewing money as a tax-driven government monopoly. Second, I met Michael Hudson at a seminar at the Levy Economics Institute, who provided the key to help unlock what Keynes had called his "Babylonian Madness" period—when he was driven crazy trying to understand money's origins in Mesopotamia. Hudson argued that money was an invention of the authorities to be used for accounting purposes. So, over the next decade I worked with a handful of people to put the state into monetary theory. This is what became Modern Money Theory.

As we all know, the mainstream wants a small government, with a central bank that follows a rule (initially, a money growth rate but now some version of inflation targeting). The fiscal branch of government is treated like a household that faces a budget constraint. But this conflicts with Institutionalist theory as well as Keynes's own theory. As the great Institutionalist J. Fagg Foster—who preceded me at the University of Denver (my first teaching position)—put it: whatever is technically feasible is financially feasible. How can we square that with the belief that sovereign government is financially constrained? And if private banks can create money endogenously—without limit—why is government constrained?

My second book, in 1998 (*Understanding Modern Money*), provided a different view of sovereign spending. I also revisited the origins of money. By this time I had discovered the two best articles ever written on the nature of money—by A. Mitchell Innes.[1] Like WarrenMosler, Innes insisted that the dollar's value is derived from the tax that drives it. And he argued this has always been the case. This was also consistent with what Keynes claimed in the *Treatise*, where he said that money has been a state money for the past four thousand years, at least. I called this "modern money" with intentional irony—and titled my 1998 book *Understanding Modern Money* as an inside joke. It only applies to the past 4000 years. That is "modern."

Surprisingly, this work was more controversial than the earlier endogenous money research. In my view it was a natural extension—or more correctly, it was the prerequisite to a study of privately created money. You need the state's money before you can have private money. Eventually our work found acceptance outside economics—especially in law schools, among historians, and with anthropologists.

For the most part, our fellow economists, including the heterodox ones, attacked us as crazy. Many still do, although Modern Money Theory (MMT) is now discussed in all the major newspapers and by politicians around the world.

I benefited greatly by participating in law school seminars (in Tel Aviv, Cambridge, England, and Harvard) on the legal history of money—that is where I met Chris Desan and later Farley Grubb, and eventually Rohan Grey (who helped found the Modern Money Network). Those who knew the legal history of money had no problem in adopting MMT views—unlike economists, who generally work with highly abstract mathematical models and have little understanding of history, law, or the real world.

As a student I had read a lot of anthropology—as most Institutionalists do. So, I knew that money could not have come out of tribal economies based on barter exchange. David Graeber's[2] highly popular book insisted that anthropologists have never found any evidence of barter-based markets. Money preceded market exchange.

Studying history also confirmed our story, but you must carefully read between the lines. Most historians adopt monetarism because the only economics they know is Milton Friedman—who claims that money causes inflation. Almost all of them

---

[1]My third book, *Credit and State Theories of Money* (2004) republished the original articles by Innes as well as a half dozen new articles on the topic.

[2]*Debt: The First 5000 Years*, by David Graeber, Melville House Publishing 2011.

also adopt a commodity money view—gold was good money and fiat paper money causes inflation. If you ignore those biases, you can learn a lot about the nature of money from historians.

Farley Grubb—the foremost authority on early American Colonial currency—proved that the American colonists understood perfectly well that taxes drive money. Every Colonial Act that authorized the issue of paper money imposed a Redemption Tax. The colonies burned all their tax revenue. Again, history shows that this has always been true. All money must be redeemed—that is, accepted by its issuer in payment. As Innes said, that is the fundamental nature of credit. It is written right there in the early acts by the American colonies. Even a gold coin is the issuer's IOU, redeemed in payment of taxes. Once you understand that, you understand the nature of money.

So, we were winning the academic debates, across a variety of disciplines. But we had a hard time making progress in economics or in policy circles. Bill Mitchell in Australia, WarrenMosler, Mat Forstater (my colleague at the University of Missouri-Kansas City [UMKC]) and I used to meet up every year or so to count the number of economists who understood what we were talking about. It took over decade before we got up to a dozen. I can remember telling Pavlina Tcherneva (my student at UMKC and now my colleague at Bard College) back around 2005 that I was about ready to give it up.

But in 2007, Warren, Bill, and I met to discuss writing an MMT textbook. Bill and I knew the odds were against us—we thought it would be for a small market, consisting mostly of our former students. Still, we decided to go for it. Here we are—another dozen years later—and the textbook was published. The first printing sold out immediately. Alexandria Ocasio-Cortez—America's breakout political star who is destined to become President someday—was tweeted holding up a copy of the textbook. MMT is everywhere. It was even featured in a *New Yorker* crossword puzzle in August 2018. You cannot get more mainstream than that. We originally titled our textbook *Modern Money Theory*, but we decided to just call it *Macroeconomics*. There is no need to modify that with a subtitle. What we do is Macroeconomics. There is no coherent alternative to MMT.

A couple of years ago PIMCO's[3] brains, Paul McCulley told me: "You won. Declare victory but be magnanimous about it." After so many years of fighting, both of those are hard to do. We won. Be nice.

Let me finish with 10 bullet points of what I include in MMT to set the framework for the book that follows:

1. What is money? An IOU denominated in a socially sanctioned money of account. In almost all known cases, it is the authority—the state—that chooses the money of account. This comes from Knapp, Innes, Keynes, Geoff Ingham, and Minsky.

---

[3]The biggest bond trading firm in the world.

2. Taxes or other obligations (fees, fines, tribute, tithes) drive the currency. The ability to impose such obligations is an important aspect of sovereignty; today states alone monopolize this power. This comes from Knapp, Innes, Minsky, and Mosler.

3. Anyone can issue money; the problem is to get it accepted. Anyone can write an IOU denominated in the recognized money of account; but acceptance can be hard to get unless you have the state backing you up. This is Minsky.

4. The word "redemption" is used in two ways—accepting your own IOUs in payment and promising to convert your IOUs to something else (such as gold, foreign currency, or the state's IOUs).

   The first is fundamental and true of all IOUs. All our gold bugs who want to return to a gold standard mistakenly focus on the second meaning—which does not apply to the currencies issued by most modern nations, and indeed does not apply to most of the currencies issued throughout history. This comes from Innes and Knapp, and is reinforced by Hudson's and Grubb's work, as well as by Margaret Atwood's great book: *Payback: Debt and the shadow side of wealth*.

5. Sovereign debt is different. There is no chance of involuntary default on a national government's debt so long as the state only promises to accept its currency in payment. It could voluntarily repudiate its debt, but this is rare.

6. Functional finance: Finance should be "functional" (to achieve the public purpose), not "sound" (to achieve some arbitrary "balance" between spending and revenues). Most importantly, monetary and fiscal policy should be formulated to achieve full employment with price stability. This is credited to Abba Lerner, who was introduced into MMT by Mat Forstater.

7. The Job Guarantee is a critical component of MMT. It anchors the currency and ensures that achieving full employment will enhance both price and financial stability. This comes from Minsky's earliest work on the employer of last resort, from Bill Mitchell's work on employed labor bufferstocks, and Warren Mosler's work on monopoly price setting.

8. Capitalist economies are naturally unstable—subject to boom and bust and to occasional financial crises. So we need Minsky's analysis of financial instability. Here I do not really mean just his financial instability hypothesis—for which he is justly famous. I mean his whole body of work and especially the research line that began with his dissertation written under Schumpeter up through his work on Money Manager Capitalism at the Levy Institute before he died.

9. The government's debt is our financial asset. This follows from the sectoral balances approach of Wynne Godley, who was our colleague at the Levy Institute. We have to get our macroeconomics accounting correct and Godley helps us to do that. Minsky always used to tell students: go home and do the

balances sheets because what you are saying is nonsense—you must constrain your analysis with proper accounting. Fortunately, I had learned how to do accounting from John Ranlett in Sacramento (who also taught Stephanie Kelton—advisor to Bernie Sanders—from his own money and banking textbook—it is all there, including the impact of budget deficits on bank reserves). Godley taught us about stock flow consistency and he insisted that all mainstream macroeconomics is incoherent. We need a coherent framework to formulate policy.

10. Rejection of the typical view of the central bank as independent and potent. Monetary policy is weak and its impact is at best uncertain—it might even be mistaking the brake pedal for the gas pedal. The central bank is the government's bank so it can never be independent. Its main independence is limited to setting the overnight rate target, and it is probably a mistake to let it do even that. Permanent ZIRP (zero interest rate policy) is probably a better policy since it reduces the compounding of debt and the tendency for the rentier class to take over more of the economy. I credit Keynes, Minsky, Hudson, Mosler, Eric Tymoigne, and Scott Fullwiler for much of the work on this.

That is my short list of what MMT ought to include. Some of these traditions have a very long history in economics. Some were long lost until we brought them back into discussion. We have integrated them into a coherent approach to Macroeconomics. In my view, none of these can be dropped if you want a macroeconomics that is applicable to the modern economy. There are many other issues that can be (often are) included, most importantly environmental concerns and inequality, gender, and race/ethnicity. I have no problem with that.

This framework will always be in the background throughout this book as we tackle the most important economic policy issues of our times. Many of the subjects raised in this introduction—money and finance, financial instability and crises, the appropriate role for the government in our monetary system and in our economy, the Job Guarantee versus other alternative policies for fighting unemployment, poverty and inequality—will be explored in detail in this book as we make our "Great Leap Forward," proposing progressive policy for the 21st century.

The trouble with financialization

In this first part of the book, we will examine in detail the characteristics of the stage of capitalism in which we currently live. My dissertation advisor, Hyman Minsky, called it "money manager capitalism," singling out the role played by professional money managers. Neoconservatives such as President Bush called it the "Ownership Society," while the progressive James K. Galbraith analyzed it in a book he titled *The Predator State*. Still others—mostly on the left—have called it "financial capitalism," invoking the analysis by Rudolf Hilferding of capitalism at the turn of the 20th century—what he called "finance capitalism." In many ways our economy at the beginning of the 21st century did look similar to Hilferding's capitalism: dominance of the economy by finance—especially by investment banks—and globalization of both trade and finance. The economy that Hilferding studied collapsed into the Great Depression in the 1930s. Ours collapsed into the Global Financial Crisis (GFC) of 2007. Both of these calamities lasted about a decade, with high unemployment, large financial losses, and widespread suffering.

We were pulled out of the Great Depression by the combination of New Deal and WWII spending. The New Deal also included an unprecedented array of progressive policies that included constraints placed on Wall Street as well as protections for labor along with a strong social safety net. Together, the high aggregate demand created by Big Government spending and social protection set the stage for sustained and rapid growth of living standards after WWII.

The postwar period has often been called capitalism's "Golden Era"—or at least a "practical best"—as both the developed and the developing world grew faster than they ever had before. We enjoyed a new phase of capitalism—one with unprecedented rising living standards, and—even more notably—one in which prosperity was widely shared. Minsky called it "managerial welfare-state capitalism"; many in Europe called it "social democracy"; and economists called it the "mixed economy" in which big government, big business, and big labor shared the economic reins. Importantly, finance was downsized and constrained, letting government and industry run the show.

The recovery from the GFC took a decade in the United States and was even more sluggish in Europe. It was far less robust than the recovery from the Great Depression, and even after a dozen years of "recovery" there was no sign that a new Golden Era lay on the horizon. Indeed, many economists have warned that what we face instead is "secular stagnation"—slow growth for as far as the eye can see. Worse, the gains from growth go almost entirely to the very tippy top of the income distribution. For most Americans, it is difficult to see the fruits of recovery. And unlike the post-depression era, policy has not taken a progressive turn; indeed it has mostly moved to the right in most of the world as increasingly scary political movements push forward reactionary demagogues. Wall Street was rescued and the few constraints that were adopted in the aftermath of the crash are being rolled back. Wall Street has fully regained its control of the economy. Indeed, it is arguably bigger, stronger, and more dangerous than it was in Hilferding's time.

In this first part, we will argue that our current situation is worse than the precarious position in which we found ourselves on the eve of the GFC. Another "Great Crash" is inevitable. However, the purpose of this section is not to warn of a coming crisis but rather to help us to understand what is wrong with the economic system. The last "crash" was wasted—we lost the opportunity to reform the system. In large part, this is because few understood the forces that led to the collapse. Virtually none of the economists or policymakers saw the crash coming and even after it happened, they did not understand the nature of the crisis. To reform the system, we must understand what is wrong with it.

We will argue that the financial sector is far too large—it takes about a fifth of America's measure of value added. Its share of corporate profits is 40%—an outrageous portion for what should be an "intermediate" input to the production process. Along with Big Medicine, finance is the most profitable game in town. And drugs and healthcare, themselves, have been largely financialized (see Part B). There is little regulation or supervision of the "too big to fail" megabanks—with oversight largely left to "market" or even "self" supervision. All the wrong incentives are in place, however, so the lack of restraint has led to massive fraud. We will spend some time looking at a few representative cases of fraud—although this should no longer be in doubt because all the big banks have paid numerous fines. Unfortunately, while the financial institutions themselves have admitted to fraud after fraud, none of those in charge of the biggest and most fraudulent institutions have been held criminally accountable. In short, we will argue that "We're Screwed." We will close, however, on a somewhat hopeful note with some analysis of policy that might downsize finance should the opportunity arise.

I. What causes financial crises?

Before we proceed to examine the GFC, it will be useful to build an understanding of crisis.

Economists have long been concerned with the economic fluctuations that occur more or less regularly in all capitalist economies (Sherman, 1991; Wolfson, 1994). To be sure, there are different kinds of economic fluctuations—ranging from the Kitchin cycle (tied to inventory swings and lasting on average 39 months) to the Juglar cycle (lasting about 7 or 8 years and linked to investment in plant and equipment) to the Kuznets cycle of 20 years (associated with demographic changes) and finally to the Kondratieff long wave cycles attributed to major innovations (electrification, the automobile). Financial factors might play only a small role in some of these fluctuations.

Generally, economists studying financial instability have tended to focus on periodic financial crises that frequently coincide with the peak of the common business cycle, although financial crises (especially in recent years) can occur at other times during the cycle. Furthermore, an economy might be financially unstable but manage to avoid a financial crisis. It is best to think of financial instability as a tendency rather than as a specific event, although the typical financial crisis might be the result of unstable financial processes generated over the course of a business cycle expansion. In this section, we will be concerned primarily with economic instability that has at its roots a financial cause, with less interest in either economic fluctuation that is largely independent of finance or in isolated financial crises that do not spill over to the economy as a whole.

A variety of explanations of the causes of financial instability have been offered. One possible cause could be a speculative "mania" in which a large number of investors develop unrealistic expectations of profits to be made, borrowing heavily to finance purchases of assets and driving their prices to absurd levels. Eventually, the mania ends, prices collapse, and bankruptcies follow (Kindleberger, 1989). The tulip mania of 1634, the South Sea bubble in 1719, or the Dot-com boom of the late 1990s might be cited as examples of speculative manias. Speculative booms often develop, and are fueled by, fraudulent schemes. Recent examples of financial crises in which fraud played a large role include the collapse of the Albanian national pension system (1990s) as well as the American Savings and Loan fiasco (1980s) (Mayer, 1990).

Other explanations have tended to focus on a sudden interruption of the supply of money or credit that prevents borrowing and forces spending to decline, precipitating a cyclical downturn. The modern monetarist approach attributes financial instability and crises to policy errors by central banks. According to monetarist doctrine, when the central bank supplies too many reserves, the money supply expands too quickly, fueling a spending boom. If the central bank then overreacts to the inflation this is believed to generate, it reduces the money supply and causes spending to collapse (Friedman, 1982).

Others advance a "credit crunch" thesis according to which lenders (mostly banks) suddenly reduce the supply of loans to borrowers—either because the lenders reach some sort of institutional constraint or because the central bank adopts restrictive monetary policy (as in the monetarist story) (Wojnilower, 1980; Wolfson, 1994). Finally, one could add exchange rate instability and foreign indebtedness as a precipitating cause of economic instability, especially in developing nations since the breakup of the Bretton Woods system (Huerta, 1998).

Other analyses have identified processes inherent to the operation of capitalist economies (Magdoff and Sweezy, 1987). In other words, rather than looking to fundamentally irrational manias or to "exogenous shocks" emanating from monetary authorities, these approaches attribute causation to internal or endogenous factors. Karl Marx had claimed that the "anarchy of production" that is an inevitable characteristic of an unplanned economy in which decisions are made by numerous individuals in pursuit of profit is subject to "disproportionalities" of production such that some of the produced goods cannot be sold at a price high enough to realize expected profits. Key to his explanation was the recognition that production always begins with money, some of which is borrowed, used to purchase labor and the instruments of production in order to produce commodities for sale. If, however, some of the commodities cannot be sold at a sufficiently high price, loans cannot be repaid and bankruptcies occur. Creditors then may also be forced into bankruptcy when their debtors default because the creditors, themselves, will have outstanding debts they cannot service. In this way, a snowball of defaults spreads throughout the economy generating a panic as holders of financial assets begin to worry about the soundness of their investments. Rather than waiting for debtors to default, holders of financial assets attempt to "liquidate" (sell) assets to obtain cash and other safer assets. This high demand for "liquidity" (cash and marketable assets expected to hold nominal value) causes prices of all less liquid assets to collapse, and at the same time generates reluctance to spend as all try to hoard money. Thus, the financial crisis occurs in conjunction with a collapse of aggregate demand (Sherman, 1991; Marx, 1990, 1991, 1992).

Some of the elements of Marx's analysis were adopted by Irving Fisher in his "debt deflation" theory of the Great Depression, as well as by John Maynard Keynes in his General Theory. While Fisher devised a theory of special conditions in which markets would not be equilibrating, in Keynes's theory these were general conditions operating in monetary economies. Briefly, Fisher attributed the severity of the Great Depression to the collapse of asset prices and the ensuing financial crisis that resulted from an avalanche of defaults (Fisher, 1933; also Galbraith, 1972).

Adopting Marx's notion that capitalist production begins with money on the expectation of ending with more money later, Keynes developed a general theory of the determination of equilibrium output and employment that explicitly incorporated expectations (Keynes, 1964). He concluded there are no automatic, self-righting forces operating in capitalist economies that would move them toward full employment of resources. Indeed, he described destabilizing "whirlwinds" of optimism and pessimism, in striking contrast to the Smithian notion of an "invisible hand" that would guide markets toward stable equilibrium. Also, like Marx, Keynes identified what he called the "fetish" for liquidity as a primary destabilizing force that erects barriers to the achievement of full employment. Most relevantly, rising liquidity preference lowers the demand for capital assets, which leads to lower production of investment goods and thus falling income and employment through the multiplier effect.

Hyman Minsky, arguably the foremost 20th-century theorist on the topic of financial instability, extended Keynes's analysis with two primary contributions (Minsky, 1975, 1986). First, Minsky developed what he labeled "a financial theory of investment and an investment theory of the cycle," attempting to join the approaches of those who emphasized financial factors and those who emphasized real factors as causes of the cycle by noting that the two are joined in a firm's balance sheet (Papadimitriou and Wray, 1998). As in Keynes's approach, fluctuations of investment drive the business cycle. However, Minsky explicitly examined investment finance in a modern capitalist economy, arguing that each economic unit takes positions in assets (including, but not restricted to, real physical assets) that are expected to generate income flows by issuing liabilities that commit the unit to debt service payment flows.

Because the future income flows cannot be known with certainty (while the schedule of debt payments is more or less known), each economic unit operates with margins of safety, collateral, net worth, and a portfolio of safe, liquid assets to be drawn upon if the future should turn out to be worse than expected. The margins of safety, in turn, are established by custom, experience, and rough rules of thumb. If things go at least as well as expected, these margins of safety will prove in retrospect to have been larger than what was required, leading to revisions of operating rules. Thus, a "run of good times" in which income flows are more than ample to meet contracted payment commitments will lead to reductions of margins of safety. Minsky developed a classification scheme for balance sheet positions that adopted increasingly smaller margins of safety: hedge (expected income flows sufficient to meet principal and interest payments), speculative (near-term expected income flows only sufficient to pay interest), and Ponzi (expected income flows not even sufficient to pay interest, hence, funds would have to be borrowed merely to pay interest).

This leads directly to Minsky's second contribution, the financial instability hypothesis (Minsky, 1992b). Over time, the economy naturally evolves from one with a "robust" financial structure in which hedge positions dominate, toward a "fragile" financial structure dominated by speculative and even Ponzi positions. This transition occurs over the course of an expansion as increasingly risky positions are validated by the booming economy that renders the built-in margins of error superfluous—encouraging adoption of riskier positions. Eventually, either financing costs rise or income comes in below expectations, leading to defaults on payment commitments. As in the Marx-Fisher analyses, bankruptcies snowball through the economy. This reduces spending and raises planned margins of safety. The recession proceeds until balance sheets are "simplified" through defaults and conservative financial practices that reduce debt leverage ratios.

Central to Minsky's exposition is his recognition that development of the "big bank" (central bank) and the "big government" (government spending large relative to GDP) helps to moderate cyclical fluctuation. The central bank helps to attenuate defaults and bankruptcies by acting as a lender of last resort; countercyclical budget deficits and surpluses help to stabilize income flows. The problem, according to Minsky, is that successful stabilization through the big bank and the big government creates moral hazard problems because economic units will build into their expectations the supposition that intervention will prevent "it" (another great depression) from happening again.

Thus, risk-taking is rewarded and systemic fragility grows through time, increasing the frequency and severity of financial crises even as depression is avoided. While there may be no ultimate solution, Minsky believed that informed and evolving regulation and supervision of financial markets is a necessary complement to big bank and big government intervention. Like Keynes, Minsky dismissed the belief that reliance upon an invisible hand would eliminate financial instability; indeed, he was convinced that an unregulated, small government capitalist economy would be prone to great depressions and the sort of debt deflation process analyzed by Irving Fisher.

Late in his career, Minsky changed course and focused on the longer term transformation of the financial system. Rather than looking at the processes that generate the usual financial crisis, he developed an analysis of the evolution of capitalism from a robust financial system in which crises are transitory and rather easily resolved to a capitalism with a fragile financial system that could be vulnerable to another "Great Crash" like the one we suffered in the 1930s. Looking at the evolution of the US financial system over the entire postwar period, by the 1990s he began to worry that "It Could Happen Again"—another deep depression with a cataclysmic financial crisis. He died in 1996, 10 years before "it" arguably Did Happen Again. In the following sections, we begin to analyze the evolution from the robust system that existed in the early postwar period to the fragile system that collapsed in 2007.

II. The rise of financialization, neocons, and the ownership society

James K. Galbraith's great book, *The Predator State* (2008) introduces Thorstein Veblen's idea of predatory behavior into John Kenneth Galbraith's (his father) theory of the "New Industrial State" to produce a theory of the "predator state." According to Galbraith, senior, the postwar period saw the rise of a managed economy with cooperation by big government, big corporations, and big labor. Galbraith, junior, argues that his father's vision was already outdated by the time the Bretton Woods system collapsed in the early 1970s. The demise of the New Industrial State was brought about by the rise of finance, which took control over industry as well as government. Jamie argues that the state is run by "predators"—in their own interest. In this section, I discuss the transformation of the economy from what Minsky called "paternalistic capitalism" toward a new form of financial capitalism called "money manager capitalism" run by financial market participants in predatory pursuits.

This takeover was under the cover of a claimed return to "laissez-faire" capitalism in which "free markets" would unleash the entrepreneurial spirit to restore growth and end the stagflation of the 1970s. In truth, all economies are always and everywhere planned, as Jamie Galbraith insists. The only question is who does the planning. As we shifted to money manager capitalism, it was finance that took over the planning process. Government still played a role, but it was run by the predators in the interest of Wall Street. There were many regulatory changes that helped the money managers take over the state.

Deregulation often has both push and pull components. Financial markets approach sympathetic politicians and administration officials with close connections to financial institutions (Larry Summers, Alan Greenspan, Hank Paulson, Bob Rubin, Barney Frank, Christopher Dodd) with wish lists of legislative changes that would increase their profits—which are then pushed through Congress. On the other hand, much deregulation is in response to financial innovations that have rendered New Deal era constraints either moot or problematic. For example, the New Deal regulations limited the interest rates that banks and thrifts could pay on deposits, but the rise of "nonbank" competitors not subject to these rules meant that deposits were flowing out of the banks and into new institutions such as money market mutual funds. When one constraint was removed, this would shift the balance of power in the financial sector, leading to further deregulation in an attempt to restore balance. Ultimately, this was futile as the stream of innovations kept generating winners and losers.

However, the ultimate result of the deregulation movement was to allow for greater leverage ratios, more risk, less transparency, less oversight and regulation, and the rise of powerful "too big to fail" institutions that operate across the full range of financial services, combining commercial banking, investment banking, insurance, and risk hedging. Political candidates willing to support Wall Street were able to generate huge campaign contributions. During the administration of President Clinton, the Democratic Party was brought into Wall Street's folds. In the international sphere, there was a movement toward "self-supervision" that went beyond deregulation to allow the biggest international banks to supervise themselves because they had become so complex and sophisticated that no government could regulate them. This fit well into the "free market" ideology as the self-interest of these institutions was supposed to ensure that they operate to protect shareholder's interests.

This transformation of the role of the state fits well with President Bush Junior's promotion of the "ownership society"—the notion that government's proper role is to promote and protect private property interests. As his website proclaimed: "Since becoming President of the United States in 2001, President Bush has worked with the Congress to create an ownership society and build a future of security, prosperity, and opportunity for all Americans."

While much of the deregulation took place under President Clinton, it was President Bush who better articulated the neocon's goal of overturning the postwar consensus that had created the "mixed economy" or what Minsky called "managerial welfare-state capitalism": the goal was nothing short of replacing it with the *Ownership Society*.

The supporters of the president's reform agenda claimed that ownership promotes responsibility, good citizenship, active participation in society, and care of the environment. As the Cato Institute's David Boaz explained, "People who are owners feel more dignity, more pride, and more confidence. They have a stronger stake, not just in their own property, but in their community and their society" (Boaz, 2005). Owners have a permanent stake in America that "renters" and transient "users" of resources do not.[1] Public ownership of resources, or public provision of services, encourages abuse—as in Garrett Hardin's "tragedy of the commons" (Hardin, 1968)—and, worse, removes the incentive for individuals to behave in their own long-term interest.

The uncertainty associated with relying on publicly owned and provided services arises from the fact that politicians can (and do) change the rules regarding access to them. This reinforces the short view and a lack of responsibility. Hence, only private

---

[1] As Boaz argues, "There is a good deal of historical evidence… as well as abundant contemporary evidence, that ownership tends to encourage self-esteem and healthy habits of behavior, such as acting more for the long term, or taking education more seriously" (Boaz, 2005).

ownership can empower individuals and provide the discipline and real freedom to induce Americans to take control of their healthcare, education, and retirement. "Talking with staff, Bush emphasizes that he wants to use these policies to move from an 'anything-goes culture' to a 'responsibility culture.' By giving individuals control of their own retraining, their own savings, and their own homes, he hopes to inculcate self-reliance, industriousness, and responsibility" (Brooks, 2003). Americans can then respond efficiently to market signals and self-interest.[2]

This perspective has a long pedigree. The father of economics, Adam Smith, proclaimed: "Civil government, so far as it is instituted for the security of property, is in reality instituted for the defense of the rich against the poor, or of those who have some property against those who have none at all" (Smith, 1937, p. 674). John Locke expressed the same sentiment: "Government has no other end but the preservation of property"; and Locke's editor quotes James Tyrell to the effect that the "main end of [government] is to maintain the Dominion or Property before agreed on" (Locke, 1988, p. 329). Even clearer was Governor Morris: "Property was the main object of Society. The savage state was more favorable to liberty than the Civilized; and sufficiently so to life. It was preferred by all men who had not acquired a taste for property; it was only renounced for the sake of property which could only be secured by the restraints of regular Government" (quoted in Nedelsky, 1990, p. 68). This stance was advocated by other propertied framers of the Constitution, including the more moderate James Madison, who argued, "The first object of government is the protection of the different and unequal faculties of acquiring property."[3]

While Madison also recognized the importance of protecting the rights of people, he put the rights of property first because he feared that in America the majority might tyrannize the wealthy few—that is, the best government would be one "ruled by propertied elites and insulated from direct popular control."[4]

In this view, property is not only the origin of society and the reason for government, but also a hallmark of civilization.[5] The push for an ownership society by President Bush and the neocons must be placed within this broad historical and ideological

---

[2] While more extreme than Clinton's promise to "end welfare as we know it" in order to promote individual responsibility, the truth is that most of the early postwar social protections had already been removed or at least subjected to unrelenting criticism long before Bush took office.

[3] Madison in "Federalist No. 10," quoted in McCann (1991, pp. 53–57).

[4] McCann (1991, p. 53). McCann goes on to quote Nedelsky that Madison's vision was one where the "people as a whole would be relegated to the margins of politics, but guaranteed the freedom and security to pursue their private interests—which was the real purpose of government." This, according to Nedelsky, explains Madison's opposition to redistributive policies, including debt relief.

[5] Gouverneur Morris explains: "This Conclusion results that the State of Society is perfected in Proportion as the Rights of Property are secured." The Founders' Constitution (Kurland and Lerner, 1987) sums up the views of many of the founders: "Proprietorship is a condition for entry and full participation in political life, a prerequisite for the necessary independence that would guard the citizenry from becoming the mere instruments of the powerful and ambitious, a token of the seriousness of one's commitment to stability and order, and a claim to a full voice in the disposition of the community's affairs, especially as those bear on the enjoyment of one's own."

framework. Government policy ought to promote the interests of owners, who will act as responsible stewards of privatized resources, while protecting the owning classes against the nonowning classes, who tend to make excessive demands for entitlements and legal protection. The ownership-society movement represents a conservative reaction to what many see as the erosion of the rights of the propertied over the past two centuries.

"Reforms" pushed by neocons included privatization of Social Security, tightening bankruptcy law, replacing income and wealth taxes with consumption taxes, transferring healthcare burdens to patients, devolution of government responsibility, substituting "personal reemployment and training accounts" for unemployment benefits, "No Child Left Behind" and school vouchers legislation, elimination of welfare "entitlements," bridling "runaway trial lawyers," transformation of private pensions to defined contribution plans, the movement against government "takings," and continuing attempts to hand national resources over to private exploiters.[6]

In addition, "freeing" financial markets and money managers played a critical role in (temporarily) increasing homeownership—the most visible "success" of the ownership society policy. While supporters held out the promise that access to wealth would be broadened, I have argued that such policies actually *increased* inequality, which undermines an important justification for policies that aim to promote ownership[7] (Wray, 2005a, 2005b). Again, the most telling evidence is that by early spring 2009, homeownership rates had already returned to the pre-Bush levels, with millions more foreclosures expected and with many more millions of America's homeowners "underwater" (mortgage debt exceeds value of their homes).

The case for existence of an ownership society really rests on homeownership, since owner-occupied homes represent the only significant asset held by families across all income and wealth percentiles. However, about half the home "owners" have mortgages against their properties and that debt rose quickly—from 40% of personal disposable income in 1984 to 100% at the peak of the boom. Indeed, recent years have seen a tendency to cash out equity—the housing "ATM" phenomenon—contributing to rising debt ratios and high default rates. Further, while financial assets and net worth are heavily skewed toward the richest households, debts are more "democratically" shared—

---

[6] Space constraints do not permit a thorough exploration of the links between these policies and neoconservative ideology and the interests of money managers (see Wray, 2005a).

[7] Supporters claim that ownership promotes responsibility, citizenship, active participation in society, and care of the environment. As the Cato Institute's David Boaz explains, "People who are owners feel more dignity, more pride, and more confidence. They have a stronger stake, not just in their own property, but in their community and their society" (Boaz, 2005). Owners have an interest in America that "renters" and transient "users" of resources do not. Public ownership of resources or provision of services encourages abuse—as in Garrett Hardin's "tragedy of the commons" (Hardin, 1968). Uncertainty associated with relying on publicly owned and provided services arises because politicians can (and do) change access rules. Only private ownership can empower individuals and provide the discipline and real freedom to induce Americans to take control of their healthcare, environment, education, and retirement. Hence, elimination of New Deal and other obstacles is said to democratize access to wealth.

with the bottom half of the wealth distribution "enjoying" more debt relative to income, and absolutely higher levels of debt in some cases.

With little or no equity cushion, even a slight downturn in real estate prices—or a decline in household income—would lead to foreclosures. The repercussions of a slowdown in real estate markets would be far-reaching, given the level of household debt, given that the family home represents a huge chunk of typical household wealth and given how important the housing bubble was for job creation. It is ironic that the 30-year mortgage brought to us by New Deal government guarantees— making homeownership possible for working Americans for the first time— morphed into a speculation-fueling, debt-pushing casino that buried homeowners in a mountain of liabilities. Creditors would emerge as owners of the foreclosed houses *and* with claims on debtors, who will be subject to a form of perpetual debt bondage (bankruptcy "reform" does not allow relief from debt on a first home— this was seen as a "credit enhancement" that made securitized subprime mortgages safer—but it still allows relief for those rich enough to own more than one home).[8] Many "home owners" merely occupy, manage, and improve homes really owned by the *true* owner class—those with lots of wealth, particularly financial wealth.

Thus, the neocon policies created a sharper division between a small class of owners and a much larger class of nonowners—including the highly indebted putative owners of homes. When neocon predators captured the state, this became inevitable because government policy was increasingly directed by and for the owners. With rising inequality, the true ownership class was actually shrinking in number (but gaining in wealth) and government policy was directed by a handful of predators for the benefit of that elite. The fallout was home price appreciation; when prices finally collapsed under an unserviceable debt load, the economy crashed, unemployment exploded, and the nation's real wealth became even more concentrated in the hands of predators.

There was thus a fortuitous synergy: government policy promoted "ownership," "free markets" that actually generated rising inequality, innovations that increased risk and—as we will see later—esoteric instruments that made homeownership less affordable. The result was rising debt that would eventually lead to collapse of the financial system.

III. The dark recesses of the financial system: why no one saw "it" coming

Ah, the Eternal Sunshine of the Recessed Mind!

---

[8] Widespread homeownership is beneficial, and for at least some of the reasons enumerated by promoters of the ownership society. However, to equate holding a mortgaged family home with membership in a class of "citizen investors" (as neocons do) borders on delusion.

In the aftermath of the GFC, mainstream economists attempted to explain what went wrong. The biggest problem for them is that they never saw it coming. Indeed, in the run up to the crash, they mostly functioned as cheerleaders for the deregulation and financial practices that guaranteed a crisis would occur. Afterward, economists from Alan Greenspan on the right (who presided over the Fed during most of the period that Wall Street's riskiest practices were "innovated) to Paul Krugman on the left acknowledged that they had it all wrong. Let us look at a particularly hilarious mea culpa by Olivier Blanchard—that follows in main outline Krugman's excuse (Blanchard, 2014; Krugman, 2014).

Here is the Cliffs Notes version (paraphrased):

Yes, we didn't see anything coming. But that isn't our fault. The Global Financial Crisis—the biggest calamity since 1929—was invisible to us because it had been lurking in the dark corners of the financial system. Meanwhile, we had been creating highly sophisticated economic models in which there were no financial institutions—at least nothing like those in the real world. Ours were transparent and honest. They were well-capitalized. Their risks were perfectly hedged. There was no uncertainty. There was no chance of financial instability because the market forces always—inevitably—drove toward equilibrium. We had very nicely behaved DSGE[9] models—models with no default risk. Where everyone was civilized and played nice. No one ever missed a payment. All debts were always paid. On time. In our world, even Lake Woebegone would have been impossibly unruly.

In the world that Blanchard and other mainstreamers modeled, deviation from equilibrium was "essentially self correcting. The problem is that we came to believe that this was indeed the way the world worked."

Blanchard goes on: Our models "made sense only under a vision in which economic fluctuations were regular enough so that, by looking at the past, people and firms (and the econometricians who apply statistics to economics) could understand their nature and form expectations of the future, and simple enough so that small shocks had small effects and a shock twice as big as another had twice the effect on economic activity."

In other words, like the drunks who look for their keys under the street lights, Blanchard and other mainstream economists preferred to model impossible worlds because the math was easier. The world—obviously—is not linear, but the math skills of economists were not sufficient to model real, nonlinear worlds.

Blanchard admits he was warned: "The late Frank Hahn, a well-known economist who taught at Cambridge University, kept reminding me of his detestation of linear models, including mine, which he called 'Mickey Mouse' models."

Yep, the mainstream used Mickey Mouse models to reach the conclusion that we had entered what Chairman Bernanke called the "Era of the Great Moderation"—

---

[9] Dynamic Stochastic General Equilibrium models that are mathematically complicated but that model impossibly simple worlds—usually with no money or financial institutions in them.

where nothing can possibly go wrong because we have got Uncle Ben at the Fed and the Invisible Hand of the Market to protect us.

Paul Krugman's mea culpa went like this:

> *It is true that economists failed to predict the 2008 crisis (and so did almost everyone). But this wasn't because economics lacked the tools to understand such things—we've long had a pretty good understanding of the logic of banking crises. What happened instead was a failure of real-world observation—failure to notice the rising importance of shadow banking. This was a case of myopia—but it wasn't a deep conceptual failure. And as soon as people* did *recognize the importance of shadow banking, the whole thing instantly fell into place: we were looking at a classic financial crisis.*

How were they supposed to see those darned shadow banks that operated in the dark out of their sight?

The dark cornered cobwebs of their minds made it impossible for the mainstream to see the instability building—on trend since 1966! They failed to notice the crises of the early 1970s (commercial paper, Franklin National), the crises of the early 1980s (Developing country debt, commercial real estate), the crises of the mid-1980s (S&Ls, REITs, LBOs),[10] or the late 1980s (all of the biggest US banks were probably insolvent by 1990) or the 1990s (developing countries—again—as well as the LTCM and Dot-com fiascos).[11] They missed the residential real estate bubble that was obvious by 2000. They never noticed that the shadow banking system had grown to be much larger than the chartered banks. And they never understood that the setup of the EMU guaranteed a Euro area crisis.

Nope, those dark recesses of their minds made it impossible to see anything coming.

Yet, according to Blanchard, they have now learned from their mistakes. We should listen to them now.

Maybe not.

Here is a better idea. Ignore those who never saw that last crisis coming. You can be sure that they will miss the next one, too. Nothing will penetrate the dark corners of those minds.

IV. The global financial crisis explained

As Hyman Minsky put it, "The main reason why our economy behaves in different ways at different times is because financial practices and the structure of financial

---

[10] The Saving and Loan crisis, the Real Estate and Investment Trust crisis, and the Leveraged Buy-out crisis (remember Michael Milken?).

[11] Long-Term Capital Management went bust and the Dot-com bubble burst soon afterward.

commitments change." (Minsky, 1986). If we are going to understand our economy well enough to reform it, we need to understand how our financial system works.

Mainstream economists have developed theories in which financial markets are "efficient," in pricing financial assets according to fundamental values. Indeed, if finance is efficient in the manner described by orthodoxy, it does not even matter. This is a logical extension of the neoclassical theory's conclusion that markets efficiently allocate real resources to the financial sector—so that it is "just the right size" to provide the optimal amount of finance to the real sector. In the form of rational expectations, it led to the conclusion that no individual or regulator could form a better idea of equilibrium values than the market.

This led to Chairman Greenspan's famous excuse for not intervening into the serial bubbles that preceded the GFC that began in 2007.[12] And it was this theory that provided the intellectual underpinning of the behavior of market participants as well as regulators that led to the crisis in financial markets.

Yet, it is clear that financial "markets" did not "efficiently" price assets. The prolonged crisis—by far the worst since the Great Depression—makes it clear that "finance" does matter. This is now recognized by virtually all observers. However, after the crisis, most policymakers were simply focused on "getting finance flowing" again—as if we just needed to take a big plunger to a blocked financial toilet—and on ensuring that asset prices more correctly reflect fundamental market values.

Ronald Coase had long ago argued that while free markets might be the most efficient form of economic organization, many economic transactions take place outside the market, which calls into question the role of markets as the organizing structure of capitalism. Thus, following the example previously set by Keynesians and institutionalists, even Coase left an opening for institutions, including the state, in formulating rules and providing regulation and supervision. These institutions will not arise endogenously out of market processes; they must be imposed on the market. One could go even further and argue that the market, itself, is an institution—created and regulated through human agency.

These objections are even more relevant to the sphere of finance. At the most basic level, banking is concerned with building a relationship that allows for careful underwriting (assessing creditworthiness) and for ensuring that payments are made as they come due. Long-term relations with customers increase the possibility of success, by making future access to bank services contingent upon meeting current commitments.

Further, within the bank itself, a culture is developed to provide and enforce rules of behavior. Relations among banks are also extra-market, with formal and informal agreements that are necessary for mutual protection—banks are often forced to "hang together, or all will be hung separately" because of the contagion effects of runs on their liabilities.

---

[12] However, Greenspan himself repudiated that view after the crash when he testified in Congress, arguing that his entire world view had been wrong.

Social policy has long promoted the use of bank liabilities as the primary means of payment. This is not something that arose naturally out of markets but was imposed on them. A well-functioning payments system requires par clearing—the United States's long and sordid history of nonpar clearing by "free" banks (in the 19th century) stands out as singularly unsuccessful. For that reason, par clearing was finally ensured with the Federal Reserve Act of 1913, which created a central bank for the United States whose original primary purpose was to ensure par clearing of bank demand deposits. However, there was a glitch in the system because the Fed's role was limited to lending to solvent banks against good assets. Hence, the payments system collapsed in the 1930s, when runs on banks returned as depositors rightly feared insolvent banks would never make good on their promises.

For that reason, Congress created the Federal Deposit Insurance Corporation (FDIC) to "insure"[13] deposits (with similar guarantees on deposits at thrifts and some other types of institutions). This effectively eliminated runs on banks (although later runs returned on other types of bank liabilities, such as brokered CDs (certificates of deposits in amounts above insured limits), and in the GFC on commercial paper issued by banks).

The combination of access to the Fed as lender of last resort, par clearing, and deposit insurance provided very cheap and stable sources of finance for banks. In addition, Regulation Q limited interest on deposits (set at zero for demand deposits) to keep interest costs down. Banks could charge fees to handle deposit accounts. All of this made it possible for banks to operate the payments system while shifting most costs to consumers and government. Further, because these bank liabilities are guaranteed, bad underwriting leads to socialization of most losses as the FDIC makes the deposits good. (Owners of "bad" banks could lose their equity—although in practice that usually does not occur in the case of the biggest "too big to fail" banks.)

Clearly, operation of the payments system has not been left to "free markets." While it now seems natural to run payments through nominally private banks, there was no reason to combine lending (predominately commercial lending) and the payments system in this manner. An alternative arrangement would have been to separate the two—with the government operating the payments system as a public utility (for example, through a postal savings system) and banks focusing on underwriting loans while financing positions in assets by issuing a combination of short-term and long-term liabilities.

If bank liabilities were not the basis of the payments system, there would have been no reason for the bank liabilities to maintain par—nor even any reason for

---

[13] While FDIC was set up as an insurance system (banks pay premiums that in principle are used to cover payouts to depositors when banks fail), the "full faith and credit" of the US Treasury is presumed to stand behind FDIC. If FDIC's reserves cannot cover losses, Congress is expected to provide funding. In that sense, FDIC goes well beyond insurance—it is really an "assurance" that promises Uncle Sam stands behind the deposits (up to the legislated limit on each account), no matter how big the losses faced by FDIC. That is better than "insurance."

them to circulate. In other words, they would not have received or required a government backstop.

Bad underwriting would first hit equity holders and then would reduce the value of the liabilities. Losses would not be automatically socialized. There might then have been some discipline on banks to do good underwriting.

Of course, Glass-Steagall did segregate a portion of the financial sector from the payments system: investment banks were allowed freer rein on the asset side of their balance sheets, but they could not issue deposits. Their creditors could lose. Creditors were protected mostly by the Securities and Exchange Commission (SEC)—which provided regulations primarily on the "product" or liability side. Investment banks (and other non–deposit-taking financial institutions) were largely free to buy and hold or trade any kinds of assets they deemed appropriate. They were required to "mark-to-market" and to provide reports to creditors. Other than rather loose rules requiring them to ensure that the products they marketed were "suitable" for those who purchased them, it was expected that "markets" would discipline them.

That did not work, even for the less protected institutions that did not have bank charters. And when the financial system collapsed, the remaining investment banks (that is, the ones that were chosen for rescue—some were allowed to fail) were handed charters so that they could access the payments system.

Over the past half century, there has been a trend toward reducing relationship banking in favor of supposedly greater reliance on "markets." This is reflected in the rise of "shadow banks" that are relatively unregulated, that in many cases are required to "mark-to-market," and that have successfully eroded the bank share of the financial sector. It is also reflected in the changing behavior within banks, which largely adopted the "originate to distribute" model that is superficially market-based. This shift was spurred by a combination of innovation (new practices that were not covered by regulations), competition from shadow banks with lower costs, and deregulation (including erosion of and finally repeal of Glass-Steagall).

This trend also reflects the growing faith in the efficacy of markets. However, the move to increase reliance on markets is more apparent than real. The new innovations such as asset-backed securities (ABSs) increased institutional linkages even as they reduced the free market competitive pressures imagined by orthodoxy. The prices to which asset values are marked reflect neither "fundamentals" nor "markets"—rather, they result from proprietary models developed (mostly) in-house and that reflect the culture and views of teams working within institutions.

At the same time, these trends reduced "social efficiency" of the financial sector, if that is defined along Minskyan lines (Minsky, 1992a) as Minsky always insisted that the role of finance is to promote the "capital development of the economy," defined as broadly as possible. Minsky would agree with institutionalists that the definition should include enhancing the social provisioning process, promotion of equality and democracy, and expanding human capabilities.

Instead, the financial sector has promoted several different kinds of inequality as it captured a greater proportion of social resources. It has also promoted boom and bust cycles, and proven to be incapable of supporting economic growth and job creation except through the promotion of serial financial bubbles. And, finally, it has imposed huge costs on the rest of society, even in the booms but especially in the crises.

Indeed, the post-GFC attempts to rescue the financial sector (especially in the United States) have laid bare the tremendous social costs created by the way finance dominates the economy. If anything, the various bailouts have actually strengthened the hands of the financial sector, increasing concentration in the hands of a small number of behemoth institutions that appear to control government policy. Meanwhile the "real" economy suffered, as unemployment, poverty, and homelessness rose, but policymakers claimed we cannot afford to deal with these problems. Their only hope was to gently prod Wall Street to lend more—in other words, to bury the rest of the economy under even more debt. The rescue of Wall Street displaced other fiscal policy that would have led to a more robust and fair recovery.

In sum, the financial sector has not been operating like a neoclassical market. In spite of the rhetoric that deregulation improved efficiencies by replacing government rules with market discipline, markets have not and cannot discipline financial institutions. Rather, we reduced regulation and supervision by government that was supposed to direct finance to serve the public interest. This was replaced by self-supervision for private profit that generated huge social costs. Financial institutions do not even pursue "market" interests (of shareholders, for example). Instead, they have been largely taken over by top management with personal enrichment as the goal.

In the next two sections, we will examine the consequences.

V. The role of lender fraud

We have long known that lender fraud was rampant during the real estate boom. The FBI began warning of an "epidemic" of mortgage fraud as early as 2004. We know that mortgage originators invented "low doc" and "no doc" loans, encouraged borrowers to take out "liar loans," and promoted "NINJA loans" (no income, no job, no assets, no problem!). All of these schemes were fraudulent from the get-go. Across most of the United States, it is illegal to give a loan to someone you expect cannot meet the terms. The "low" and "no" doc and NINJA loans were designed to offer a thin patina of protection to lenders who provided loans on a "don't ask don't tell" basis—"we do not want to see any documents that prove that we know you cannot possibly qualify for the loan." This was fraud. And if you did enter income data that disqualified you, the mortgage brokers used "white out" to doctor the documents and boost your income to whatever level was required.

Property appraisers were involved, paid to overvalue real estate. That is fraud. The securitizers packaged trashy mortgages into bundles that rating agencies blessed with the triple A seal of approval. By their own admission, raters worked with securitizers to provide the rating desired, without examining the loan tapes to see what they were rating. Fraud. Trustees at the investment banks provided false "representations and warranties" that the trash mortgages met required standards for securitization. Fraud. Venerable investment banks like Goldman Sachs packaged the trashiest securities into collateralized debt obligations (CDOs) at the behest of hedge fund managers—who were allowed to choose the most toxic of the toxic waste—then sold the CDOs on to their own customers and allowed the hedge funds to bet against them. More fraud. It was all fraud.

Now we know that it was not just the mortgage brokers, and the appraisers, and the ratings agencies, and the accountants, and the investment banks that were behind the fraud. It was the securitization process itself that was fraudulent. Indeed, the securities themselves are fraudulent. Many, perhaps most, maybe all of them.

Indeed, the largest financial institutions were run by their management as what my former UMKC colleague Bill Black calls "control frauds" (Black, 1995). That is, the banks used accounting fraud to manufacture fake profits so that they could pay huge bonuses to top management. Even after the GFC and the bailout, the data on Wall Street bonuses indicated that these institutions were still run as control frauds, with record bonuses paid.

In the aftermath of the crisis, many called for a national moratorium on foreclosures. Even some of the banks that have been run as control frauds voluntarily stopped foreclosing. And yet President Obama, ever the centrist, took sides with the Securities Industry and Financial Markets Association, which warned that "it would be catastrophic to impose a system-wide moratorium on all foreclosures and such actions could do damage to the housing market and the economy."

No, it would expose the securities industry, itself, as the chief architect of perhaps the biggest scandal in human history.

This is the mother of all frauds, and it will be etched into the history books for all time. Let us look in some detail at the frauds.

VI. The four developments that precipitated the crisis

There are four important developments that need to be recognized.[14]

a. Managed money

First, there was the rise of "managed money"—pension funds (private and public), sovereign wealth funds, insurance funds, university endowments, and other savings that are placed with professional money managers seeking maximum returns.

Also important was the shift to "total return" as the goal—yield plus price appreciation. Each money manager competes on the basis of total return, earning fee income and getting more clients if successful. Of course, the goal of each is to be the

---

[14] I thank Frank Veneroso for lengthy discussions that led to some of the ideas expressed in this section.

best—anyone returning less than the average return loses clients. But it is impossible for all to be above average—generating several kinds of behavior that are sure to increase risk (Wray, 2011). Money managers will take on riskier assets to gamble for higher returns. They will innovate new products, using marketing to attract clients. Often these are purposely complex and opaque—the better to dupe clients and to prevent imitation by competing firms. And, probably most important of all, there is a strong incentive to overstate actual earnings—by failing to recognize losses, by overvaluing assets, and through just plain fraudulent accounting.

This development is related to the rising importance of "shadow banks"—financial institutions that are not regulated as banks. Recall the New Deal's Glass-Steagall Act imposed functional separation, with heavier supervision of commercial banks and thrifts. Over time, these lost market share to institutions subject to fewer constraints on leverage ratios, on interest rates that could be paid, and over types of eligible assets. The huge pools of managed money offered an alternative source of funding for commercial activities. Firms would sell commercial paper or junk bonds to shadow banks and managed money rather than borrowing from banks. And, importantly, securitization took many types of loans off the books of banks and into affiliates (special investment or purpose vehicles—SIVs and SPVs) and managed money funds. Banks continually innovated in an attempt to get around regulations, while government deregulated in a futile effort to keep banks competitive (Wray, 2008a, 2008b; Kregel, 2010). In the end, government gave up and eliminated functional separation in 1999.

Note that over the previous two or three decades, there had been increased "outsourcing" with pension, insurance, and sovereign wealth fund managers hiring Wall Street firms to manage assets. Inevitably this led to abuse, with venerable investment houses shoveling trashy assets like ABSs and CDOs onto portfolios of clients. Firms like Goldman then carried it to the next logical step, betting that the toxic waste they sold to clients would crater. And, as we now know, investment banks would help their clients hide debt through opaque financial instruments, building debt loads far beyond what could be serviced—and then bet on default of their clients using credit default swaps (CDSs). This is exactly what Goldman did for Greece. When markets discovered that Greece was hiding debt, this caused CDS prices to climb, raising Greece's finance costs and causing its budget deficit to climb out of control, fueling credit downgrades that raised its interest rates in a vicious death spiral. Goldman thus benefited from the fee income it got by hiding the debt and by gambling on the inside information that Greece was hiding debt!

Such practices appear to have been normal at global financial institutions, including a number of European banks that also used CDSs to bet against Greece. Wall Street also extended the practice to betting on US state and local governments. For example, Goldman encouraged clients to bet against the debt issued by at least 11 US states—while collecting fees from those states for helping them to place debt.

These are among the tools used by money managers to distribute the rewards of the financial system to themselves. They have next to nothing to do with financing desirable economic activity. And, as we will see, they became weapons of fraud.

b. Investment banks

This bring us to the second transition: the investment banks went public.

During the 1929 boom, Wall Street partners could not benefit directly from rising stock values (they could only earn fee income by placing equities and bonds, or by purchasing shares in traded firms)—hence they created traded subsidiaries. In the "irrational exuberance" of the late 1990s, Wall Street firms again lamented that they could not directly benefit from the boom. Hence Wall Street firms went public, issuing traded shares. In this way, top management's bonuses would include stocks and options to be sold at huge profit if share prices rose. Just as they did in 1929, management could manipulate share prices by overreporting earnings, selectively leaking well-timed rumors, and trading on inside information. They became richly rewarded. Related to this was the substitution of profit maximization of underlying firms by "total return to shareholders" (dividends plus share price appreciation) as the goal of a corporation. This increased the focus on stock prices—which can be easily manipulated for short-term gain, both serving as the justification for big rewards and also as the means to enrichment for management holding options.

So in 1999, Goldman and the other partnerships went public to enjoy the advantages of stock issue in a boom. Top management was rewarded with stocks—leading to the same pump-and-dump short-term incentives that drove the 1929 boom. To be sure, traders like Robert Rubin (later, Treasury Secretary under President Clinton) had already come to dominate firms like Goldman. Traders necessarily take a short view—you are only as good as your last trade. More importantly, traders take a zero-sum view of deals: there will be a winner and a loser, with the financial firm pocketing fees for bringing the two sides together. Better yet, the firm would take one of the two sides—the winning side, of course—and pocket the fees and collect the winnings.

You might wonder why anyone would voluntarily become the client of an investment bank, knowing that the deal was ultimately zero-sum and that the bank would have the winning hand. No doubt there were some clients with an outsized view of their own competence or luck, but most customers were wrongly swayed by the bank's reputation that was being exploited by hired management.

Note that before it went public, only 28% of Goldman's revenues came from trading and investing activities. That is now about 80% of revenue. While many think of Goldman as a bank, it is really a huge hedge fund, albeit a very special one that now holds a bank charter—giving it access to the Fed's discount window and to FDIC insurance. That, in turn, lets it borrow at near-zero interest rates. Indeed, in 2009, it spent only a little over $5 billion to borrow, versus $26 billion in interest expenses in 2008—a $21 billion subsidy, thanks to its bank charter. It was also widely believed to be "backstopped" by the government—under no circumstances would it be allowed to fail, nor would it be restrained or prosecuted—keeping its stock price up.

Essentially both the research arms of the big financial firms as well as the supposedly unbiased reporting of the financial media (especially television) became little more than marketers for the products and shares of Wall Street banks. All of this irreversibly changed the incentive structure of investment banking—away from placing equities and bonds of industrial corporations and toward a frenzy of trading in complex financial instruments whose values were determined mostly by "marking to model" or even "marking to myth"—that is, value was set by the seller in "over the counter," unregulated and opaque markets. In the new environment, traders rose to the top of firms like Goldman (and then on to head the Treasury in the case of Robert Rubin and Henry Paulson). It is no wonder that "originate to distribute" securitization and trading replaced careful underwriting (assessment of borrower risk) and lending as the primary focus of financial institutions.

c. Deregulation and desupervision

The previous two fueled the third transition, deregulation and desupervision, which actually began in the United States in the late 1960s and built up steam through the 1980s and 1990s.

We gradually allowed financial institutions to take riskier positions—holding riskier assets, taking illiquid positions (mismatched maturities of assets and liabilities, for example), increasing leverage (and moving assets off balance sheet where they would not count toward capital requirements), and using internal models to assess risk and asset values. This should be more properly called "self-supervision" rather than deregulation and desupervision. The theory was that financial institutions could better evaluate risks than could government supervisors, and that relying on private credit raters and accounting firms would provide more flexibility. We also let managed money such as pension funds "diversify" portfolios—into new and complex financial instruments that promised higher and uncorrelated returns that would supposedly reduce systemic risk (Nersisyan and Wray, 2010a, 2010b, 2010c). At the end of the 1990s, we ended the functional separation of financial institutions, allowing a single holding company to engage in the full range of financial services—one-stop financial supermarkets that were mostly free of government intervention.

The completion of this transformation occurred with the collapse of Lehman, Bear, and Merrill, when the last two remaining investment banks (Goldman and Morgan Stanley) were handed commercial banking charters so that they would have access to cheap and government-insured deposits—as mentioned above—made necessary because they could not raise funds any longer in financial markets that were shaken by the collapse of three investment banks. Now the riskiest of the financial institutions were playing with "house money"—government-insured deposits that could be gambled, with government absorbing almost all losses (at a capital ratio of 12:1, government incurs losses of 92 cents of each dollar blown in bad bets) (Tymoigne and Wray, 2009).

d. The rise of fraud as normal business procedure

The fourth and, for our purposes, final transformation was the inevitable result of these three changes just examined: the rise of fraud as normal business procedure.

In early spring 2010, a court-appointed investigator issued a report on the failure of Lehman, accusing the firm of engaging in a variety of "actionable" practices (potentially prosecutable as crimes). Interestingly, it hid debt using practices similar to those employed by Goldman to hide Greek debt. The investigator also showed how the prices on Lehman's assets were set—and subject to rather arbitrary procedures that could result in widely varying values. But most importantly, the top management as well as Lehman's accounting firm (Ernst & Young) signed off on what the investigator said was "materially misleading" accounting. The question is why would a top accounting firm as well as Lehman's CEO, Richard Fuld, risk prison in the post-Enron era (similar accounting fraud brought down Enron's accounting firm, and resulted in Sarbanes-Oxley legislation that requires a company's CEO to sign off on company accounts)? There are two answers. First, it is possible that fraud became so widespread that no accounting firm could retain top clients without agreeing to overlook it. Second, fraud may be so pervasive, and enforcement and prosecution thought to be so lax that CEOs and accounting firms have no fear. It appears that both answers are correct.

In the aftermath of the 1980s savings and loan crisis in the United States, 1000 top managers of failed institutions went to jail. Investigations found fraud in virtually every failed institution examined (Wray, 1994; Black, 1995). Interestingly, the FBI warned of an "epidemic" of fraud in mortgage lending as early as 2004. Subsequent detailed investigation of randomly selected MBSs has found evidence of fraud in virtually every one. William Black (who worked in thrift supervision during the 1980s crisis and blew the whistle on the worst S&L crook, Charles Keating—remembered for his association with five US senators, including John McCain)—has convincingly argued that what we really have is a criminogenic environment that fueled the worst kind of fraud, control fraud. This is where the top management—in this case, of a financial institution—turns a firm into a weapon of fraud in the interest of enriching top management.

The easiest example to understand is a pyramid or Ponzi scheme (named after a famous pyramid run by Charles Ponzi), with Bernie Madoff of recent note. Many of the failed savings and loans of the 1980s—and all of the most expensive failures—were control frauds. However, these are small potatoes compared with the failures of AIG or Lehman. If (and the mounting fines imposed seems to indicate that fraud was indeed pervasive and indeed continues[15]) the large financial institutions responsible for the GFC are still hiding "actionable" practices approved by top management and external auditors, then we remain in the midst of the biggest control fraud in history

---

[15] In 2018, Wells Fargo was still being assessed new penalties totaling billions of dollars—some for fraud that took place over a decade after the frauds that led to the GFC. House Financial Services Committee Chairwoman Maxine Waters, D-Calif., called Wells Fargo "a recidivist financial institution.... Wells Fargo's ongoing lawlessness and failure to right the ship suggests the bank—with approximately $1.9 trillion in assets and serving one in three U.S. households is simply too big to manage." Daniella Cheslow NPR March 12, 2019 "Ceo says Wells Fargo Has transformed after scandals, Lawmakers are skeptical."

a decade after the end of the GFC. In any case, it is likely that fraud worthy of incarceration was rampant. To date, however, there has been almost no investigation and no prosecution of top officials at any of the big banks.

VII. Fraud as a business model

In mid-April 2010, the SEC announced a civil fraud lawsuit against Goldman Sachs. (Goldman agreed to pay a fine of $550 million, without admitting guilt, although it did admit to a "mistake.")[16] The details of the SEC's case will be familiar to anyone who knows about Magnetar. This hedge fund sought the very worst subprime MBSs to package as CDOs. The firm nearly single-handedly kept the subprime market afloat after investors started to worry about Liar and NINJA loans, since Magnetar was offering to take the very worst tranches—making it possible to sell the higher-rated ("safer") tranches to other more skittish buyers. And Magnetar was quite good at identifying trash: According to an analysis commissioned by ProPublica, 96% of the CDO deals arranged by Magnetar were in default by the end of 2008 (vs. "only" 68% of comparable CDOs). The CDOs were then sold on to investors, who ultimately lost big time. Meanwhile, Magnetar used CDSs to bet that the garbage CDOs they were selling would go bad. Actually, that is not a bet. If you can manage to put together deals that go bad 96% of the time, betting on bad is as close to a sure thing as a financial market will ever find. So, in reality, it was just pickpocketing customers—in other words, a looting.

Magnetar was a hedge fund, and as they say, the clients of hedge funds are "big boys" who are supposed to be sophisticated and sufficiently rich so that they can afford to lose. Goldman Sachs, by contrast, is a 140-year-old firm that operates a revolving door to keep the US Treasury and the NY Fed well-stocked with its alumni. As Matt Taibi has argued, Goldman has been behind virtually every financial crisis the United States has experienced since the Civil War. In John Kenneth Galbraith's *The Great Crash*, a chapter that documents Goldman's contributions to the Great Depression is titled "In Goldman We Trust." As the instigator of crises, it has truly earned its reputation. And it has been publicly traded since 1999—an unusual hedge fund, indeed. Furthermore, Treasury Secretary Geithner handed it a bank charter to ensure it would have cheap access to funds during the financial crisis. This gave it added respectability and profitability—one of the chosen few anointed by government to speculate with Treasury funds. So, why did Goldman use its venerable reputation to loot its customers?

In the particular case prosecuted by the SEC, Goldman created synthetic CDOs that placed bets on toxic waste MBSs. A synthetic CDO does not actually hold any

---

[16] The following discussion is based on reports by Louise Story (2010), Gretchen Morgenson and Louise Story (2009, 2010a, 2010b), Joe Nocera (2010), Christine Harper (2010), and Peter Henning and Seven Davidoff (2010).

mortgage securities—it is simply a pure bet on a bunch of MBSs. The purchaser is betting that those MBSs will not go bad, but there is an embedded CDS that allows the other side to bet that the MBSs will fall in value, in which case the CDS "insurance" pays off. Note that the underlying mortgages do not need to go into default or even fall into delinquency. To make sure that those who "short" the CDO (those holding the CDS) get paid sooner rather than later, all that is required is a downgrade by credit rating agencies. The trick, then, is to find a bunch of MBSs that appear to be overrated and place a bet they will be downgraded. Synergies abound! The propensity of credit raters to give high ratings to junk assets is well known, indeed assured by paying them to do so. Since the underlying junk is actually, well, junk, downgrades are also assured. Betting against the worst junk you can find is a good deal—if you can find a sucker to take the bet.

The theory behind shorting is that it lets you hedge risky assets in your portfolio, and it aids in price discovery. The first requires that you have actually got the asset you are shorting, the second relies on the now thoroughly discredited belief in the efficacy of markets. In truth, these markets are highly manipulated by insiders, subject to speculative fever, and mostly over the counter. That means that initial prices are set by sellers. Even in the case of MBSs—that actually have mortgages as collateral—buyers usually do not have access to essential data on the loans that will provide income flows. Once we get to tranches of MBSs, to CDOs, squared and cubed, and on to synthetic CDOs, we have leveraged and layered those underlying mortgages to a degree that it is pure fantasy to believe that markets can efficiently price them. Indeed, that was the reason for credit ratings, monoline insurance, and CDSs. CDSs that allow bets on synthetics that are themselves bets on MBSs held by others serve no social purpose whatsoever—they are neither hedges nor price discovery mechanisms.

The most famous shorter of MBSs was John Paulson, who approached Goldman to see if the firm could create some toxic synthetic CDOs that he could bet against. Of course, that would require that Goldman could find chump clients willing to buy junk CDOs—a task for which Goldman was well placed. According to the SEC, Goldman allowed Paulson to increase the probability of success by allowing him to suggest particularly trashy securities to include in the CDOs. Goldman arranged 25 such deals, named Abacus, totaling about $11 billion. Out of 500 CDOs analyzed by UBS, only two did worse than Goldman's Abacus. Just how toxic were these CDOs? Only 5 months after creating one of these Abacus CDOs, the ratings of 84% of the underlying mortgages had been downgraded. By betting against them, Goldman and Paulson won—Paulson pocketed $1 billion on the Abacus deals; he made a total of $5.7 billion shorting mortgage-based instruments in a span of 2 years. This is not genius work—84% to 96% of CDOs that are designed to fail will fail.

Paulson has not been accused of fraud—while he is accused of helping to select the toxic waste, he has not been accused of misleading investors in the CDOs he bet against. Goldman, on the other hand, never told investors that the firm was creating these CDOs specifically to meet the demands of Paulson for an instrument to allow him to bet against. The truly surprising thing is that Goldman's patsies actually met with Paulson as the deals were assembled—but Goldman never informed them that Paulson was the shorter of the CDOs they were buying! Goldman's defense amounted to little more than the argument that (1) these were big boys and (2) Goldman also lost money on the deals because it held a lot of the Abacus CDOs. If that is not exploitation of reputation by Goldman's management, one wonders what would qualify.

Remember the AIG bailout, of which $12.9 billion was passed-through to Goldman? AIG provided the CDSs that allowed Goldman and Paulson to short Abacus CDOs. So AIG was also duped, as was Uncle Sam—although that "sting" required the help of the New York Fed's Timmy Geithner. Even Goldman claimed to suffer losses on the deal. It must be remembered that when Hank Paulson ran Goldman, it was bullish on real estate; through 2006 it was accumulating MBSs and CDOs—including early Abacus CDOs. It then slowly dawned on Goldman that it was horribly exposed to toxic waste. At that point it started shorting the market, including the Abacus CDOs it held and was still creating. Thus, while it might be true that Goldman could not completely hedge its positions so that it got caught holding junk, that was not for lack of trying to push the risks onto its clients. Apparently, the market crashed before Goldman found a sufficient supply of buyers to allow it to short everything it held. Even vampire squids can get caught holding garbage.

Even if Goldman has been cleared of criminal activities (although along with the other "TBTF" institutions, it has paid huge fines for its activities), it does not do "God's work" as Goldman's CEO, Lloyd Blankfein famously claimed in 2009.

As another example, JPMorgan Chase suckered the Denver public school system into an exotic $750 million transaction that went horribly bad. In the spring of 2008, struggling with an underfunded pension system and the need to refinance some loans, it issued floating rate debt with a complicated derivative. Effectively, when rates rose, that derivative locked the school system into a high fixed rate. Morgan had put a huge "greenmail" clause into the deal—the school system is locked into a 30-year contract with a termination fee of $81 million. That, of course, is on top of the high fees Morgan had charged up front because of the complexity of the deal.

To add insult to injury, the whole fiasco began because the pension fund was short $400 million, and subsequent losses due to bad performance of its portfolio since 2008 wiped out almost $800 million—so even with the financing arranged by Morgan the pension fund is back even deeper in the hole in which it began with the school district levered in debt that it cannot afford but probably it also cannot afford to refinance on better terms because of the termination penalties. This experience was repeated all across America—the Service Employees International Union estimates that between 2008 and 2010, state and local governments have paid $28 billion in termination fees to get out of bad deals sold to them by Wall Street (see Morgenson and Story, 2010a, 2010b).

VIII. The Wall Street bailout

Just as the behavior of the financial institutions smells like fraud, the bailout by the Treasury and the Fed was problematic. A report details how Geithner's New York

Fed allowed Lehman Brothers to use an accounting gimmick to hide debt. The report, which runs to 2200 pages, was released by Anton Valukas, the court-appointed examiner. It actually makes the AIG bailout—that also was eye-brow raising—look tame by comparison.

In the depths of the crisis, the New York Fed arranged for AIG to pay 100 cents on the dollar on bad debts to its counterparties—benefiting Goldman Sachs and a handful of other favored Wall Street firms.[17] The purported reason is that Geithner (President of the NY Fed at the time) so feared any negative repercussions resulting from debt write-downs that he wanted Uncle Sam to make sure that Wall Street banks could not lose on bad bets. Geithner told Congress that he has never been a regulator. That might be an honest assessment of his job performance, although it is completely inaccurate as a description of his duties as President of the NY Fed. Geithner has denied that he played any direct role in the AIG bailout—a somewhat implausible claim given that he was the President of the NY Fed and given that this was a monumental and unprecedented action to funnel government funds to AIG's counterparties.

Later, we found that Geithner's NY Fed supported Lehman's efforts to conceal the extent of its problems (Smith, 2010). Not only did the NY Fed fail to blow the whistle on flagrant accounting tricks, it also helped to hide Lehman's illiquid assets on the Fed's balance sheet to make its position look better.

Note that the NY Fed had increased its supervision to the point that it was going over Lehman's books daily; further, it continued to take trash off the books of Lehman right up to the bitter end, helping to perpetuate the fraud that was designed to maintain the pretense that Lehman was not massively insolvent (Dash, 2010, *NYT*). Lehman executives claimed they "gave full and complete financial information to government agencies," and that the government never raised significant objections or directed that Lehman take any corrective action. In fairness, the SEC also overlooked any problems at Lehman (Smith, 2010).

But here is what is so astounding about the gimmicks: Lehman used "Repo 105" to temporarily move liabilities off its balance sheet—essentially pretending to sell them although it promised to immediately buy them back. The abuse was so flagrant that no US law firm would sign off on the practice, fearing that creditors and stockholders would have grounds for lawsuits on the basis that this caused a "material misrepresentation" of Lehman's financial statements. The court-appointed examiner hired to investigate the failure of Lehman found "materially misleading" accounting and "actionable balance sheet manipulation" (De la Merced, 2010, *NYT*). But just as Arthur Andersen had signed off on Enron's scams, Ernst & Young found no problem with Lehman (Nasiripour, 2010, *HP*). In short, this looks like an Enron-style sort of fraud. Lehman's had been using this trick since 2001. It looked fine to Geithner's

---

[17] See Wray on NEP here: https://neweconomicperspectives.org/2010/02/worst-revelation-yet-in-on-going.html and https://neweconomicperspectives.org/2009/11/why-is-obama-championing-bushs.html.

Fed, which extended loans allowing Lehman to flip bad assets onto the Fed's balance sheet.

More generally, this revelation drives home three related points. First, the scandal continued long after the crisis began. Point number two: Lehman used an innovation, "Repo 105" to hide debt. The whole Greek debt fiasco was abetted by Goldman et al., who helped hide government debt.[18] Whether legal or illegal, Wall Street has for many years been producing financial instruments designed to mislead shareholders, creditors, and regulators about the true financial position of its clients. Note that Lehman's counterparties in this fraud included JPMorgan and Citigroup (who precipitated Lehman's final failure when they finally called in their loans). It always takes at least three to tango: the firm that wants to hide debt, the counterparty that temporarily takes it off their books, and the accounting firm that provides the kiss of approval. Worse, after aiding and abetting such deception, Goldman and other Wall Street institutions then place bets (using another nefarious innovation, CDSs) against their clients, wagering that they will not be able to service the debts—which are greater than the market believes them to be. Does that sound something like insider trading? How can regulators permit such actions?

Third point: To the extent that debt is hidden, financial institution balance sheets present an overly rosy picture—of course, that is the purpose of the financial "innovations." Enron did it; AIG did it; Lehman did it. We now know that the New York Fed subjected Lehman to three wimpy "stress tests," all of which it failed. Geithner's Fed then allowed Lehman to construct its own sure-to-pass "stress" test. (We know, of course, that the test was absolutely meaningless because, well, Lehman passed the test and then immediately failed *spectacularly*.) Geithner then let the biggest banks run their own stress tests, which they (surprise, surprise) managed to pass.

To be clear, we are not saying that the crisis was caused by fraud. There has been a long-term transformation to create an environment in which fraud was encouraged. Incentives matter: deregulation and reliance on self-supervision were important; a long period without a great depression as well as prompt intervention by government to attenuate crises helped to reduce perceptions of risk; and globalization linked balance sheets so that a crisis in the United States would infect the entire world.

Further, there is the long-term growth of debt, especially household debt that made the entire economy more vulnerable. That is a complex issue that I have examined elsewhere (Wray, 2005a, 2005b), but in short it was encouraged not only by "democratization" of access to credit, but also by greater social acceptance of indebtedness (again in large part by absence of an experience like the Great Depression), and by stagnant growth of median real income in the United States (inequality of income and wealth reached and perhaps exceeded the 1929 record by 2009). Unions lost power, workers lost high paying jobs, unemployment (including those not counted in official statistics) and underemployment trended higher, and support

---

[18] See Wray on NEP "Memo To Greece: Make War Not Love With Goldman Sachs" and "Interview with Randall Wray about Greece's Debt Crisis."

for the poor declined—all of this increased reliance on debt to maintain livelihood even as it increased uncertainty that made people behave in what might appear to be irrational and self-destructive ways—but it really amounted to desperation.

So in short, the crisis resulted from a number of related factors and trends, and was a long-time coming. The Queen famously asked why economists did not see it coming. But some did. Minsky saw it coming by the late 1950s! He began writing about money manager capitalism in the 1980s. There are also many publications at the Levy Institute (by Godley and others) from the late 1990s and early 2000s that projected this collapse and in general outline captured many of the forces that brought it on. And there is plenty of evidence that traders on Wall Street also (accurately) foresaw the bust. However, each trader thought he would be able to sell out positions just in time to avoid losses. Of course, when all traders tried to sell, they all found that liquidity disappeared. Only the Fed and Uncle Sam would buy, or lend against, assets.

IX. Why we are screwed: it will happen again

After 1990, we removed what was left of financial regulations following the flurry of deregulation of the early 1980s that had freed the thrifts so that they could self-destruct. And we were shocked, *SHOCKED*! that thieves took over the financial system.

Nay, they took over the whole economy and the political system lock, stock, and barrel. They did not just blow up finance, they oversaw the swiftest transfer of wealth to the very top the world has ever seen. They screwed workers out of their jobs, they screwed homeowners out of their houses, they screwed retirees out of their pensions, and they screwed municipalities out of their revenues and assets.

Financiers forced schools, parks, pools, fire departments, senior citizen centers, and libraries to shut down. They forced national governments to auction off their cultural heritage to the highest bidder. Everything had to go in fire-sales at prices rigged by traders at the biggest institutions.

And since they have bought the politicians, the policymakers, and the courts, no one will stop it. Few will even discuss it, since most university administrations have similarly been bought off—in many cases, the universities are even headed by corporate "leaders"—and their professors are on Wall Street's payrolls.

We are screwed.

Bill Black joined me in the economics department at the University of Missouri-Kansas City in 2006. At UMKC (and the Levy Economics Institute) we had long been discussing and analyzing the coming crash that we *knew* was going to hit (with warnings issued as early as 1997), using the approaches of Hyman Minsky and Wynne Godley. Bill insisted we were overlooking the most important factor, fraud. To be more specific, as mentioned above, Bill calls it control fraud, where top corporate management runs an institution as a weapon to loot shareholders and customers to the benefit of top management. Think Bob Rubin, Hank Paulson,

Bernie Madoff, Jamie Dimon, and Jon Corzine. Long before, I had come across Bill's name when I wrote about the S&L scandal, and I had listed fraud as the second most important cause of that crisis. While I was open to his argument back in 2006, I could never have conceived of the scope of Wall Street's culpability and even depravity. The crisis was like Shrek's Onion, with fraud in every layer.

The fraud cannot be reduced much less eliminated. First, there are too few regulators to stop it, the regulations that exist are far too weak, and even where fraud is exposed, prosecutors rarely try to punish it. But, far more importantly, fraud *is* the business model—even if a financial institution tried to buck the trend it would fail. As Bill says, fraud is always the most profitable game in town. So Gresham's law dynamics ensure that fraud is the *only* game in town—to compete, you must engage in fraud.

As Robert Sherrill said, without regulation, capitalism is thievery. We essentially stopped regulating the financial system, so thieves took over.

A century ago, Thorstein Veblen analyzed religion as the quintessential capitalist undertaking. It sells an inherently ephemeral product that cannot be quality tested. Most of the value of that product exists only in the minds of the purchasers, and most of that value cannot be realized until death. Dissatisfied customers cannot return the purchased wares to the undertakers (Adam Smith's term for entrepreneurs—which is also French for undertaker) who sold them—there is no explicit money-back guarantee and in any event, most of the dissatisfied have already been "undertaken." The value of the undertaker's institution is similarly ephemeral, mostly determined by "goodwill." Aside from a fancy building, very little in the way of productive facilities is actually required by the religious undertaker.

But modern finance has replaced religion as the supreme capitalistic undertaking. Again, it has no need for production facilities—maybe a fancy building, a few Bloomberg screens, greasy snake oil salesmen, and some rapacious traders is all that is required to separate widows and orphans from their lifesavings and homes. Religious institutions only want 10%; Wall Street currently gets 20% of all the nation's output (and 40% of profits), but will not stop until it gets everything.

There is rarely any recourse for dissatisfied customers of financial institutions. Few customers understand what it is they are buying from Wall Street's undertakers. The product sold is infinitely more complicated than the Theory of the Trinity advanced by Theophilus of Antioch in 170 AD, let alone the Temple Garments (often called Magic Underwear by nonbelievers) marketed today. That makes it so easy to screw customers and to hide fraud behind complex instruments and deceptive accounting.

A handful of traders running a modern Wall Street firm might run up a trillion dollars in ephemeral assets whose worth is mostly determined by whatever value the traders assign to them.

And that is just the start. They also place tens of trillions of dollars of bets on "CDS" derivatives whose value is purely "notional." The financial sector gets paid when something goes wrong—the death of a homeowner, worker, firm, or country triggers payments on Death Settlements, Peasant Insurance, or CDSs (see below on these kinds of instruments). To ensure that death comes sooner rather than later, the undertaker works with the likes of John Paulson to handpick the most sickly households, firms, and governments to stand behind the derivative bets.

And the value of the Wall Street undertaker's firm is largely determined by euphemistically named "goodwill"—as if there is any good will in betting on death.

With these undertakers running the show, it is no wonder that we are buried under mountains of crushing debt—underwater mortgages, home equity loans, credit card debt, student loans, healthcare debts, and auto-related finance. Simply listing the kinds of debts we owe makes it clear how far along the path of financialization we have come: everything is financialized as Wall Street has its hand in every pot.

Thirty years ago we could still write of a dichotomy—industry versus finance—and categorize General Electric and General Motors as industrial firms, with Goldman Sachs as a financial firm. Those days are gone, with GM requiring a bailout because of its financial misdealings (auto production was a sideline business helpful in burdening households with debt owed to GMAC, the main business line), and Goldman Sachs buying up warehouses to run up commodities prices in a speculative bubble. Even the Democrats' greatest achievement of the past decade—Obamacare—simply fortifies the FIRE (finance, insurance, and real estate) sector's control of the healthcare industry as it inserts its strangling tentacles[19] into every facet of life.

Food? Financialized. Energy? Financialized. Healthcare? Financialized. Homes? Financialized. Government? Financialized. Death? Financialized. There no longer is a separation of the FIRE and the non-FIRE sectors of the economy. It is all FIRE.

Everything is complexly financed. In the old days a municipal government would sell a 20-year fixed rate bond to finance a sewage system project. Now they hire Wall Street to create complex interest rate swaps (or even more complex constant maturity swaps, "swaptions," and "snowballs") in which they issue a variable rate municipal bond and promise to pay Wall Street a fixed rate while Wall Street pays them a floating rate linked to LIBOR—which is rigged by the biggest banks to ensure the municipality gets screwed. Oh, and the municipal government pays upfront fees for the sheer joy of getting screwed by Wall Street's finest.

The top four US Banks hold $171 trillion worth of derivative deals like this. Derivatives are really just bets by Wall Street that we will lose—it is all "insurance" that pays off when we fail. Everything is insured—by them against us.

What is healthcare "insurance," really? You turn over a portion of your salary to Wall Street in the hope that should you need healthcare, Wall Street's insurance sector will allow your "service provider" to provide it. But when you need the service, Wall Street will decide whether it can be provided.

Oh, and Wall Street's undertakers have also placed a bet that you will die sooner than you expect, so it wins twice by denying the coverage.

---

[19] Cite to Matt Taibbi's vampire squid, "The Great American Bubble Machine" Rolling Stones April 5, 2010.

Finally, US real estate—the RE of the FIRE—underlies the whole kit and caboodle. That is the real story behind the GFC: given President Clinton's budget surpluses and the simultaneous explosion of private finance, there simply was not enough safe federal government debt to collateralize all the risky debt issued by financial institutions to one another back in the mid-1990s. Wall Street needed another source of collateral.

You see, the top financial institutions are dens of traders with questionable morals, and traders know better than to trust one another. So lending to fellow traders has to be collateralized by safe financial assets—which is the traditional role played by US Treasury bonds. But there were not enough of those to go around so Wall Street securitized home mortgages that were sliced and diced to get tranches that were supposedly as safe as Uncle Sam's bonds. And there were not enough quality mortgages, so Wall Street foisted mortgages and home equity loans onto riskier borrowers to create more products—dicey "subprime" mortgages that were securitized.

Never content, in order to suck more profit out of mortgages, Wall Street created "affordability" products—mortgages with high fees and exploding interest rates—that it knew would go bad. Even that was not enough, so Wall Street created derivatives of the securities (CDO) and then derivatives squared and cubed—and then we were off and running straight toward the GFC.

Wall Street bet your house would burn, then lit a firebomb in the basement.

Mortgages that were designed to go bad would go bad. CDOs that were designed to fail would fail.

Suddenly, there was no collateral behind the loans Wall Street's finest had made to one another. Each Wall Street trader looked in the mirror and realized everything he was holding was crap because he knew all of his own debt was crap.

Hello Uncle Sam, Uncle Timmy,[20] and Uncle Ben,[21] we have got a problem. Can you spare $29 trillion to bail us out?

It worked—at least for Wall Street. The rest of us? Not so much. And that is why we are screwed.

I see two scenarios playing out. In the first, we continue to allow Wall Street to carry on its merry way, as the foreclosure crisis continues and Wall Street seizes homes, packaging them into bundles to be sold for pennies on the dollar to hedge funds. Since it was hard to get another housing bubble going, Wall Street applied all the same practices to all our other debts: student loans, auto loans, and credit card debt—all packaged, securitized, tranched, CDO-ed, and CDS-ed. The crash is inevitable, only the timing is uncertain.

All wealth will continue to be redistributed to the top 1% who will become modern-day feudal lords with the other 99% living at their pleasure on huge feudal estates.

---

[20] Geithner, head of the NY Fed and then Secretary of the Treasury.
[21] Ben Bernanke, head of the Board of Governors of the Fed.

You can imagine for yourselves just what you are going to have to do to pleasure the lords.

This will take years, maybe even decades, but it is the long march Wall Street has formulated for us. To be sure, "formulated" should not be misinterpreted as intention. No one sat down and planned the creation of Western European feudalism when Rome collapsed. Now, the modern-day feudal lords on Wall Street certainly conspire—to rig LIBOR and muni bond markets, for example—and each one individually wants to take as much as possible from customers and creditors and stockholders. But they are not planning and conspiring for the restoration of feudalism. Still, that is the default scenario—the outcome that will emerge in the absence of action.

In the second scenario, the 99% occupy, shut down, and obliterate Wall Street. There is no chance that will happen before the next GFC. Wall Street's power was restored with the bailout.

However, GFC Round Two will offer up the opportunity once again—an opportunity the fledgling Obama administration refused to seize when it had the chance. The only hope is to follow the lead of the Roosevelt administration—which upon taking office immediately declared a "banking holiday" and took over the financial system.

Next time, Wall Street must be hit when it is down. "Reform" is impossible after a rescue.

X. Did we learn anything from the crisis?

In a word, no.

Or, at least, not much.

Here is what we *should have learned*, as we mark the dozen-years anniversary of the event that sparked the crisis.

1. The crisis exposed the dangerous and lawless culture prevailing at the world's biggest financial institutions. We now know, beyond any doubt, that it was fraud from bottom to top. For example, every single step in the MBS business was fraudulent. The mortgage originations were fraudulent—with the originators lying to borrowers about the terms, and then crudely doctoring the paperwork to make the terms even worse after borrowers had signed. The property appraisers falsified the home values. The investment banks misrepresented the quality of the mortgages as they were securitized. The trustees lied to the buyers of the securities about possession of the proper paperwork. At the urging of the industry's creation, MERS, the banks lost or destroyed the property records, making it impossible to know in the case of many homes who owns what and who owes whom. The mortgage servicers "lost" payments and illegally foreclosed using documents forged by "robo-signers," wrongly evicting even homeowners who owed no mortgage. Those homes were sold in huge blocks to

hedge funds at cents on the dollar so that they can be rented back to the former owners. It is not too much to say that foreclosure and dispossession was the desired result of what President Bush had called the "ownership society": move all wealth to the top 1%. This is just one example—you will find a similar level of deception in every line of business undertaken by the biggest banks, from manipulating bond markets to setting LIBOR rates, from manipulating commodity prices to front-running stocks and trading on insider information. Over the decade following the crisis, the biggest banks were fined time after time for these frauds.

2. The crisis demonstrated that real reform can only be undertaken in the depths of a crisis. Once Wall Street had been rescued behind closed doors by the US Fed and Treasury (it took $29 trillion!) (Felkerson, 2011), there was no hope of reform. The biggest institutions just got bigger. They are back to doing the same things they were doing in 2007. Even the very weak Dodd-Frank reforms were not and will never be fully implemented—Wall Street put together armies to delay, water-down, and eventually prevent implementation of changes that would constrain the financial practices that caused the crisis. Franklin Roosevelt did it the right way in the 1930s: declare a banking "holiday," demand resignations from all top management, and refuse to allow banks to open until they had a plan that would lead to solvency. Almost all the New Deal financial sector reforms were enacted in the heat of the crisis. The important lesson that should have been learned: in the next crisis, we cannot let the Fed and Treasury meet behind closed doors to rescue the "vampire squids" that are destroying the economy. We must drive the stake through their hearts when they are weakest.

3. The crisis brought into public view the longer term trend toward "financialization" of the entire economy. The FIRE sector gets 40% of corporate profits and 20% of value added. That is, quite simply, crazy. Everything has become financialized—from college education (student loans are nearing a trillion and a half dollars) to homes, healthcare (Obamacare makes this worse), and even death (so-called death settlements and peasant insurance in which employers bet that workers will die early). Wall Street has financialized energy and even crops. It has turned worker's pensions against them, by using their own retirement funds to bid up the price of gasoline at the pump and bread at the grocery store. Just wait until they use pension funds to drive up the price of water at the meter!

In a very important sense it is wrong to label what happened following Lehman's bust a crisis. Life at the top has improved tremendously since 2007, as high unemployment has softened labor even as income and wealth gushed toward the top 1%.

Of course, for the bottom 99% it is a crisis, but not a financial crisis. And it did not begin in 2007, but rather in the early 1970s. It is a long-term jobs crisis. It is a long-term wage crisis. It is a long-term education, housing, and healthcare crisis, as necessities are priced beyond the reach of most workers.

So what needs to be done?

Mayer, M., 1990. The Greatest-Ever Bank Robbery: The Collapse of the Savings and Loan Industry. Charles Scribner's Sons, New York.

Minsky, H.P., 1975. John Maynard Keynes. Columbia University Press.

Minsky, H.P., 1986. Stabilizing An Unstable Economy. Yale University Press.

Minsky, Hyman, 1996. Uncertainty and the Institutional Structure of Capitalist Economies, 155. Levy Economics Institute, WP, p. 4. April.

Minsky, H.P., 1992a. The Capital Development of the Economy and the Structure of Financial Institutions. WP 72. Levy Economics Institute of Bard College.

Morgenson, G., Story, L., 2010a. Investor who made billions is not target of suit. New York Times. April 16.

Morgenson, G., Story, L., 2010b. SEC accuses Goldman of fraud in housing deal. New York Times. April 16.

Minsky, H.P., 1992b. The Financial Instability Hypothesis. WP 74. The Levy Economics Institute of Bard College.

Morgenson, G., Story, L., 2009. Banks bundled bad debt, bet against it, and won. New York Times. December 24.

Nasiripour, S., November 2010. Lehman bankruptcy report: Top officials manipulated balance sheets, JPMorgan and citi contributed to collapse. The Huffington Post. https://www.huffpost.com/entry/lehman-bankruptcy-report_n_495668?guccounter=2link. last accessed Aug 31,2019.

Nedelsky, J., 1990. Private Property and the Limits of American Constitutionalism: The Madisonian Framework and Its Legacy. University of Chicago Press, Chicago, p. 68.

Nersisyan, Y., Wray, L.R., 2010a. The Global Financial Crisis and the Shift to Shadow Banking. WP 587. Levy Economics Institute.

Nersisyan, Y., Wray, L.R., 2010b. Deficit Hysteria Redux? Why We Should Stop Worrying About U.S. Government Deficits. Economics Public Policy Brief Archive ppb_111. Levy Economics Institute.

Nocera, J., 2010. A Wall Street invention let the crisis mutate. New York Times. April 16.

Nersisyan, Y., Wray, L.R., 2010c. The global financial crisis and the shift to shadow banking. European Journal of Economics and Economic Policies: Intervention (Edward Elgar Publishing).

Papadimitriou, D.B., Wray, L.R., 1998. The Economic Contributions of Hyman Minsky: Varieties of Capitalism and Institutional Reform. Macroeconomics 9802018. University Library of Munich, Germany.

Smith, Adam, 1937. An Inquiry into the Causes of the Wealth of Nations. The Modern Library, New York, p. 674.

Sherman, H., 1991. The Business Cycle: Growth and Crisis under Capitalism. Princeton University Press, Princeton, NJ.

Smith, Yves, March 2010. "NY Fed under Geithner implicated in Lehman accounting fraud allegation" Naked Capitalism last accessed Aug 31, 2019. https://www.nakedcapitalism.com/2010/03/ny-fed-under-geithner-implicated-in-lehman-accounting-fraud.html.

Story, L., 2010. Investment firm agrees to settle kickback inquiry. New York Times. April 15.

Tymoigne, E., Wray, L.R., 2009. It Isn't Working: Time for More Radical Policies. Economics Public Policy Brief Archive ppb_105. Levy Economics Institute.

Wojnilower, A., 1980. The central role of credit crunches in recent financial history. Brookings Papers on Economic Activity (2), 277−326.

Wolfson, M., 1994. Financial Crises: Understanding the Postwar U.S. Experience. M.E. Sharpe, Armonk, New York and London.

Wray, L.R., 1994. The political economy of the current US financial crisis. International Papers in Political Economy 1 (3), 1—51.

Wray, L.R., 2005a. Manufacturing a Crisis: The Neocon Attack on Social Security. Policy Note 2005/2. The Levy Economics Institute.

Wray, L.R., 2005b. The Ownership Society: Social Security Is Only the Beginning. Public Policy Brief No. 82. Levy Economics Institute.

Wray, L.R., 2008a. Financial Markets Meltdown: What Can We Learn from Minsky. PPB 94. Levy Economics Institute of Bard College, Annandale-on-Hudson, NY.

Wray, L.R., March 2011. Minsky's money manager capitalism and the global financial crisis" WP 661. Levy Economics Institute of Bard College, p. 6.

Wray, L.R., 2008b. The Commodities Market Bubble: Money Manager Capitalism and the Financialization of Commodities. Public Policy Brief 96. Levy Economics Institute of Bard College, Annandale-on Hudson, NY.

Further reading

Black, W.K., 2009. Why Is Obama Championing Bush's Financial Wrecking Crew? New Economic Perspectives.

Ferguson, T., Johnson, R., 2009. Too big to bail: the 'Paulson Put', presidential politics and the global financial meltdown, Part 1: from shadow financial system to shadow bailout. International Journal of Political Economy 38 (1).

Matt, P., November 9, 2009. Goldman Sachs' Blankfein on banking: doing god's work. The Wall Street Journal.

Minsky, H.P., 2008a. [1975] John Maynard Keynes. McGraw Hill, New York.

Minsky, H.P., 2008b. [1986] Stabilizing an Unstable Economy. McGraw Hill, New York.

Nersisyan, Yeva, Wray, L. Randall, March 2010. The Global Financial Crisis and the Shift to Shadow Banking, 587. Levy Economics Institute, WP.

Sherrill, R., October 9, 2008. "Thievery is what unregulated capitalism is all about" "S&Ls, big banks and other triumphs of capitalism". The Nation.

Tymoigne, E., 2010. The Financial Crisis: Subprime or Systemic? In: Gregoriou, G.N. (Ed.), The Banking Crisis. Taylor and Francis, London.

Veblen, T., 1958. The Theory of Business Enterprise. A Mentor Book. The New American Library of World Literature, New York.

Wray, L.R., 2006. Can Basel II Enhance Financial Stability? Public Policy Brief No. 84 Levy Economics Institute.

Wray, L.R., 2009. The rise and fall of money manager capitalism: a Minskian approach. Cambridge Journal of Economics 33, 807—828.

Wray, L.R., 2010a. Memo to Greece: Make War not Love with Goldman Sachs. New Economic Perspectives; Interview with Randall Wray about Greece's Debt Crisis. New Economic Perspectives, 2010.

Wray, L.R., 2010b. Worst Revelation Yet in the On-Going Goldman-AIG-NY Fed Scandal. New Economic Perspectives.

The road to social progress

B

In this part we examine policy to enhance social and economic security. On January 6, 1941 President Roosevelt laid out his vision for promoting social progress:

In the future days, which we seek to make secure, we look forward to a world founded upon four essential human freedoms. The first is freedom of speech and expression—everywhere in the world. The second is freedom of every person to worship god in his own way—everywhere in the world. The third is freedom from want ... everywhere in the world. The fourth is freedom from fear ... anywhere in the world. That is no vision of a distant millennium. It is a definite basis for a kind of world attainable in our own time and generation.

On June 12, 2019, in the early days of the 2020 campaign for president, Bernie Sanders gave a speech that invoked the words of FDR as he laid out the challenges faced by America and the world:

My friends, we are in the midst of a defining and pivotal moment for our country and our planet. And, with so many crises converging upon us simultaneously, it is easy for us to become overwhelmed or depressed—or to even throw up our hands in resignation. But my message to you today is that if there was ever a moment in the history of our country where despair was not an option, this is that time.

Over eighty years ago Franklin Delano Roosevelt helped create a government that made transformative progress in protecting the needs of working families. Today, in the second decade of the 21st century, we must take up the unfinished business of the New Deal and carry it to completion.

As FDR stated in his 1944 State of the Union address: "We have come to a clear realization of the fact that true individual freedom cannot exist without economic security and independence."

In this Part we will focus on FDR's third freedom—freedom from want—although we recognize that satisfaction of this want is inextricably linked with the other three freedoms. If the basic wants—including adequate food, clothing, shelter, education, and healthcare—are not met, the others cannot be fully realized either. We will address policy related to old age security and universal access to healthcare in Part B. In Part C we will examine employment for all who want to work and the challenges we face due to rising inequality. In Part D we will address the challenges facing our species, and indeed, our planet, due to climate change.

A Great Leap Forward. https://doi.org/10.1016/B978-0-12-819380-8.00002-6

I. Aging, social security, and pensions

a. Demographics and infinite horizon calculations of burdens

Demographers agree that we are aging—individually and collectively, nationally and globally. An aging population results from the twin demographic forces of fewer children per family and longer lives. Most experts recognize the burden that aging causes as the number of retirees supported by each worker rises. This trend is reinforced by the graying of the baby boom generation, but burdens will continue to rise even after the boomers are buried—albeit at a slower pace.

Three key statistics are commonly quoted to reinforce the extent of the demographic and economic challenges that lie ahead. First, the rising "real burden" is most directly highlighted by noting that the ratio of workers to retirees will fall from three to two during the next 75 years.

Second, we can get some idea of the future "financial burden" by projecting the year in which total Social Security revenues will first fall short of benefit payments, at which time benefits purportedly will have to be cut or tax burdens on workers increased.[1] Based on current projections, benefit levels, and tax rates, that happens sometime in the 2040s.[2]

Finally, in recent years it has become fashionable to estimate projected Social Security shortfalls infinitely far into the future, based on the argument that this provides a better idea of the financial burden of the program imposed on all future generations (Kotlikoff and Burns, 2005).This is called "intergenerational accounting", which calculates the program's expected spending and revenue over an infinite number of years and then discounts the shortfall by an assumed interest rate. In 2004 Kotlikoff estimated the infinite horizon shortfall of US "entitlement programs" to equal $51 trillion. Most of that was due to Medicare, with Social Security accounting for $10 trillion. However, a dozen years later he put the total shortfall of government entitlements at a staggering $210 trillion (Mauldin, 2017).

Projections covering a period as long as 75 years—let alone projections through eternity—are of necessity quite uncertain. Such forecasts require assumptions about future fertility rates, longevity, inflation, interest rates, labor productivity, GDP and wage growth, immigration, disability rates, labor force participation and unemployment rates, and so on.

Who would have imagined back in the early 1960s—when the typical American family had 3.7 children and the typical Chinese family had 6 kids,[3] causing

---

[1] Here, total revenue includes payroll tax revenues, interest earned on the trust fund, and sales of trust fund assets.

[2] As most baby boomers will be dead by the 2040s, this drives home the point that the problem is the general aging of the population, not the postwar baby bulge.

[3] See "The Effects of China's universal two-child policy", www.thelancet.com, vol. 388, October 15, 2016, pp. 1930−1938. By 1979, when the two-child policy was implemented, the fertility rate had fallen to about 3 children and continued to fall to just 1.7 by 2004—which is well below replacement rate (implying an eventually falling population).

demographic experts to worry about the "population bomb"[4]—that by the 21st century birthrates among native born American females would fall to about two, so low that we would have to rely on immigration (and higher birthrates among immigrants) to avoid a shrinking population? Who would have predicted China's "one child" policy that was so successful that it had to be reversed because of a dearth of young people and the prospect of a shrinking population?

How many kids will the typical household have in 2094? What will be the labor force participation rate of married women in the 2060s? Will the rate of productivity growth in the 2070s be higher or lower than it was in the 1970s? No honest economist would pretend to know the answers.

Back in 2006 I asked one of the foremost proponents of the use of infinite-horizon calculations to leave to the side all of these uncertainties. I suggested that he imagine he had received divine confirmation that all the "intermediate cost" assumptions used by the Social Security Trustees in their long-range, 75-year projections will turn out to be accurate. Is there anything we might do today, I asked, that would reduce the real burden of supporting retirees in the year 2081? After a thoughtful silence, he provided an impeccably reasoned, two-word, response: "more capital."

To an economist, this means a combination of more human capital (education and training), more public capital (infrastructure such as roads, public buildings, and airports), and more private capital (productive plant and equipment, farms, telecommunications, infrastructure, etc.).Of course, no economist could disagree: more capital would mean greater productive capacity available to reduce the burden of providing for tomorrow's elders.

But is it that simple?

No one doubts that the United States would reap current and future benefits from improvements to our educational system, which is presumably the main source of improvements to human capital. While our universities are widely considered to be the best in the world, and while the percent of our population that has attended at least 2 years of college is rising inexorably, experts concede that large segments of our population are inadequately educated for our current economy—much less for the economy of the future. High school dropout rates remain high (for a rich country), dooming too many young people to sporadic work in low-paying jobs—or worse, to life on the margins of society, often under the control of the criminal justice system (Pigeon and Wray, 1999).

The problem is that while there are innumerable proposals to enhance education and training, we are far from consensus on what works: More money? Stay-in-school programs? No Child Left Behind? More testing? Less testing? School vouchers? Integration? Community-based schools? Magnet schools? Afrocentric education? While we can agree that "more human capital" will reduce future

---

[4] See Paul Ehrlich, *The Population Bomb* 1968; the book predicted worldwide famine in the 1970s and 1980s due to overpopulation.

burdens of aging, that statement tells us nothing about which policy initiatives will bring about the desired result.

More fundamentally, let us suppose that we did not have an aging society—that the age distribution would not change, or even that the nation would become younger. Would we then oppose "more human capital"? Of course, we would not. We need a more productive labor force today and into the future—whether we have more elderly people to support or not.

Hence, even if we knew that the projections of the trustees would turn out to be correct, it is hard to see why that should change the level of human capital desired. The only difference that such divine confirmation would make is about the type of human capital developed.

For example, an aging society will presumably require more healthcare (specifically, more eldercare) workers. However, we do not need to know the age distribution of the population in 2081, or even in 2041, to realize that policy needs to encourage human capital investment in these areas. We already have critical shortages of such workers, which are only partially relieved through immigration. It is obvious that current policy in this area is woefully inadequate—irrespective of distant demographic trends.

Public infrastructure can increase the quality of life and reduce the burden on future workers by enhancing private sector productivity. Further, at least some types of public infrastructure are exceedingly long-lived. With proper maintenance, dams, highways, levees, bridges, water delivery systems, and waste management systems can remain serviceable for half a century or more. Thus, "more public infrastructure" certainly appears to be good advice for an aging society.

Still, there is great uncertainty involved in projecting infrastructure needs for the far distant future. Will workers and seniors in 2081 still rely on individual internal combustion—propelled transportation devices that ride on rubber in contact with asphalt? Will the greatest need for expansion of water treatment facilities over the next 75 years occur in North Dakota or in Rhode Island? Assuming we will need new bridges in Florida to handle traffic flows in 2060, do we begin now, or wait until 2055?

Moreover, if the population were not aging, should we forgo increased public infrastructure investment? Again, no one would (or, at least, should) adopt that line of argument. As with the case of human capital, the aging of society does not change the need for more public investment, although aging changes the nature of the needed infrastructure. We need more senior housing, more long-term care facilities, and more senior citizen recreational centers—just to take care of today's seniors.

These types of public investments can be long-lived. Further, some of the existing capital stock (hospitals, apartment buildings, schools) can be renovated as needed to accommodate growing numbers of seniors. Hence, it makes sense to increase the supply of infrastructure that serves elders through new construction as well as rehabilitation of existing facilities. And the time to begin is now.

Again, we do not need high-powered think tanks to tell us that public investment in infrastructure construction and maintenance has been inadequate for the past three or four decades—whether we are aging or not. Just ask the victims of hurricanes Katrina, Rita, Irma, and Michael.

The American Society of Civil Engineers provides an annual estimate of the infrastructure deficit, which now amounts to about a $2.0 trillion 10-year investment gap (2017)—and the report card gives the United States a D+ for its infrastructure. My own crude estimate of the discounted value of that deficit from now until the sweet hereafter amounts to a gazillion dollars. It is truly amazing that Social Security "reformers" have spent so much time calculating the supposed infinite-horizon financial shortfall of that program (which has run huge fiscal surpluses since the Reagan years), while ignoring the very real, obvious, and current infrastructure deficit that burdens everyone today.

Finally, we turn to private investment in plant, equipment, provision of services, and farming. Fifty years ago, economists liked to pretend that investment was like "putty"—highly pliable, so that it could be adapted to any technology and produce any type of output.[5] In truth, most private capital is inflexible in both respects: hard to upgrade and designed to produce specific products or services. The longer the horizon, the more difficult it becomes to adapt plant and equipment to new technologies and new products.

Thus, even if capital put in place today could continue to produce output over the next 75 years, it is highly unlikely that it would be appropriate to our needs at that time. Many of the problems I raised with regard to investing in public infrastructure today for the elderly persons of 2095 apply with much greater force to private investment.

Further, private investment is undertaken with a view to making a profit. Government could conceivably build a dam today that will not be needed until 2045. No private firm would build plant and equipment today on the expectation that it will find a demand for its output in 2030—let alone 2095. Hence, even if we removed all uncertainty over future technologies and baskets of goods consumers will demand, firms will not invest today to meet demand by seniors even a relatively few years down the road.

The problem, then, is not simply uncertainty about the future, or even the problem of finite lives of capital goods. "More capital" cannot be a recommended solution to far distant burdens because firms will invest more today only if demand for the relevant products is forthcoming today (or in the very near future).

The benefits of increasing private investment, and thus raising productive capacity, are no less obvious than recommendations to increase human capital and public

---

[5] This was the tactic adopted by those who took the neoclassical side in the "Capital Controversy" debates of the 1960s (Samuelson, Solow) against the Keynesians (Joan Robinson). The neoclassicals lost the debate although they continued to preach the discredited marginal productivity views. See https://harvardlawreview.org/2014/12/the-laws-of-capitalism/ for a recent update of the critique.

infrastructure. But, again, it is easy to support this course of action even if the society were not aging. And, again, it is very difficult to come up with actual private investment projects that will reduce the burden on workers of supporting retirees even 25 years into the future, let alone 75 years into the future. Certainly, we will need greater production of pharmaceutical products, wheelchairs and other mobility devices, private eldercare facilities, aged-friendly vehicles, and so on. Indeed, we need that today. What is holding back private investment is—mostly—insufficient demand today for such products, which is due, at least in part, to insufficient income of today's seniors.

Nor is it the business of business to plan for demographic events that might occur in a half century. If any institution ought to plan that far ahead, it should be the federal government.

The favored solution to insufficient private investment is "more saving." Indeed, many of the proposed "reforms" to Social Security have always included some sort of tax incentive scheme to promote more saving. If we lived in an economy that suffered from chronic supply constraints—say, the former Soviet Union before its breakup—this might make some sense. We would want to encourage consumers to reduce their spending, thus freeing up resources that could be redirected by economic planners to produce investment goods that would lead to increased production of products needed by our aging population.

But the United States is not the USSR! Investment in the private production of products for today's, and tomorrow's, seniors is rarely—if ever—restrained by inability to purchase resources, including labor. What constrains investment is demand for the output that will be produced by the new private capital as soon as it comes on line. And if we got consumers to cut consumption, that would discourage investment, not encourage it.

Finally, even according to the conventional estimates made by advocates of tax-advantaged savings plans, the effects of such schemes on savings, investment, and growth are too small to make much difference. Inasmuch as today's investment has to be related to perceived demand for output either today or in the very near future, we are left with the conclusion that any proposal to resolve future burdens of aging through "more saving" will at best amount to "much ado about nothing".

Ironically, the economist who recommended "more capital" as the solution to the rising burden of caring for the elderly also argued that faster economic growth would worsen the Social Security crisis! His analysis was complex, rigorous, and correct—on its own terms. To put it simply, given low birth rates, rising longevity, and the way that Social Security benefits are calculated (based on earnings),the discounted financial gap between total benefits paid out and payroll tax revenues received, calculated over an infinite horizon, will be *higher* if GDP and wages grow faster. Hence, those who rely on infinite horizon calculations must argue against economic growth as a solution to our aging problem!

This conflict between his intuition that more capital (and hence more real output) would reduce future burdens and the results from his infinite-horizon model, which implied that more growth makes things worse, should have led him to drop the model in favor of common sense. What matters is the real burden, not any "financial burden" implied by "actuarial gaps". Ability to produce more real stuff in the future is the key to reducing the real burden of taking care of more elderly people. But common sense can be a scarce resource among economists.

Actually, the projected increase of the real burden resulting from aging is far too small to mount a serious challenge to our nation's ability to produce enough output so that workers, retirees, and other dependents will have a significant and steady increase of real living standards (Wray, 2005; Papadimitriou and Wray, 1999a). On current projections, the number of workers per retiree falls from about three today to about two in the future; however, worker productivity is projected by Social Security's Trustees to quadruple over the same period. We will have so much more real stuff produced that both our workers and our retirees of the future will enjoy much more real consumption than we do today.

Further, the workers of the future will have fewer children to support (on current projections), so that the total dependency ratio (elderly plus young relative to working-age populations) will rise only to the level we already achieved back in the mid-1960s. Our workers of the 1960s not only handled the burden of supporting more dependents than we do today, but they also enjoyed rapidly rising living standards themselves. Since then, the dependency ratio fell (due to fewer young people per worker) and is now growing slowly (due to rising numbers of elderly people) to a peak just below where it already has been. And remember that workers of the future will be 4 times more productive than they are today. That cannot represent a catastrophic rise of the "real" burden!

Further, even the financial burden will not rise much; on current projections, the share of national GDP that will have to be shifted to Social Security benefits rises by only 2% points (from about 4.5% to about 6.5% of GDP)—and we have already achieved shifts that large twice since the program was enacted. Again, that cannot represent an insurmountable burden. In any case, many supporters of Social Security have come up with numerous easy fixes that will allow us to maintain a balance between benefits and revenues, if such is desired. (In the next section we return to the issue of "financial fixes".)

In this section we have sought only to answer a seemingly simple question: given that the real burden will rise, is there anything we can begin to do today to attenuate that increase? The answer seems to be that we should essentially follow the same policy prescriptions that would make sense even if our society were not aging: (1) more human capital: more years of schooling, fewer dropouts, higher quality schooling, and enhanced apprenticeship and training programs; (2) more public investment: new and improved public infrastructure, better maintenance of existing infrastructure, and reduction of adverse environmental impacts; and (3) more private investment: new and improved private production facilities to enhance growth.

The last item will almost certainly require maintenance of higher aggregate demand today and over the near future in order to encourage private investment. All of this is quite sensible, although it bears no relation to the ongoing debate in Washington about "reforming" Social Security. That misguided debate focuses almost exclusively on the "financing gap" and on "financial fixes"—such as private accounts that are supposed to grow with the stock market at a pace so fast that tomorrow's seniors will have the financial wherewithal to buy what they need. In truth, if there really were a looming crisis in Social Security's future, any financial fixes would amount to nothing more than rearranging deck chairs on the Titanic, unless they reduce future real burdens.

However, no one has made a strong case that financial fixes can reduce future real burdens. To do so the reforms would have to reduce the number of future elders, increase the number of future workers, or increase the productivity of future workers. Yet Social Security's "reformers" have yet to provide an argument that their reforms would (Heaven forbid!) shorten the lives of tomorrow's seniors, nor that they would increase birthrates—indeed, most policymakers would reject out of hand any proposals to accomplish either of these outcomes. Hence, all reforms must be geared toward increasing productivity, which comes down to encouraging more capital formation.

Yet, as we have argued here, that advice provides virtually no useful guidance to policymakers. Further, the types of investments that can be made today to reduce burdens in the distant future are in human capital and public infrastructure. That is to say, the investments must be undertaken primarily by government. Yet the reformers seek to reduce the role of government and increase reliance on the market—which by its very nature is focused on the here and now, not on infinite horizons.

To move forward in the discussion about aging, in general, or Social Security, in particular, each reformer should be forced to outline in detail how his or her proposals will generate "more capital" specifically suited to the projected needs in 2045, 2095, and beyond. Any reform that fails to provide specifics should be dismissed as "much ado about nothing." To be sure, we can expect our society to continue to age (although growth of the ratio of aged to those of working age will slow considerably before we reach the end of the 75 "long range" forecast), and that will mean fewer workers per retiree. Although it amounts to "something", the rise of real burdens is small given projected productivity increases, and there is not a lot that can be done, or needs to be done, in the foreseeable future, anyway.

b. How to pay for social security: truth and fictions

There is no question that Social Security has been under attack by well-organized and well-funded opponents for the past half century, and that this has paid off in terms of stoking fear among the young that they may never collect a dime. In this section we examine the development of the narrative that the program will run out of money.

Social Security turns 85 in 2020. While our nation's most successful social program, and among its longest lived, has allowed generations of Americans to live with dignity in retirement, many think it is time to retire Social Security itself. They claim it is necessary to shift more responsibility to individuals and to scale back the promises made to the coming wave of retiring baby boomers. Of course, Social Security has always had its enemies—who have long seen it as pinko socialism or even red communism. However, a new wave of concern focuses instead on Social Security's finances—it is said to be running out of money.

On current projections, Social Security's income falls short of spending on benefits in 2020 for the first time since the early 1980s when the Reagan administration had boosted payroll taxes. That means the Trustees will begin to sell bonds from its Trust Funds to finance the shortfall. By 2035 Social Security will have exhausted its savings; with no more bonds to sell it faces a financial gap of about a fifth of its spending. As Fox News put it, "Social Security will run out of money in 2035".

Even the nonpartisan Social Security Administration has been enlisted in the effort to lower expectations, posting on its website the following caution:"Unless changes are made, when you reach age 62 in 2041, benefits for all retirees could be cut by 26 percent and could continue to be reduced every year thereafter. If you lived to be 100 years old in 2079 (which will be more common by then), your scheduled benefits could be reduced by 32 percent from today's scheduled levels." Private accounts, lower benefits, and—perhaps—higher taxes are the prescribed remedy for "unfunded" trillions of commitments we have made to tomorrow's seniors.

As Max Skidmore has documented, the enemies of the program have been there from the beginning, but they had little success until the 1980s and 1990s (Skidmore, 1999). Originally, the program was criticized on the basis that it was socialistic. However, the framers of the Social Security Act anticipated such claims and consequently formulated the program as if it were an insurance plan, with payroll taxes that could be counted as "contributions" and "benefit payments" that bore some relation to the contributions. Americans came to believe that they earned benefits because they "paid into" the program. And because the program was never means tested, it enjoyed wide support. Hence, rather than socialistic welfare, the program has been viewed as little different from a pension plan. For several decades, this misconception effectively quashed criticism, so the program was expanded over the years, rather than cut—providing more generous benefits to dependents, survivors, and people with disabilities (Wray, 2001). However, beginning in the 1980s, the critics seized on an apparent weakness. Slower economic growth after 1970, lower birth rates, longer life spans, and especially the coming retirement of a wave of baby boomers all supposedly threatened the long-run financial viability of Social Security.

The enemies of the program formulated a two-pronged attack. First, they began a campaign to convince younger people that because of shaky finances they would never collect benefits equal to what they paid into the program (Skidmore, 1999). This became an increasingly easy sell for younger, high-income workers because the redistributive aspects of the program provide fairly low "money's worth" returns for the "pension" provided by Social Security.[6] (Note that the debate mostly ignored all the "nonpension" aspects of the program, such as disability and survivors' benefits, which make it a good deal for just about all Americans.)

Second, the Greenspan Commission was formed in 1983 with an aim of resolving supposed long-run financial problems with "reforms" that included large payroll tax increases and a gradual rise of the normal age of retirement (Papadimitriou and Wray, 1999b). These changes reinforced the claim that Social Security was a bad deal for younger workers, who were already seeing take-home pay fall during a period in which organized labor was under attack by the Reagan administration.

After the Greenspan Commission had purportedly "solved" the financial problems, the Social Security Administration adopted increasingly pessimistic assumptions for its long-run forecasts, even as it ran huge surpluses—as documented by (Skidmore 2001) and by actuary (David Langer 2000). Not surprisingly, a "looming financial crisis" reappeared, and hysteria about reforming Social Security was revived. Taxes would have to be raised, benefits would have to be cut, and, more importantly, the return on Trust Fund assets would have to be increased. As the stock market performed well throughout most of the 1980s and then picked up the pace in the 1990s, the enemies saw a chance to privatize the program while playing the role of savior. The system would be "privatized", with payroll taxes handed over to Wall Street to increase returns.

At the same time, the "friends" of Social Security, mostly Democrats and Big Labor, also saw a chance to exploit popular fears. They would play along with the enemies, pretending there really was a financial problem, so that they could "save" Social Security from the imaginary shortfalls and thereby win votes. Polls consistently showed that voters trusted Democrats more on Social Security; hence, given a choice between Republican schemes to "save" the program through privatization or Democratic plans to "save" it by boosting the Trust Funds, the voters would choose the Democrats.

I have been writing about Social Security since the late 1980s, and in 1990, I published a critique of *Can America Afford to Grow Old?* a book by Henry Aaron, Barry P. Bosworth, and Gary Burtless that argued that the only way to take care of baby boomers would be to immediately increase national saving (Wray, 1990−1991; Aaron et al., 1989; Aaron, 1990−1991). This could be done, according to the authors, by running budget surpluses, adding to national savings, and increasing the

---

[6] Money's worth calculations add up the payroll taxes paid by the individual, assume a market return is paid on these "savings" and then compare that to the promised benefits to be paid over the individual's retirement years. The "money's worth" calculations are more favorable for those with low income (because benefits are paid out in a progressive manner) and less favorable for individuals with high wage income (who could get a higher return by "investing" their payroll taxes in the stock market). However, this ignores the other benefits offered by Social Security, including automatic cost of living adjustments (benefits go up with inflation), and benefits paid to spouses and children if the worker dies, as well as benefits paid to those with short working lives due to disabilities.

size of the Trust Fund. Hence, this book could be seen as a road map for the evolving Democratic Party position during the Clinton years.

However, I argued at the time that a larger Trust Fund could not in any way provide for future retirees, nor would it add to national savings. (See the next subsection on subway tokens.) Rather, the Trust Fund represents a leakage that lowers aggregate demand; all else being equal, this lowers economic growth and thus makes it more difficult to take care of future retirees. Aaron responded to my piece, arguing that he had thought that such "vulgar Keynesianism" was "blessedly extinct" (Aaron, 1990–1991). According to Aaron, running budget surpluses to add to the Trust Fund would indeed increase saving and lower interest rates, thus stimulating investment and economic growth, making it easier to take care of retirees.

As we now know, the Clinton budget did turn sharply toward surplus, and those surpluses were projected at the time to continue for at least a generation. A number of economists advocated "saving" this surplus for future retirees. As laid out earlier in the plan by Aaron et al., President Clinton proposed to take a portion of each year's surplus and add it to the Trust Fund (Papadimitriou and Wray, 1999b, 1999c). Essentially, this would allow double counting of the surplus run by Social Security, since most of the budget surpluses accrued during the Clinton years were due to payroll taxes that far exceeded program benefits. The proposal essentially amounted to nothing more than an accounting trick. If you could double count, why not quadruple count the surplus and lock all that away for safekeeping?

During the 2000 presidential race, candidate (and Vice President) Al Gore used Social Security "lockboxes" as a primary campaign issue, confusing an internal bookkeeping operation (as Social Security's assets in the Trust Fund equal the Treasury's liabilities to Social Security, this is a case of the government owing itself) with availability of "finance" for the government as a whole. A wide variety of economists (including Aaron) joined the bandwagon, proclaiming that this was "good economics", going so far as to sign a petition in support of the plan (Wray, 1999).

At the time, I was told by economic advisors to top Democrats and big unions that they realized lockboxes were nonsense but believed it was politically pragmatic to endorse irregular accounting as a means to "save" the program. I responded that there was no need to run budget surpluses in order to credit Social Security's Trust Fund; the government can immediately credit the Trust Fund with trillions of dollars of assets, offset by the Treasury's commitment to make timely benefit payments when and as necessary (Wray, 1999). Most importantly, I worried about the long-term damage that would be done to the program by creating a false crisis and then proposing to resolve it with a preposterous gimmick.

Of course, the Democrats' strategy did backfire: Gore lost the election to George Bush, Jr., the Clinton budget surpluses brought down the economy and morphed into huge deficits "as far as the eye can see", and President Bush took on Social Security "reform" as a major goal of his administration. Ironically, the Republicans began to quote President Clinton whenever Democrats tried to deny that the program faces a crisis, leaving Democrats in the untenable position of either admitting they were lying in the 1990s or that they were lying now (Wray, 2005).

After taking office, President Bush appointed a Reform Commission to study the problem. The Commission claimed that Social Security was "broken" and required a "complete overhaul"; it engaged in a sleight of hand by comparing its "reforms" against "current law benefits" that were actually a quarter below those promised in the current benefit formula (none of the proposed reforms came close to providing the legislated benefits); it claimed that the present value of Social Security's shortfall was $3.2 trillion; and it proposed partial privatization and benefit cuts as the solution (Wray, 2001). Workers would be able to take part of their payroll taxes and put them into private retirement savings plans (managed of course by Wall Street), actually worsening Social Security's finances.

However, terrorism and security issues forced Social Security to the back burner during the first Bush term. After reelection, Bush felt he had a mandate to return to privatization of Social Security. At first, supporters of privatization claimed that it would resolve the "financial crisis"; eventually, the President admitted that the private accounts would worsen the program's finances (Wray, 2005). Finally, he returned to the Commission's suggestion to drop wage indexing of future benefits (at least for all but the lowest-income workers) and hinted that he would consider elimination of the cap on wages subject to taxation (Wray, 2005).

While none of these "reforms" was enacted during the Bush administration (nor later during the Obama years), they are still the subject of conversation. If ever enacted, these changes would substantially erode the support of middle- and upper-income earners, who would face huge cuts to benefits and higher taxes. Partial privatization would almost certainly lead to lower retirement payments for many lower-income workers (with management fees eating up the returns on their small accounts). Further, as many middle- and upper-income workers would opt for the privatization alternative, the amount of benefits received directly from Social Security by them would fall toward insignificance (Krugman, 2005). Over the long haul, the nonprivatized portion of Social Security would be converted to a "welfare" program, important only to low-income people. This could be the last straw for what has long been America's most successful and popular government program.

The truth is that Social Security does not, indeed cannot, face any financial crisis. It is a federal government program and as such cannot become insolvent. Social Security benefits are paid in the same way that the federal government makes expenditures for all its other programs: by cutting a Treasury check or, increasingly, by directly crediting a bank account. Social Security is an unusual program only in that we pretend the payroll taxes "pay for" benefits; in reality, trying to maintain a balance between these flows is purely a politically inspired accounting procedure. Any federal government spending must be accounted for, but spending cannot be financially constrained by specific or even by general tax revenues.

Further, the Trust Fund does not and cannot provide finance for Social Security. So long as the full faith and credit of the US government stands behind the promised benefits, they can and will be paid, whether the Trust Fund has a positive or negative balance. None other than Alan Greenspan (whose Commission changed Social Security to an "advanced funding" system that would accumulate billions of dollars of reserves) admitted this:

> *The notion that we have a trust fund is nonsense—that trust fund has no meaning whatsoever. The trust fund is a meaningless instrument that has no function.*
>
> *(Greenspan, 2015)*

The actual effect of raising payroll taxes in 1983 to accumulate a huge Trust Fund was to reduce support for the program because it unnecessarily raised taxes without boosting benefits. Many proponents of the current system who understand this economic reality still want to accumulate a Trust Fund on the argument that it provides political protection. Perhaps the Trust Fund provided cover at one time, but it no longer serves even that purpose. It is precisely because there is a Trust Fund that the privatizers are making headway: if there were no Trust Fund, there would be nothing to privatize. Indeed, some of the privatizers see the trillion and a half dollars in the Trust Fund as a potential boost to equity markets.

More importantly, the projected eventual "exhaustion" of the Trust Fund—that is now said to occur in 2035—provides ammunition for the "reformers" who propose to increase returns on assets through privatization. Hence, the irregular accounting only hinders development of a clear understanding of the issues involved.

Social Security provides a substantial measure of security for aged persons, survivors, and disabled persons—and their dependents. It has never missed a payment, nor will it ever do so, as long as the full faith and credit of the US government lies behind the program. Reform might be desired, and might even be necessary, but not because of any mythical looming financial crisis. Our nation is undergoing slow but important demographic changes that probably warrant informed discussion of the future shape of Social Security. While the baby boomers receive all the attention, other demographic and economic changes may be more important, including a greater proportion of female-headed households, higher immigration and the rising proportion of "minority" populations (already a majority in several states), and increasing economic inequality. All of these trends mean that a greater proportion of our elderly population relies on insufficient Social Security benefits.

Combined with the disappearance of employer-provided defined benefit pension plans and reduced employment security, these trends strengthen the arguments for more generous and secure publicly provided safety nets—not for benefit cuts and privatization. As Bernie Sanders has argued, we need to increase the generosity of benefits for those with lower lifetime earnings; Social Security must be strengthened, not cut.

However, none of the challenges faced by Social Security rises to the level of a programmatic crisis; we will have years and even decades to make adjustments to Social Security should we decide they are necessary.

c. Social security, subway tokens, and pizza coupons

Let us look at the Trust Fund issue from another perspective.

There is a widespread belief that Social Security surpluses must be "saved" for future retirees. Most analysts believe that this can be done by accumulating a Trust Fund and ensuring that the Treasury does not "spend" the surplus. The "saviors" of Social Security thus insist that the rest of the government's budget must remain balanced, for otherwise the Treasury would be forced to "dip into" Social Security reserves.

But can a Trust Fund really help to provide for future retirees? Let us first look at the case of subway tokens and then turn to pizza coupons.

Suppose the New York Metro Transit Authority (MTA) decided to offer subway tokens as part of the retirement package provided to employees—say, 50 free tokens a month after retirement.[7] Should the city therefore attempt to run an annual "surplus" of tokens (collecting more tokens per month than it pays out) today in order to accumulate a trust fund of tokens to be provided to tomorrow's MTA retirees? Of course not. When tokens are needed to pay future retirees, the City will simply issue more tokens at that time. Not only is accumulation of a hoard of tokens by the City unnecessary, it will not in any way ease the burden of providing subway rides for future retirees. Whether or not the City can meet its obligation to future retirees will depend on the ability of the transit system to carry the paying customers plus MTA retirees.

Note, also, that the MTA does not currently attempt to run a "balanced budget", and, indeed, consistently runs a subway token deficit. That is, it consistently pays-out more tokens than it receives, as riders hoard tokens or lose them. Attempting to run a surplus of subway tokens would eventually result in a shortage of tokens, with customers unable to obtain them. A properly run transit system would always run a deficit—issuing more tokens than it receives.

As we will see, accumulation of a Social Security Trust Fund is neither necessary nor useful. Just as a subway token surplus cannot help to provide subway rides for future retirees, neither can the Social Security Trust Fund help provide for baby boomer retirees. Whether the future burden of retirees will be excessive or not will depend on our society's ability to produce real goods and services (including subway rides) at the time that they will be needed. Nor does it make any sense for our government to run a budget surplus—which simply reduces disposable income of the private sector. Just as an MTA token surplus would generate lines of token-less people wanting rides, a federal budget surplus will generate jobless people desiring the necessities of life (including subway rides).

Your local pizza restaurant issues coupons for free pizzas. It knows that many of these will never return for redemption before they expire. But when a coupon does come in, the restaurant must bake a pizza. The outstanding coupons represent

---

[7] The MTA shifted from use of tokens to Metrocards some years ago.

liabilities of the restaurant and assets of the holders. Each coupon is worth a pizza until the expiration date, after which its value immediately drops to zero. When a coupon is presented to the restaurant for redemption, it is torn and tossed in the recycling bin. Only a misguided restaurant manager would lock them up in a safe deposit "lockbox" thinking they are valuable assets. The manager knows they represent claims and thus potential costs in terms of labor, ingredients, and fuel involved in pizza production. It would be silly to accumulate them to be counted as assets that would help defray the costs of meeting the future demand of customers for pizzas.

Social Security's Trust Fund is by law limited to accumulating Uncle Sam's treasury bonds. (They are special bonds that cannot be sold in secondary markets, and the interest rate paid is set by policy.) Each year that Social Security runs a surplus (revenue comes mostly from the payroll tax—plus interest on the Trust Fund) this adds to the stock of treasury bonds held. When Social Security runs a deficit, it redeems bonds to the Treasury in the amount of the deficit. In some years the Social Security surplus has been enough to more than offset the deficits on the rest of the Treasury's spending. That allowed the Treasury to record a surplus on its "unified" budget—and led to celebration during the Clinton years for a well-managed budget.

However, in most years the Social Security surplus is too small to offset the deficits in the rest of the budget. In those years, the Treasury issues bonds equal to the overall deficit plus the surplus in Social Security's budget. The Trust Fund represents a debt of one branch of government (Treasury) to another branch (Social Security). This is really just an internal accounting procedure.

Beginning in 2020 Social Security will begin to run deficits that add to the deficits on the rest of the budget. As the Trust Fund redeems bonds, the Treasury's debt to the Trust Fund declines—the government owes itself less. However, since the Treasury must issue bonds equal to the total deficit (Social Security's deficit plus the deficit on the rest of the government's budget) Treasury will issue additional debt equal to the debt that Social Security redeems, plus the rest of the government's deficit. In other words, the retirement of bonds held by Social Security is matched by the issue of bonds held outside the government. Instead of owing itself, the government will owe others. And instead of paying interest to itself, the government will pay interest to others.

What would happen if Social Security did not have any Trust Fund? The Treasury would issue bonds equal to the combined deficits of the program plus all other government programs. In that case, the amount of Treasury debt issued would be the same—regardless of whether or not Social Security had accumulated surpluses over the years between 1983 and 2018. Thus, the Trust Fund makes no difference to the accounting for budget deficits of the government taken as a whole. Trust Fund assets represent nothing more than internal accounting—record keeping. They do not provide any "wherewithal" to finance Social Security.

While it is true that the overall stance of the unified government budget looked "better" (smaller deficits) between 1983 and 2018 because of the surpluses run by Social Security, from the perspective of that program payroll tax rates were higher than necessary for 35 years on the misguided belief that the Trust Fund assets would help to "pay for" the retirement of baby boomers. Yet the accumulation of bonds in the Trust Fund over those 35 years does not in any way reduce the government's "need" for finance when Social Security starts redeeming the bonds.

Accumulating treasury bonds in Social Security's Trust Fund is like accumulating pizza coupons in the restaurant's safe. They do not in any way make it easier to provide for baby boomer retirements—just as pizza coupons will not help the restaurant bake more pizzas for future customers who will present coupons in payment. The treasury bonds accumulated by Social Security are functionally identical to the free pizza coupons locked away by a confused restaurant manager—debts (not assets) of the government and restaurant, respectively.

d. Private pensions: an introduction

In the final topic of this Part, we examine the financialization of worker's pensions. Together with private savings and Social Security, this is the third leg of the retirement stool. Social Security was never meant to provide—by itself—for a decent retirement, and it does not. That said, far too many workers do rely almost exclusively on Social Security benefits that are inadequate. Less than half of American workers have a pension. Two-thirds of government workers do, as well as 70% of union workers—but pensions are far less common among other workers (Ghilarducci, 2008). Most of those who do have pensions now have "defined contribution" rather than the traditional "defined benefit" plans. The "legacy" pensions of the old megacorps like General Motors promised decent retirement pay based on time worked for the firm as well as income earned—with the benefits "defined" and contractual. The typical plan pays about $35,000 per year for life after retirement.

In recent years, employers have largely shifted from defined benefit to defined contribution. This is a huge topic, but the change puts most of the risk on the employee. In a defined benefit plan, the employer uses a formula to calculate one's pension—related to income earned (usually in the last few years of work) and years employed. The more one earns and the longer one works for the firm, the higher the retirement pay. For the firm, this becomes a large and very long-term liability; the so-called "legacy" firms (auto manufacturers and airlines) have large numbers of retired workers they must support and find it hard to compete with upstart competitors with no such "legacy". For the worker, there is the uncertainty over the prospect that the employer might go bankrupt and default on the promised pension (the Pension Benefit Guarantee Corporation provides some insurance but often forces a conversion of the defined benefits to defined contributions—a bad deal for the worker). Further, it can tie the worker to a firm—raising the perceived cost of switching jobs.

Defined contribution plans could work well for both firm and employee—the firm contributes some fixed percent of the worker's wage to a managed fund, with the worker also contributing. Workers can often take their accumulated pension with them when they switch jobs. But there are several possible hitches: workers often do not contribute up to the maximum permitted (so when they retire, their benefits are inadequate); workers often "cash in" their pensions when they switch jobs rather than rolling them into another retirement fund; and performance of the managed fund determines the return on the retirement savings. If one needs to retire in a financial markets slump, the annuity that can be purchased to pay retirement benefits is reduced. Finally, at retirement many workers (wrongly) opt for a lump sum payment rather than an annuity—often in the misguided belief that they will die early.

The new normal is often voluntary participation that commits the worker to setting aside part of her salary (sometimes matched by the employer) to be professionally managed. On retirement, the worker will receive an income based on accumulated earnings—which depends in turn on how much was set aside, plus how well the savings were managed. The ideal defined contribution plan could pay even more than the typical defined benefit plan, but the problem is that very few workers or money managers live up to the ideal. Hence the typical real-world defined contribution plan only pays $6000 per year for life after retirement. Clearly not much of a supplement to Social Security. As Ghilarducci laments, there is no evidence, anywhere, that a typical worker can accumulate enough savings (either personally or in a defined contribution plan) to provide a comfortable retirement. This is why most workers rely largely—or even entirely—on Social Security for their retirement years.

Experts now recommend that an individual should accumulate about $230,000 of retirement savings for each $1000 of monthly earnings desired after retirement—or about $1 million to get $4000 a month. However, the average Social Security retirement pay is about $1000 a month, so that million dollar retirement saving would give you about $5000 per month or $60,000 a year. This is barely adequate for a comfortable retirement—particularly since the private retirement funding is unlikely to be inflation-indexed, unlike Social Security, which is. To reach this goal is very tough for the average worker. If you are now 40 years old and earn $45,000 a year, you will need to save $27,000 of that per year—obviously unattainable for most. If you start at age 30 years, you would need to save $16,000 a year—again not something that most would be able to achieve. The average middle-class American aged 47–55 years had only $186,000 of personal assets plus a pension worth $113,000, according to Ghilarducci. That was before the Great Recession hit in 2008, which dropped the median wealth for the "pre-retired" age group of 50–64 years from $259,000 to just $143,000 by 2013. This shows that even with good planning, bad luck can wipe out your retirement savings and impoverish you in your old age. Many of those people had to postpone retirement, and many older people who had retired were forced back into the labor market. You still see them today, acting as "greeters" at big-box stores. Things are far worse for women and minorities—whose earnings are lower over their working lives, and who are less likely to have the good "legacy pensions"—so it is not surprising to see them overrepresented among the elderly poor with lower personal retirement savings and meager pensions.

It is important to understand how we got into this predicament. During WWII the government wanted to hold down wages to prevent inflation given that much of the nation's productive activity was oriented toward the war. Unions and employers negotiated postponed payment in the form of pensions—which pleased all three parties: big firms, big government, and big unions. Unions saw this as delayed payment of foregone wages; government saw it as a way to constrain wage and price inflation; and firms saw it as a "carrot" they could use to recruit and retain good workers.

Government supported pensions with tax advantages for contributions. Firms loved pushing costs to an indefinite future—rather than paying wages, they would promise to pay pensions 30 or 40 years down the road. Much of the promise was unfunded or met by stock in the firm. This meant that pensions could be paid only if the firm was successful for a very long time into the future.

As an aside, it is worth noting the similarities between the US healthcare system (discussed in Part B, Section C, *Health insurance diversions: the financialization of health (and everything else)* and its pension system. Firms also offered healthcare as a tax-advantaged benefit in lieu of wage increases. Over time, this became our current "managed care" highly financialized system. Like pension funds that are controlled by money managers, our healthcare is managed by highly oligopolized financial firms run by well-compensated executives. Workers have little control over their healthcare or their pensions. They are not "sovereign consumers" because they have neither the knowledge nor the ability to shop around for healthcare or pensions—in both cases, employers negotiate with providers and pass fees along to workers. With others in control, there is little to hold down costs—even as wages were sacrificed on the argument that workers were receiving valuable nonwage compensation. Both healthcare and pensions are endangered by the same Washington forces promoting ever greater financialization of our economy.

As time went on and it became apparent that "legacy" firms might not survive long enough to pay promised benefits, unions and government felt that a mere promise to pay pensions would not suffice. Either firms would have to kick in a huge amount of cash to fully fund the pensions, or government would have to guarantee the pensions. Corporations did not like the costs attached to full funding. The grand compromise was that firms would increase funding a bit, and government would provide insurance through the PBGC. Funding did increase, although the more frequent and more severe crises in the post-1970 period wiped out enough assets in each crisis to cause pension funding to dip below prudent levels. Only a financial bubble could get them back to full funding. To make matters worse, firms were allowed to reduce contributions during speculative bubbles (since asset values would be rising)—ensuring that the funds would face a crisis whenever the economy was not bubbling.

Just before the global crisis hit, pension funding was, on average, doing well—thanks to the speculative bubble as well as to some deregulation that took place at the end of the Clinton administration that allowed pensions to gamble in more exotic instruments, and in riskier markets such as commodities. Prior to 2000, pensions could not buy commodities because these are purely speculative bets. There is no return to holding commodities unless their prices rise—indeed, holding them is costly. However, Goldman Sachs and other Wall Street firms promoted investment in commodities as a hedge, on the basis that commodities' prices are uncorrelated with equities. In the aftermath of the dot-com collapse (when pensions were hard hit by plummeting stock prices), that was appealing. (In truth, when managed money flows into an asset class that had previously been uncorrelated with other assets, that asset will become correlated with other assets. Hence, by marketing commodities Wall Street ensured a commodities bubble that would collapse along with everything else.)

You may already know the rest of that story: pension funds poured into commodities and commodity futures, driving up prices of energy, metals, and food. As energy prices rose, Congress mandated addition of biofuels to gasoline—which added to pressures on food prices that contributed to starvation around the globe. The bubble popped in what is known as the great Mike Masters[8] inventory liquidation, as pension funds pulled out of commodities on the fear that Congress was coming after them. They did not want all the bad publicity that would be caused if workers knew that it was their own pension fund that was driving up gas prices at the pump. However, pensions quietly moved back into commodities after the dip of prices in 2008—and oil prices doubled (Wray, 2008).

Over the postwar period, pension funds grew to equal about three-quarters of GDP and became so large that they will bubble up any financial market they are allowed to enter—and what goes up must come down. So when they enter a new asset class, they cause its prices to rise, which induces pensions to invest a larger share of their portfolio in that asset to reap the higher expected returns. This creates a nice recursive dynamic until something causes them to stop chasing the higher returns. For example, a Congressional investigation of their speculative behavior.

But that is not the only problem with pensions, as we will see in the next subsection on reforming pensions. Maybe the entire strategy of relying heavily on private pensions and retirement savings needs rethinking.

e. Reforming pension fund and private savings strategies

After the GFC hit the economy and devastated pensions (which lost much of their accumulated wealth), I attended a financial markets conference at which some pension funds managers, as well as a former head of the Pension Benefit Guarantee Corporation (PBGC, the FDIC of the pension world), spoke. Private pensions were just over 80% funded, meaning that the value of accumulated assets fell short of meeting promised payouts of defined benefit pension plans by about a fifth,

---

[8] Mike Masters is a commodities market expert who testified before Congress that pension funds were behind the run-up of commodities prices. Fearing a backlash from union members and others with pensions, pension managers pulled out of commodities before Congress could enact controls on pension funds. Commodity prices collapsed—oil prices fell from around $150 a barrel to around $50 a barrel almost immediately.

amounting to a $400 billion shortfall. Not surprisingly, they were down considerably due to losses incurred during the financial crisis. Public pensions provided by state and local governments had a shortfall estimated to run as high as $2 trillion.

On any reasonable accounting standard, the PBGC was bankrupt because its reserves would have been wiped out by the failure of just a couple of large firms on "legacy" pensions. Most pensions had already taken the form of defined contribution plans—which means that workers and retirees take all the risks. That will likely become the outcome of any "legacy" plans that require bailouts because the PGBC typically imposes that as a condition for funding failing pension funds—they must convert from "good" defined benefit to "bad" defined contribution plans.

I always had my suspicions about the strategy followed by pension fund managers, so the conference gave me the opportunity to talk to experts. Here is what I learned. Each pension fund manager must come from the land of Lake Wobegone[9] because she/he must beat the average return or get fired.

There are two fundamental principles widely believed to operate in financial markets that make such an outcome unlikely: the *risk-return relation* and the *efficient markets hypothesis*. Higher risk is rewarded with higher returns, hence fund managers believe they must take on more risk to get the reward of above-average returns. But since the higher return only rewards higher risk, if markets really are efficient the average fund manager will only receive the risk-free return. To put this as simply as possible, the pricing of assets should be just sufficient to cover the risk; on average there is no better return to taking risk. Anything above that is due to luck. So you must get that manager from Lake Wobegone—the one who is above average. The higher returns of the brighter or luckier managers will be offset by the lower returns of the dumber and luckless money runners.

If your fund manager is not from Lake Wobegone, you would be better off investing in riskless Treasury bonds because hiring an above-average fund manager will require above-average compensation—so even those funds with B-rated managers would probably provide lower net returns than US Treasuries (which can be bought online from Treasury Direct. Gov with no fees). To be sure, there is some shuffling of the deck so that one manager with a run of good luck can beat the average for a while, but she will probably fail catastrophically and wipe out several years of winnings in one swoop as some other lucky fool takes her place in the Wall Street lottery. Only the fortunate few can permanently live in Lake Wobegone and thereby beat Treasuries over the long run.

To be clear, these two principles may not be entirely correct—or, there could be other forces at play to allow for a positive return to risk even after subtracting losses. If so, that would go against the conventional wisdom that drives Wall Street. I think it is likely that over long periods of time, markets do tend to push risk-adjusted net

---

[9] The imaginary town immortalized in public radio's "Prairie Home Companion", where "all the women are strong, all the men are good looking, and all the children are above average". http://www.garrisonkeillor.com/radio-categories/the-news-from-lake-wobegon/.

returns toward zero so that on average safe Treasuries will beat net returns on risky assets. There is, however, a positive return to taking illiquid positions. And all things equal, it is probable that longer-term maturities (long duration) receive such a premium.

Still, when all is said and done, pension managers that follow similar strategies, including taking positions in traded, liquid assets, will push risk spreads toward the point that they just compensate for losses due to risk and fees paid to the supposedly above-average managers.[10]

Each time there is a financial crisis, the funds tank and managers look for strategies to reduce risk. Enter Wall Street marketeers with an array of instruments to hedge and diversify risks. That was one of the big topics of the conference I attended. There is one sure bet when it comes to gambling: the house always wins. In financial markets, the big boys on Wall Street are the house, and they always win. Even if we leave to the side their ability to dupe and defraud country bumpkin pension fund managers, they charge fees for all the stuff they are selling. This ensures that on average pension funds will net less than a risk-free return. But wherever Wall Street intrudes, sucker bets and fraud exist. So the average return should be well below that of Treasuries, and even the managers from Lake Wobegone will probably net less than the risk-free return.

To recap: pension fund managers take on risk on the assumption that with higher risk comes higher return. Wall Street manufactures risky assets such as securitized subprime mortgages. It then convinces pension funds that they ought to diversify to reduce risk, for example by gambling on commodities. By coincidence, Wall Street just happens to be marketing commodities futures indexes to satisfy the demand it has created. It also provides a wide array of complex hedging strategies to shift risk onto better fools, as well as credit default "insurance" and buy-back assurances in case anything goes wrong.

If all of these "risk management" strategies were successful, the pension fund would achieve a risk-free portfolio. Of course, it could have achieved this if it had bypassed Wall Street entirely and gone straight to the Treasury. However, Wall Street's masters of the universe then would have had no market for the junk they were pushing, and pension fund managers would not have received their generous compensation. So workers are left with fees that drain their pension funds, and pension funds are left with massive counterparty risk as the hedges, insurance, and assurance go bad.

---

[10] Vanguard's founder, John Bogle, has long argued that investing in a broad stock index will beat actively managed funds that not only take greater risks, but also charge higher fees. He created Vanguard—the world's largest provider of mutual funds, to provide low fee index funds to small investors—and has consistently proven his hunch. "Vanguard research found that since the 1976 index fund inception, the majority of passively managed index funds outperformed their actively managed competitors. Although, part of the outperformance can be explained by the lower fees typically charged by index funds." In other words, trying to beat the average is so costly that it is not worth the expense. https://money.usnews.com/investing/funds/articles/why-its-time-to-consider-actively-managed-funds.

Strangely enough, we reward pensions with tax advantages and government guarantees that help to support the shenanigans. Before the crisis, private pension fund assets reached about 50% of GDP and state and local government pension fund assets reached almost 25%. That is a huge industry that has created a lot of well-compensated jobs for managers as well as Wall Street sales staff. The entire industry can be justified only if through skill or luck pension fund management can beat the average risk-free return by enough to pay all of those industry compensations with a margin to reward pensioners with above-average returns.

Yet, the expectation should be that pension fund managers are significantly less skilled and less "lucky" than, say, Goldman Sachs and J.P. Morgan bankers. Hence, workers would be far better off if their employers were required to fully fund pensions with investments restricted to Treasury debt. At most, each pension plan would require one lowly paid employee who would log in to www.treasurydirect.gov to transfer funds out of the firm's bank deposit and into Treasuries, in an amount determined by actuarial tables plus nominal benefits promised.

Goodbye fund managers and Wall Street sales staff!

Indeed, this raises the question: should the federal government promote and protect pensions and private retirement savings at all? Surely individuals should be free to place savings with fund managers of their choice, and each saver can try to find that manager from Lake Wobegone. But it makes no sense to promote a scheme that cannot succeed at the aggregate level—the average fund manager cannot beat the average, and on average there is no reason to believe that managed funds will provide a net return that is above the return on Treasuries. It would be far better as social policy to remove the tax advantages and government guarantees provided to pension plans, and instead allow individuals to put their savings directly into US Treasuries that are automatically government-backed and provide a risk-free return.

The US retirement system is supposed to rest on a three-legged stool: pensions, individual savings, and Social Security. Pensions are mostly employer-related and are chronically and seriously underfunded. There are also huge and growing administrative problems posed by the transformation of the US workplace—with the typical worker switching jobs many times over the course of her career, and with the lifespan of the typical firm measured in years rather than decades. And, finally, as discussed here the most plausible long-term return on managed money would be somewhat below the risk-free return on Treasuries.

So, in consequence, the shift from defined benefit to defined contribution plans has put workers in a more precarious position regarding retirement. The problem is made worse because so many workers have been forced into contingent positions—with low pay and few benefits. As a result, the private pension system part of the three-legged stool is less secure than it used to be.

The final leg is private savings—which also can receive tax advantages. The problem with private savings is that Americans do not save enough for their retirement. They never have. And even if they tried to do so, they would be duped out of their savings by Wall Street.

Further, as we argued earlier with regard to Social Security, more financial savings is not a solution to our nation's aging "problem". What we need is more investment in "capital"—private, public, and human capital—to increase tomorrow's productive capacity. More financial savings will not feed tomorrow's seniors. While saving is a virtue for individuals, it is a vice for society.

We conclude that both private pensions and private individual savings are inadequate as supplements to Social Security. Thus, the best solution would be to eliminate government support for them through tax exemptions and instead to boost Social Security to ensure that anyone who works long enough to qualify will receive a comfortable retirement. They can supplement this with private savings, according to ability and desires.

I ran these arguments by several of the pension experts at the conference. All of them agreed that this would be the best public policy. But they pleaded with me to keep it a secret because such a change would be devastating for fund managers and Wall Street.

Can you keep a secret?

We are not advocating elimination of private retirement savings or private pensions, but we have questioned the wisdom of using tax advantages to promote them. We believe it would be far more efficient and equitable to provide greater funding to Social Security so that benefits would be sufficient to provide a generous retirement. We also recommend greater regulation over the types of investments permitted for private retirement accounts and pension funds. What this would amount to is restricting Wall Street's access to the savings and pensions of Americans of modest means. The theory behind deregulation of Wall Street was that the "big boys" who deal with the likes of Goldman Sachs are capable of watching out for their own interests. The problem is that Wall Street's reach extends far beyond the big boys. We need to separate Wall Street from adequate provisioning for healthcare and retirement.

II. Health insurance versus Healthcare

In this section, we will discuss the wisdom of using the private insurance system to finance a large portion of the nation's healthcare expenses. In the first part of the section, we will examine the state of healthcare in the United States before the introduction of "Obamacare"—which tried to expand health insurance coverage to most of the US population. While it did successfully expand coverage to millions (a large portion of the expansion, however, resulted from changes to Medicaid—the program that covers low-income people by bringing them into the government-funded Medicaid program—rather than from bringing them into the private insurance system), Obamacare has not eliminated the debate about reforming healthcare provisioning. After the election of President Trump, Obamacare continued to be attacked by both the right and the left. Indeed, experience with Obamacare has helped to fuel the rise of support for expansion of Medicare to include everyone—polls in 2019 showed support for which had reached 90%.

In the final part of this section, we look at the push for a "single-payer" system—which by 2019 had been endorsed by many of the likely Democratic candidates who would challenge Trump in 2020.

a. Healthcare diversions: the elephant in the room

A 3-hour layover in a major airport in the "new South" brought into sharp focus—at least for me—the elephant in the room that no one wants to discuss.

I will not belabor the obvious point that Americans are, to put it delicately, a bit on the hefty side. But what really struck me is that many have evolved to the point that they are barely bipedal. As passengers attempted to perambulate their way from one gate to the next, it appeared that most had forgotten how to walk. I saw the most ungainly gaits—peregrination with great effort but little forward progress, the zigzag, the toe-heel-toe, the Quasimodo, the sideways roll, the zombie, the stop-start-stop again, all whilst occasionally careening off walls and other passengers. Of course, in some cases, the attire dictated the method. A few of the boys had their pants waist bands down around their knees, forcing a duck-like waddle, made even more difficult by the need to use one hand to hold onto the belt lest gravity complete its work and bring the pants down to the ankles. A lot of the girls wore PJs and flip-flops, making it impossible to do much more than shuffle along. Some 40-somethings had eight-inch stilettos in which only flamingos could parade about with grace. Still, the vast majority of passengers wore shoes marketed as sporting equipment, designed presumably for activities involving two legs and an upright posture rather than for those of the aquatic or slithering or knuckle-dragging variety. And here is an interesting factoid: the average American walks just the length of three football fields daily (Sierra Magazine, January/February 2007, p. 25). It shows. Since that is the average, it is no doubt boosted by the still considerable number of aging yuppies who manage 3k runs before breakfast, as well as by children the soccer moms idolized by Sarah Palin drive to practice. I presume that most of the airport patrons typically manage little more than a few schlepps from couch to fridge each day, taking a momentary break from their average 1600 hours in front of the TV each year (Uncle John's Bathroom Reader, 2006, p. 115).

Like many other airlines, ours had provided a welcoming speech as the plane pulled up to the gate, helpfully reminding disembarking passengers that the most dangerous part of their journey would soon begin. I had always thought that they were alluding to the fact that we would shortly be behind the wheel of our autos, taking our lives into our own unprofessional hands as we attempted to pilot 2 tons of steel on a 65 mph freeway through an obstacle course of text-messaging drivers (which studies show are twice as impaired as a drunk driver). Actually, they were referring to our more immediate mission—to walk without major mishap to the baggage claim area before returning to the relative safety of a seated or prone position in a vehicle, like the humans in the *Wall-E* movie. A few centuries ago, our ancestors here in America were able to run down buffalo, or even mastodons, and kill them with spears. Today, most Americans can, with some effort, spear a French fry—providing it is not moving too quickly and that they are seated to steady the aim.

Do not get me wrong. I am not one of the contrarians who reject the argument that lack of access to healthcare by the uninsured contributes to the United States' relatively poor ranking in terms of health outcome. Surely that explains some of our problems. But too little exercise, too much smoking, too much food, and especially too much bad food has got to be a huge factor. As Michael Pollan argues (In Defense of Food, 2008), unless we address the problem with American Food, Inc., we will not significantly improve our health no matter what we do with healthcare. According to Pollan, the cost to society of the American addiction to "fast food" (which is neither all that fast nor is it food) is already $250 billion per year in diet-related healthcare costs.

One-third of Americans born in 2000 will develop diabetes in her lifetime; on average, diabetes subtracts 12 years from life expectancy, and raises annual medical costs from $2500 for a person without diabetes to $13,000. While it is true that life expectancy today is higher than it was in 1900, almost all of this is due to reduction of death rates of infants and young children—mostly not due to the high-tech healthcare that we celebrate as the contribution of our innovative, profit-seeking system, but rather to lower tech inoculations, sewage treatment, mosquito abatement, and cleaner water. The life expectancy of a 65-year-old in 1900 was only about 6 years less than it is for a 65-year-old today—and rates of chronic diseases like cancer and type 2 diabetes are much higher (Pollan, 2008, p. 93).

Smoking causes 480,000 deaths yearly.[11] We incarcerate a far higher percentage of our population than any developed society on earth—and healthcare costs in prisons are exploding for the obvious reason that prisons are not healthy environments. Our relatively high poverty rates and high percentage of the population left outside the labor market (especially young adult males without a high school degree) all contribute to very poor health outcomes. In a very important sense that I will explore next, more health insurance coverage would no more resolve our healthcare problems than would provision of car insurance to chronic drunk drivers solve our deaths-due-to-DUI problem.

So, before ramping up healthcare insurance, how about an education program to teach people the mechanics of walking? (It is not as simple as it sounds. I speak from experience because some years ago I tore a calf muscle and after a long and painful healing process, I developed a gait that was all kinds of ugly. A physical therapist helped me to redevelop a human stride.) While we are at it, we can reintroduce Americans to food. I do not mean the corporate offal that Pollan calls "food-like

---

[11] "Cigarette smoking is responsible for more than 480,000 deaths per year in the United States, including more than 41,000 deaths resulting from secondhand smoke exposure. This is about one in five deaths annually, or 1300 deaths every day." https://www.cdc.gov/tobacco/data_statistics/fact_sheets/fast_facts/index.htm.

substances"—products derived from plants and animals but generated by breaking the original foods into their most basic molecules and then reconstituting them in a manner that can be more profitably marketed. What I mean is real food, produced by farmers and consumed after as little processing as possible. Preferably it will be local, cooked at home, eaten at a table, and will consist mostly of vegetables, grains, and fruits. And let us provide decent jobs to anyone ready to work, as an alternative to locking them up in prison. Ban smoking from all public places and regulate tobacco like the highly addictive and dangerous drug that it is. Together these policies will do far more to improve American health and to reduce healthcare costs than anything that most "reformers" were proposing in the debates surrounding Obamacare.

The benefits of extending health insurance coverage were almost certainly overstated and did not (will not) make a major dent in our two comparative gaps: we spend far more than any other nation but do not obtain better outcomes and in important areas get worse results. Nations that adopt diets closer to ours begin to suffer similar afflictions: obesity, diabetes, heart disease, hypertension, diverticulitis, malformed dental arches and tooth decay, varicose veins, ulcers, hemorrhoids, and cancer (Pollan, 2008, p. 91). Even universal health insurance is not going to lower the costs of such chronic afflictions that are largely due to the fact that we eat too much of the wrong kinds of food and get too little exercise. It makes more sense to attack the problem directly by increasing exercise, reducing caloric intake, and minimizing consumption of corporate food-like substances that make us sick than to provide insurance so that those who suffer the consequences of our lifestyle can afford costly care.

Let me be as clear as possible: it is neither rational nor humane to deny healthcare to any US resident. Further, I accept the arguments contending that early treatment through primary care is far more cost-effective than waiting for emergency care—and it is obviously more humane. But, access to health insurance does not address the bigger issue of health problems created by the way we live. Without fundamental changes to American lifestyles, better access to prevention, and reduction of the costs of our healthcare payments system, the proportion of US GDP devoted to healthcare will remain about double that of our peers.

b. Health insurance diversions: we need less health insurance, not more

In this subsection I will argue that we do not need more health insurance, rather, we need less. This is why Obamacare was the wrong solution to what ails us.

Here is the point. Healthcare is not a service that should be funded by insurance companies. An individual should insure against expensive and undesirable calamities: tornadoes, fires, auto accidents. These need to be insurable risks or insurance will not be made available. This means the events need to be reasonably random and relatively rare, with calculable probabilities that do not change much over time.

Further, as discussed in more detail below, we need to make sure that the existence of insurance does not increase the probability of insured losses. This is why we do not let you insure your neighbor's house. Insurance works by using the premiums paid in by all the insured to cover the losses that infrequently visit a small subset of them. Of course, insurance always turns out to be a bad deal for almost all the insured—the return is hugely negative because most of the insured never collect benefits, and the insurance company has to cover all costs and earn profits on its business. Its operating costs and profits are more or less equal to the net losses suffered by its policy holders.

Ideally, insurance premiums ought to be linked to individual risks; if this changes behavior so that risk falls, so much the better. That reduces the costs to the other policy holders who do not experience insured events, and it also increases profitability of the insurance companies. Competition among insurers will then reduce the premiums for those whose behavior modifications have reduced risks.

In practice, people are put into classes—say, over age 55 years with no accidents or moving violations in the case of auto insurance. Some people are uninsurable—risks are too high. For example, one who repeatedly wrecks cars while driving drunk will not be able to purchase insurance. The government might help by taking away the driver's license, in which case the insurer could not sell insurance even if it were willing to take on the risks. Further, one cannot insure a burning house against fire because it is, well, already afire. And even if insurance had already been purchased, the insurer can deny a claim if it determines that the policyholder was at fault.

The insured try to get into the low-risk, low-premium classes; the insurers try to sort people by risk and try to narrow risk classes. To be sure, insurers do not want to avoid all risks—given a risk/return trade-off, higher risk individuals will be charged higher premiums. Problems for the insurer arise if high-risk individuals are placed in low-risk classes, thus, enjoy inappropriately low premiums. The problem for many individuals is that appropriately priced premiums will be unaffordable. At the extreme, if the probability of an insurable event approaches certainty, the premium that must be charged equals the expected loss plus insurance company operating costs and profits. However, it is likely that high-risk individuals would refuse insurance long before premiums reached that level.

Of course, insured risks change over time—which means premiums charged might not cover the new risks. Some changes reduce risks, but others increase risks. Cars become safer. More people wear seat belts. Fire-resistant materials become standard and firefighting technologies improve. But global warming produces more frequent and perhaps more severe hurricanes and tornadoes. In general, these changes are generally sufficiently slow that premiums and underwriting standards can be adjusted. Obviously, big and abrupt changes to risks would make it difficult to properly price premiums. Worryingly, it seems that the risks of climate change may rise so fast that insurance will not be able to handle the changing risk environment.

In any event, once insurance is written, the insurer does its best to deny claims. Insurers will look at the fine print, try to find exclusions, and uncover preexisting conditions (say, faulty wiring) that invalidate claims. All of that is good business practice. Regulators are needed to protect the insured from overly aggressive denials of claims, a responsibility mostly of state government.

Let us examine the goal of universal health insurance from this perspective. It should now be obvious that using health "insurance" as the primary payment mechanism for healthcare is terribly inappropriate.

From the day of our birth, each of us is a little bundle of preexisting conditions—congenital abnormalities and genetic predispositions to disease or perhaps to risky behavior. Many of these conditions will only be discovered much later, probably in a doctor's office. The health insurer will likely remain in the dark until a bill is submitted for payment. It then must seek a way to deny the claim. The insurer will check the fine print and patient records for exclusions and preexisting conditions. Often, insurers automatically issue a denial, forcing patients to file an appeal. This burdens the insured and their caregivers with mountains of paperwork. Again, that is just good business practice—exactly what one would expect from an insurer.

And, again, it would be best to match individual premiums to risk, but usually people are placed into groups, often (for historical reasons) into employee groups. Insurers prefer youngish, urban, well-educated, professionals—those jogging yuppies with good habits and enough income to join expensive gyms with personal trainers. Naturally, the insurer wants to charge premiums higher than what the risks would justify, and to exclude from coverage the most expensive procedures.

Many individuals are not really insurable, due to preexisting conditions or risky behavior. However, many of these will be covered by negotiated group insurance due to their employment status. The idea is that the risks are spread and the healthier members of the group will subsidize the least healthy. This allows the insurer to escape the abnormally high risks of insuring high-risk individuals. It is, of course, a bum deal for the healthy employees and their employers.

This is not the place for a detailed examination of the wisdom of tying health insurance to one's employer. It is very difficult to believe that any justification can be made for it, so no one tries to justify it. It is simply accepted as a horrible historical accident. It adds to the marginal cost of producing output since employers usually pick up a share of the premiums. It depresses the number of employees while forcing more overtime work (since healthcare costs are fixed per employee, not based on hours worked) as well as more part-time work (since insurance coverage usually requires a minimum number of hours worked, part-time workers are excluded from the insurance plan and thus cheaper). And it burdens "legacy firms" that offer life-time work as well as healthcare for retirees.

Finally, and obviously, it leaves huge segments of the population uncovered because they are not employed, because they are self-employed, or because they work in small firms. In short, one probably could not design a worse way of grouping individuals for the purposes of insurance provision. Would anyone reasonably propose that the primary means of delivering drivers to auto insurers would be through their employers? Or that auto insurance premiums ought to be set by the insurable loss experience of one's coworkers? That is too ridiculous to contemplate—and so we do not—but it is what we do with health insurance.

Extending coverage to a diabetic against the risk of coming down with diabetes is like insuring a burning house. An individual with diabetes does not need insurance— she/he needs quality healthcare and good advice that is followed in order to increase the quality of life while reducing healthcare costs. Accompanying this healthcare with an insurance premium is not likely to have much effect on the healthcare outcome because it will not change behavior beyond what could be accomplished through effective counseling. Indeed, charging higher premiums to those with diabetes is only likely to postpone diagnosis among those whose condition has not yet been identified. Getting people with diabetes into an insured pool increases costs for the other members of the pool. Both the insurer as well as the other insured members have an interest in keeping high-risk individuals out of the pool.

Experience shows that healthcare costs follow an 80/20 pattern: 80% of healthcare costs are incurred due to treatment of 20% of patients.[12] If only a fraction of those high-cost individuals can be excluded, costs to the insurer can be cut dramatically.

Before Obamacare was passed, we had nearly 50 million individuals without health insurance. Most health "reform" proposals put forward at that time would somehow insure many or most of these people—mostly by forcing them to buy insurance. All of those without coverage had preexisting conditions (we all do!), many of which are precisely the type that if known would make them uninsurable if insurance companies could exclude them. While it is likely that only a fraction of the uninsured before Obamacare had been explicitly excluded from insurance because of existing conditions (many more were excluded because they could not afford premiums)—but every one of them had numerous existing conditions and one of the main goals of "reform" was to make it more difficult for insurers to exclude people with existing conditions. In other words, "reform" needed to require people who do not want to buy insurance to buy it and to require insurers who do not want to extend insurance to them to provide it. That is not a happy situation even in the best of circumstances—as President Trump continued to remind us when he campaigned for an end to the individual mandate to buy insurance.

So back in 2009 I put forward what I thought the outcome of any attempt to extend private health insurance to all would look like. Individuals will be forced to buy insurance against their will, often with premiums set unaffordably high. Government will provide a subsidy so that insurance can be provided. Insurance companies will impose high copayments as well as deductibles that the insured cannot afford. In this way, they will minimize claims and routine use of healthcare services by the nominally insured. When disaster strikes—putting a poorly covered

---

[12] See Roger Bybee's interview of Dr. Steffie Woolhandler "More Than a Prayer for Single Payer".

individual into that 20/80 high cost class of patients—the insurer will find a way to dismiss claims. The "insured" individual will then be faced with bankrupting uncovered costs.

That was not a farfetched prediction. Before Obamacare, two-thirds of household bankruptcies were due to healthcare costs. Surprisingly, most of those who were forced into bankruptcy had health insurance—but lost it after treatment began, or simply could not afford the out-of-pocket expenses that the insurer refused to cover. As Woolhandler wrote, in 2007 an individual in her 50s would pay an insurance premium of $4200 per year, with a $2000 deductible. Many of those without insurance would not be able to pay the deductible, meaning that the health insurance would not provide any coverage for routine care. Only an emergency or development of a chronic condition would drive such a patient into the healthcare system; with exclusions and limitations on coverage, the patient could find that even after meeting the $2000 deductible plus extra spending on copayments, bankruptcy would be the only way to deal with all of the uncovered expenses. Of course, that would leave care providers with the bill—which is more or less what happens without the universal insurance mandate.

To be sure, Obamacare did offer fairly generous subsidies for low-income households and it prohibited exclusion of "preexisting" conditions. However, insurers were not required to participate and as time went on many chose to withdraw from participation. This left consumers with less choice, sometimes with no choice at all as only one insurer would be left. Routine denials of claims remain common, and high deductibles and copayments continue to discourage the insured from seeking medical attention. Even if we admit that Obamacare on balance was an improvement, all of the weaknesses of running much of the healthcare system through for-profit insurers remained—as I had predicted.

To put things in perspective, in 2013, before Obamacare began, there were 44 million nonelderly people without insurance who would qualify; as of 2017, there remained over 27 million without insurance.[13] Thus, there was a reduction of about 17 million uninsured after Obamacare. A total of 12 million got insured through the Medicaid expansion and about 10 million enrolled in Obamacare's "Marketplace" plans. In addition, Obamacare improved coverage for millions more due to provisions that required employers to offer plans and due to expanded coverage in plans. However, while Obamacare represents an improvement over the situation in 2013, it has not (yet) succeeded in extending insurance to cover all Americans.

Further, President Trump's "tax reform" of 2017 ended the individual mandate to purchase insurance by reducing the penalty to $0 as of 2019. Trump's attack on

---

[13] "Those most at risk of being uninsured include low-income individuals, adults, and people of color. The cost of coverage continues to be the most commonly cited barrier to coverage." About 45% of those without insurance are either low income people in states that opted out of expanded Medicaid insurance, are immigrants who do not qualify for Obamacare or have income too high to obtain Federal subsidies. The rest do not seem to have a good reason for staying outside the program—except that they perceive costs to be too high (KKF Report, 2019).

immigrants will likely reduce the number who seek insurance. He has also reduced some of the Federal subsidies provided to private insurers and made it easier for states to limit Medicaid coverage. For all these reasons, it is likely that the number of uninsured will grow.[14]

In truth, insurance is a particularly bad way to provide payments for healthcare. Insurance is best suited to covering unexpected losses that result from acts of god, accidents, and other unavoidable calamities. But except in the case of teenagers and young adult males, accidents are not a major source of healthcare costs. In other words, the costs to the insurer are not the equivalent of a tornado that randomly sets its sights on a trailer park. Rather, chronic illnesses, sometimes severe, and often those that lead to death, are more important. Selling insurance to a patient with a chronic and ultimately fatal illness would be like selling home insurance on a house that is slowly but certainly sliding down a cliff into the sea. Neither of these is really an insurable risk—rather each represents a certain cost with an actuarially sound premium that must exceed the loss (to cover operating costs and profits for the insurer). So if the policy were properly priced, no one would have an economic incentive to purchase it.

Another significant healthcare cost results from provision of what could be seen as public health services—vaccinations, mother and infant care, and so on. And a large part of that has nothing to do with calamity but rather with normal life processes: pregnancy, birth, well child care, school physicals, and certification of death at the other end of life. Treating a pregnancy as an insurable loss seems silly—even if it is unplanned. It does not make much sense to finance the healthcare costs associated with pregnancy and birth in the same way that we finance the costs of repairing an auto after a wreck—that is, through an insurance claim. Many of these expenditures have public goods aspects; while there are private benefits, if the healthcare cannot be covered through private insurance or out of pocket, the consequences can lead to huge public sector costs. For this reason, it does not make sense to try to fund all private benefits of such care by charges to the individuals who may—or may not—be able and willing to pay for them. Nor does it make sense to raise premiums on one's coworkers to cover expected pregnancies as young women join a firm.

Healthcare is not similar to protecting a homeowner against losses due to natural disasters. The risks to the health insurer are greatly affected by the behavior of the covered individuals, as well as by social policy. Discovering cures and new treatments can greatly increase, or reduce, costs. To a large extent that is outside the control of the insurer or the insured—if a new treatment becomes standard care, there will be pressures on insurers to cover it. Death might be the most cost-effective way to deal with heart attacks, but standard practice does not present that as a standard treatment—nor would public policy want it to do so. In other words, social

---

[14] See footnote 13. Under Trump, the number of uninsured had grown by 7 million by 2019. https://www.vox.com/2019/1/23/18194228/trump-uninsured-rate-obamacare-medicaid.

policy dictates to a large degree the losses that insurers must cover; acts of congress are not equivalent in their origins to acts of god—although their impacts on insurers are similar.

People currently pay most healthcare expenses through health insurance (see graph below). But they need healthcare services on a routine basis—and not simply for unexpected calamities. We have become so accustomed to health insurance that we cannot understand how absurd it is to finance healthcare services in this manner. Healthcare "reform" through Obamacare forced us to turn over a larger portion of our income to insurance companies—who then do their best to ensure that any healthcare services we need will not be covered by the plan we are forced to buy. Unlike a broken toaster that can just be thrown out when the warranty fails to cover repairs, we do not, and do not want to, throw out people whose insurance coverage proves to be inadequate.

THE NATION'S HEALTH DOLLAR ($3.5 TRILLION), CALENDAR YEAR 2017: WHERE IT CAME FROM

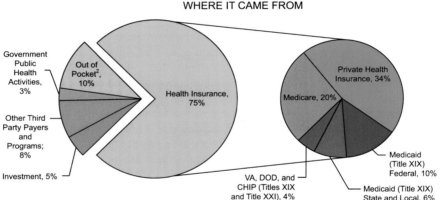

Source: https://www.cms.gov/Research-Statistics-Data-and-Systems/Statistics-Trends-and-Reports/ NationalHealthExpendData/Downloads/PieChartSourcesExpenditures.pdf.

It is worthwhile to step back to look at the costs of providing healthcare payments through insurers. As the figure above shows, about three-quarters of our healthcare dollar flows through health insurance (about 10% is paid out of pocket), and about a third of that goes to the private insurance sector (about $900 billion in 2017—a quarter of all spending).

According to Woolhandler, about 11 cents of each dollar goes to administrative overhead and profit of the healthcare providers. Much of that is due to all the paperwork required to try to get the insurance companies to pay claims (there are 1300 private insurers, with nearly as many different forms that healthcare providers must fill out to file claims); it is estimated that $350 billion a year could be saved on paperwork if the United States adopted a single-payer system. (Matt Taibi,

"Sick and Wrong", *Rolling Stone*, September 3, 2009). Hence, a large part of all healthcare spending in the United States results from the peculiar way that we finance our healthcare system—relying on insurance companies for a fundamentally uninsurable service. Getting insurance companies out of the loop would go a long way toward "paying for" provision of healthcare services to all of those who currently have inadequate access—including the underinsured.

In sum, using insurers to provide funding is a complex, costly, and distorting method of financing healthcare. Imagine sending your weekly grocery bill to an insurance clerk for review, and having the grocer reimbursed by the insurer to whom you have been paying "food insurance" premiums—with some of your purchases excluded from coverage at the whim of the insurer. Is there any plausible reason for putting an insurance agent between you and your grocer? Why do we put an insurer between you and your healthcare provider?

c. Health insurance diversions: the financialization of health (and everything else)

In the previous two subsections I have argued that extending private insurance is neither desirable nor would it significantly reduce healthcare costs. Indeed, healthcare insurance is a particularly bad way to provide funding of the provision of healthcare services. In this subsection I argue that extension of healthcare insurance represents yet another unwelcome intrusion of finance into every part of our economy and our lives. In other words, the "reforms" adopted in Obamacare simply complete the financialization of healthcare that is already sucking money and resources into the same black hole that swallowed residential real estate.

In Part A we have examined the financialization of houses and commodities and even lives. In all of these cases, Wall Street packages assets (home mortgages, commodities futures, and life insurance policies) so that gamblers can speculate on outcomes. If you lose your home through a mortgage delinquency, if food prices rise high enough to cause starvation, or if you die an untimely death, Wall Streeters win. Health insurance works out a bit differently: they sell you insurance and then the insurer denies your claim due to preexisting conditions or simply because denial is more profitable and you probably do not have sufficient funding to fight your way through the courts. You then go bankrupt (according to Steffie Woolhandler, two-thirds of US bankruptcies are due to healthcare bills) and Wall Street takes your assets and garnishes your wages.

Here is the opportunity that helped to push Obamacare through Congress: there was a huge untapped market of nearly 50 million people who are not paying insurance premiums—and the number was growing every year because employers were dropping coverage and people could not afford premiums. Solution? Health insurance "reform" that requires everyone to turn over their pay to Wall Street. Cannot afford the premiums? That is OK—Uncle Sam will kick in a few hundred billion to help out the insurers. Of course, do not expect more healthcare or better health outcomes because that has little to do with "reform". Washington was more concerned about Wall Street's insurers, who saw a missed opportunity. They will collect the extra premiums and deny the claims. This is just another bailout of the financial system because the tens of trillions of dollars already committed were not nearly enough.

You might wonder about the connection between insurance and Wall Street finance. They are two peas in a pod. Indeed, we threw out the Glass-Steagall Act that separated commercial banking from investment banking and insurance with the Gramm-Leach-Bliley Act of 1999 (note how easily that rolls off the tongue) that let Wall Street form Bank Holding Companies that integrate the full range of "financial services", that provide loans and deposits, that sell toxic waste mortgage securities to your pension funds, that create commodity futures indexes for university endowments to drive up the price of your petrol, and that take bets on the deaths of firms, countries, and your loved ones.

Student loans, credit card debt, and auto leases? Financialized—packaged and sold to gamblers making bets on default. Even the weather can be financialized. You think I jest? The World Food Programme (WFP) proposed to issue "catastrophe bonds" linked to low rainfall. The WFP would pay principal and interest when rainfall was sufficient; if there was no rainfall, the WFP would cease making payments on the bonds and would instead fund relief efforts (Das, 2006). As are earthquakes— Tokyo Disneyland issued bonds that did not have to be repaid in the event of an earthquake (Das, 2006). It is rumored that Wall Street will even take bets on assassination of world leaders. Why not? Someone even set up a charitable trust called the "Sisters of Perpetual Ecstasy" as a special purpose vehicle to move risky assets off the books of its mother superior bank, to escape what passed for regulation in recent years (Das, 2006).

I once facetiously recommended the creation of a market in Martian ocean front condo futures to satisfy the cravings of Wall Street for new frontiers in risk. Obviously, I set my sights too low. The next bubble could be in carbon trading— financialization of pollution!—this time truly toxic waste will be packaged and sold off to global savers. According to Das (p. 320), traders talk about new frontiers "trading in rights to clean air, water and access to fishing grounds; basics of human life that I had always taken for granted". Yes, all the basics of life can and will be financialized.

Is there an alternative to health insurance? Leaving aside the political problems—once Wall Street has got its hands on some aspect of our lives, it is very difficult to wrest control from its grasp—healthcare is a very complex issue. It is clear that provision of routine care should not be left to insurance companies. Perhaps "single payer" (that is, the federal government) should provide basic coverage for all of life's normal healthcare needs, with individuals purchasing additional coverage for accidents. Basic coverage can be deinsured—births, routine exams and screening, inoculations, hospice and elder care.

On the other hand, a significant portion of healthcare expenses is due to chronic problems, some of which can be traced to birth. Above we discussed why these are not really insurable—they are the existing conditions that profit-seeking insurers should exclude. Others can be traced to lifestyle "choices". Some employers are already charging higher premiums to employees whose body mass index exceeds a chosen limit—with rebates provided to those who manage to lose weight. While it is doubtful that a monetary incentive will be effective in changing behavior that is certainly quite complex, this approach is probably better than excluding individuals from insurance simply because of their BMI.

Some have called for extending a Medicare-like program to all (see the discussion below). Although sometimes called insurance, basic Medicare (we will ignore the optional add-ons to traditional Medicare) is not really an insurance program. Rather it pays for qualifying healthcare of qualified individuals. It is essentially a universal payer, PAYGO system. Its revenues come from taxes and "premiums" paid by covered individuals for a portion of the program. I will not go into the details, but "PAYGO" means it is not advance funded (the concept is similar to the original setup of Social Security). While many believe that its Trust Fund could be strengthened through higher taxes now so that more benefits could be paid later as America ages, actually, Medicare spending today is covered by today's government spending—and tomorrow's Medicare spending will be covered by tomorrow's government spending. At the national level, it is not possible to transport today's tax revenue to tomorrow to "pay for" future Medicare spending. (See the discussion of Social Security's Trust Fund above.)

I realize this is a difficult concept. In real terms, however, it is simpler to understand: Medicare is PAYGO because the healthcare services are provided today, to today's seniors; there is no way to stockpile medical services for future use (although some medical machinery and hospitals can be built now to be used later, the actual health services cannot). And the real purpose of taxes and premiums paid today is to reduce net personal income so that resources can be diverted to the healthcare sector. (Many—including me—believe we already have too many resources directed to that sector—projected to reach 20% by 2020—double that of our peer nations—although too many of the resources go to insurance, paperwork, administration, and profits.)

Hence, the solution cannot be to raise taxes or premiums today in order to build a bigger trust fund to reduce burdens tomorrow. If we find that 25 years from now we need more resources in the healthcare sector, the best way to do that will be to spend more on healthcare at that time, and to tax incomes at that time to reduce consumption in other areas so that resources can be shifted to healthcare *at that time*.

Our problem *today* is that we need to allocate more healthcare services to the currently underserved, which is comprised of two different sets of people: folks with no health insurance, and those with health insurance that is too limited in coverage to provide the care they need. The Obamacare solution was to provide a subsidy to get private insurers to expand coverage. That is a waste of spending. Let us see why.

If we take my example pursued above of a person with diabetes who is excluded because of the existing condition, the marginal subsidy required to move that person into private health insurance would have to equal the expected cost of care, plus a risk premium in case that estimate turns out to be too low, plus the costs of running the insurance business, plus normal profits. If on the other hand diabetes care were directly covered by a federal government payment to healthcare providers, the risk premium, insurance business costs, and profits on the insurance business would not be necessary. In other words, using the insurance system to pay for added costs of providing care to people with diabetes adds several layers of costs. That just makes no sense.

We face four serious and complex issues that can be separately analyzed.

First, we need a system that provides healthcare services. Our current healthcare system does a tolerably good job for most people, although a large portion of the population does not receive adequate preventative and routine care, thus, is forced to rely on expensive emergency treatment. The solution to that is fairly obvious and easy to implement—if we leave payment to the side. As discussed above we must recognize that a big part of America's health expenses are due to chronic and avoidable conditions that result from the corporatization of food—a more difficult problem to resolve.

Second, our system might, on the other hand, provide in the aggregate too many resources toward the provision of healthcare (leaving other needs of our population unmet). Rational discussion and then rational allocation can deal with that. We do not need "death panels" (which we already have—run by the insurance companies), but we do need rational allocation. I expect that healthcare professionals can do a far better job than Wall Street will ever do in deciding how much care and what type of care should be provided. Individuals who would like more care than professionals decide to be in the public interest can always pay out of pocket or can purchase private insurance. Maybe the cost of Botox treatments is an insurable expense? Obviously, what is deemed to be necessary healthcare will evolve over time—it, like human rights is "aspirational"—and someday might include nose jobs and tummy tucks for everyone.

Third, Americans pay far more for both drugs and care than do other rich nations—about twice as much for similar products and services. In the case of drugs this is because of patents that prevent competition as well as due to reluctance on the part of the government (a buyer of many of the drugs through its role as provider of Medicaid and Medicare) to negotiate for lower prices. A clear example of pricing power in the pharmaceutical sector was Martin Shkreli's fraud, arrested for price gouging in 2018. In the case of provisioning of care, it is due to high compensation of doctors—who are paid twice as much as doctors abroad—that is due in part to restrictions on entry (and, surprisingly, to unwillingness or inability of insurers to constrain reimbursement rates). We need to tackle these problems through government resolve to negotiate lower prices of pharmaceuticals and through government promotion of more training of and entry of doctors into the profession.

Fourth, we need a way to pay for healthcare services. For routine healthcare and for preexisting conditions the only logical conclusion is that the best risk pool is the population as a whole. It is in the public interest to see that the entire population receives routine care. It is also in the public interest to see that our little bundles of preexisting conditions (otherwise known as infants) get the care they need. There is no obvious advantage to involving private insurance in the payment system for this kind of care. If we decided to have more than one insurer, we would have to be sure that each had the same risks, hence, the same sort of insured pool. It is conceivable that competition among private insurers could drive down premiums, but it is more likely that competition would instead take the form of excluding as many claims as possible. We would thus get high premiums and lots of exclusions—exactly what we have got now.

We could instead have a single national private insurer pursuing the normal monopoly pricing and poor service strategy (remember those good old days when you could choose from among one single telephone service provider?), but in that case we would have to regulate the premiums as well as the rejection of claims. Regulation of premiums cannot be undertaken without regulating the healthcare costs that the insurer(s) would have to cover. If we are going to go to all the trouble of regulating premiums, claim rejections, and healthcare prices, we might as well go the whole hog and have the federal government pay the costs. Difficult and contentious, yes. Impossible? No—we can look to our fellow developed nations for examples, and to our own Medicare system—which is highly efficient.

Finally, there may still be a role for private insurers, albeit a substantially downsized one. Private insurance can be reserved for accidents, with individuals grouped according to similar risks: hang-gliders, smokers, and texting drivers can all be sorted into risk classes for insurance purposes. If it is any consolation to the downsized insurers, we also need to downsize the role played by the whole financial sector. Finance will not like that because it has become accustomed to its outsized role. In recent years it has been taking 40% of corporate profits. It takes most of its share off the top—fees and premiums that it receives before anyone else gets paid. Rather than playing an auxiliary role, helping to ensure that goods and services get produced and distributed to those who need them, Wall Street has come to see its role as primary, with all aspects of our economy run by the Masters of the Universe.

As John Kenneth Galbraith's *The Great Crash* shows, that was exactly the situation our country faced in the late 1920s. It took the Great Depression to put Wall Street back into its proper place. The question is whether we can get it into the backseat without another great depression.

d. Selling death

When Wall Street's commodities bubble crashed in 2008, I wondered whether the next bubble might be in securitized body parts. Wall Street would search the world for transplantable organs, holding them in cold storage as collateral against securities sold to managed money such as pension funds.

Of course, it was meant to be an apocryphal story about unregulated banksters gone wild. But as a 2009 article in the NYT reports (Anderson, 2009), Wall Street really was moving forward to market bets on death. The banks would purchase life insurance policies, pool and trench them, and sell securities that allow money managers to bet that the underlying "collateral" (human beings) will die an untimely death. You cannot make this stuff up.

This is just the latest Wall Street scheme to profit on death, of course. It has been marketing credit default swaps that allow one to bet on the death of firms, cities, and even nations. And the commodities futures speculation pushed by Goldman caused starvation and death around the globe when the prices of agricultural products exploded (along with the price of gasoline) between 2004 and 2008. But now Goldman will directly cash in on death.

Here is how it works. Goldman and other Wall Street firms will package a bunch of life insurance policies of individuals with an alphabet soup of diseases: AIDS, leukemia, lung cancer, heart disease, breast cancer, diabetes, and Alzheimer's. The idea is to diversify across diseases to protect "investors" from the horror that a cure might be found for one or more afflictions—prolonging life and reducing profits. These policies are the collateral behind securities graded by those same ratings agencies that thought subprime mortgages should be as safe as US Treasuries. Investors purchase the securities, paying fees to Wall Street originators. The underlying collateralized humans receive a single payout. Securities holders pay the life insurance premiums until the "collateral" dies, at which point they receive the death benefits. Naturally, managed money hopes death comes sooner rather than later.

Moral hazards abound. There is a fundamental reason why you are not permitted to take out fire insurance on your neighbor's house: you would have a strong interest in seeing that house burn. If you held a life insurance policy on your neighbor, you probably would not warn him about the loose lug nuts on his Volvo. Heck, if you lost your job and you were sufficiently ethically challenged, you might even loosen them yourself.

Imagine the hit to portfolios of securitized death if universal healthcare were to make it through Congress. Or the efforts by Wall Street to keep new miracle drugs off the market if they were capable of extending life of human collateral. Who knows, perhaps the bankster's next investment product will be gangsters in the business of guaranteeing lifespans do not exceed actuarially based estimates.

If you think all of this is far-fetched, you have not been paying attention. From Charles Keating's admonition to his sales staff that the weak, meek, and ignorant elderly widows always make good targets, to recent internal emails circulated within the major credit ratings agencies boasting about giving high ratings to toxic securities, we know that Wall Street's contempt for the rest of us knows no bounds.

Hedge funds holding CDS "insurance" fought to force the US auto industry into bankruptcy for the simple reason that they would make more from its death than from its resurrection. And the reason that most troubled mortgages could not obtain relief in the aftermath of the crash is because the firms that service the mortgages gain more from foreclosure.

It is not a big step for Wall Street and global money managers with big gambling stakes at risk to slow efforts to improve health. Indeed, it is easy to see some very nice and profitable synergies developing between Wall Street sellers of death and health insurers opposed to universal, single-payer healthcare. It would not be in the interest of securities holders or health insurers to provide expensive care that would prolong the life of human collateral—a natural synergy that someone will notice. As Alexandria Ocasio-Cortez said "Actually, we have for-profit 'death panels' now: they are companies + boards saying you're on your own bc they won't cover a critical procedure or medicine"—the private health insurers decide when to deny coverage (The Hill, 2018).

It should be amply evident that Wall Street could recreate the conditions that existed in 2005. Virtually every element that created the real estate, commodities, and CDS bubbles could be replicated in the securitization of life insurance policies. If Wall Street went forward with this scheme, it could bankrupt the life insurance companies (premiums are set on the assumption that many policyholders will cancel long before death—but once securitized, the premiums will be paid so that benefits can be collected). But it is likely that the bubble will be popped long before that happens, at which point Wall Street will look for the next opportunity. Securitized pharmaceuticals? Body parts?

This perverse logic could be extended to healthcare more generally. Longevity is a big additional cost for the healthcare industry; ideally, you need to create incentives to ensure that people die younger. More people dead at age 55 years and Presto!—there go the waiting lists for hip replacement surgery, and payouts to holders of life settlement products soar.

While we understand that there is a real need for some terminally ill patients to cash out their life insurance policies (to cover care expenses, for example), securitization is a path fraught with danger. Radical reform is needed. Ideally, instruments such as credit default swaps and life settlement securities ought to be banned, since they operate against the public interest.

At a minimum, the sale of CDS "protection" should be limited to those with an economic interest in default, such as the holders of bonds, mortgages, or other assets that might be "insured." No one should be permitted to buy "insurance" to bet on another person's calamity. Further, all such contracts should be executed on exchanges—and declared to be unenforceable if they are not. Why should we extend the protection of enforcement by US courts of law to contracts, made in secret, that increase systemic risk?

Here is the problem. There is still—even after massive losses in the last crisis—far too much managed money chasing far too few returns. And there are far too many "rocket scientists" looking for the next newest and best financial product. Each new product brings a rush of funds that narrows returns; this then spurs rising leverage ratios using borrowed funds to make up for low spreads by increasing volume; this causes risk to rise far too high to be covered by the returns. Eventually, lenders and managed money try to get out, but delevering creates a liquidity crisis as asset prices plunge. Resulting losses are socialized as government bails out the banksters. Repeat as often as necessary.

Reform of the US financial sector is neither possible nor would it ever be sufficient. As any student of horror films knows, you cannot reform vampires or zombies. They must be killed (stakes through the hearts of Wall Street's vampires, bullets to the heads of zombie banks). In other words, the financial system must be downsized.

e. The compulsive push for single payer

Since the election of President Trump the push for a universal single-payer health-care program in the United States has gained momentum. In part, this is due to Republican plans to gut Obamacare. However, it is mostly Obamacare's surprising successes and failures that have boosted support for a single-payer system. With heavy federal government subsidies of premiums for low-income people, private insurance became more affordable for millions, while an expansion of Medicaid further reduced the ranks of the uninsured.[15] Fearing a backlash in the next election, Republicans are having trouble making good on their promise to repeal Obamacare—or even to replace it with the mean-spirited Republican version that would kick tens of millions off insurance.

But, as Stephanie Woolhandler laments, *"the Affordable Care Act has been vulnerable to these Republican attacks, because people look at their own situation and say, 'Even under Obamacare, under the Affordable Care Act, healthcare [is] still not affordable to me.'"* (Woolhandler 2017).

As government subsidies and out-of-pocket spending continue to rise and as insurers intensify efforts to deny submitted claims and/or withdraw from the "marketplaces," a political reaction is inevitable. Obamacare is ultimately politically unsustainable because it relies too much on a private, for-profit insurance system to pay for healthcare. It is time to abandon this overly complex and expensive payments system and reconsider a single-payer system.

For inspiration, we can look back to President Roosevelt's New Deal. As discussed, Social Security remains among the most important achievements of the Roosevelt legacy. It was sold as an insurance program to provide old-age security—with "premiums" (in the form of payroll taxes) paid over working years to cover retirement income. In truth, it never conformed to usual insurance principles (it was set up as a "redistributive" scheme in favor of low-income workers and those with shorter work histories), and it moved ever further away from an insurance model over time (as benefits were expanded to cover those with little work experience, such as people with disabilities, children, and surviving family members).

In truth, Social Security is an intergenerational assurance program: today's workers take care of today's retirees and tomorrow's workers will take care of tomorrow's retirees. There is no alternative because no matter how much we might save for our retirements, most of what we consume during our golden years will have to be produced by those still working after we retire (Wray, 2006). Old age "insurance" does not change that—what matters is our "single-payer" Uncle Sam who will provide us with the income we will need for a decent retirement. The taxes he will impose on tomorrow's workers are not really insurance premiums—payroll taxes simply assure us that workers will not purchase everything they produce, leaving something for retirees to buy.

---

[15] A subsequent Supreme Court decision allowing states to opt out of the Medicaid expansion has undermined this prong of Obamacare.

Social Security is a single-payer retirement system.

Some in the Roosevelt administration had planned to push for a national system of healthcare as part of Social Security, but backed off due to opposition by the American Medical Association (AMA)—which managed to prevent any significant advance until President Johnson succeeded in adding Medicare for the aged, prevailing over the AMA's well-financed campaign that enlisted Ronald Reagan to try to convince the population that Medicare was a communist-inspired plot to destroy the American entrepreneurial spirit (Skidmore, 1999). By this time, private insurance had a lock on the healthcare payments system for many workers through their employers. So Medicare focused on the aged. Medicaid—a federal-state partnership—was also added to provide payments for the poor.

This patchwork system left many gaps, including workers at small establishments that did not provide group coverage, the self-employed, those with too much income to qualify for Medicaid but too little to afford expensive coverage for individuals, and those living in states with inadequate Medicaid coverage. As healthcare costs rose, the problems with the patchwork system became increasingly obvious. At the time of the passage of the Affordable Care Act in 2010, approximately 50 million individuals were without healthcare insurance.

As we have discussed, US healthcare provision is far more expensive (as a percentage of GDP) than that of other developed capitalist countries, with no better outcomes—indeed, similar outcomes are obtained while spending as little as half as much. Our peers use a wide variety of methods of provisioning and paying for healthcare, ranging from full-on "socialization" with government ownership of the hospitals to market-based private ownership of medical practices. Many use a single-payer system (whether provisioning of healthcare is nationalized or privatized), with government covering the costs, while some use private insurers.

What is unique about the United States is that we rely so extensively on private for-profit insurers—in other countries that allow participation by private insurers, these are run more like heavily regulated, not-for-profit charities. Foreign health insurance plans largely exist to pay bills and improve health, not to make a profit (Reid, 2010). Not coincidentally, the United States is also the only wealthy nation with such a large segment of its population still lacking adequate health coverage—even after Obamacare.

The problems with the Obamacare model could have been foreseen, and indeed were foreseen as described above (see (Wray NEP, 2009/8)). Simple tweaking will not do. Social Security and Medicare provide a model for reform along single-payer lines. Social Security's old-age retirement plan is nearly universal, with the federal government acting as the single payer; Medicare is universal for those over age 65 years and the main part of it is single payer, with the federal government making the payments. Both of these programs impose a payroll tax, ostensibly to fund the spending—with both building reserves to provide for an aging population. As discussed above, this is simultaneously a strength ("I paid in, so I deserve the benefits; it is not welfare") and a weakness (intergenerational warriors continually foresee bankruptcy).

Critics of proposals to provide universal healthcare coverage through a single-payer system argue that it is unaffordable. Where will the government find the $3.5 trillion required to pay for the whole kit and kaboodle? While one response is that total spending would likely go down if the system were rationalized under a single payer, critics argue that taxes would still have to be raised by a lot as we shifted from private payments to government funding.

But we can look at the taxes another way, from the perspective of the economy as a whole. Taxing today's workers reduces their net income, which reduces their spending. This leaves resources that can be directed to caring for the needs of today's elderly; government spending on retirement through Social Security and on healthcare through Medicare ensure that some of the resources are directed to satisfying those needs. In other words, the purpose of the taxes is not to raise revenue but to free up resources by taking income out of the economy so that it cannot be spent.

From the aggregate perspective, it would be better to broaden the tax base beyond payrolls—since wages today account for less than half of national income. We should also tax other income sources, such as profits, capital gains, rents, and interest. Not because the government needs revenue! But to preserve resources that can be directed to the healthcare system.

What is the right balance between spending and taxes? Let us pose two extremes. In the first case, the economy has ample unemployed resources to provide healthcare for all. In this case, the single-payer government simply spends enough to provide adequate healthcare with no additional taxes required. In the second case, let us presume the economy is already at full employment of all resources. To move some of the employed resources into the healthcare sector, the government needs to impose taxes sufficient to reduce consumption and investment spending to free up resources for healthcare. It then spends to reemploy those resources in the healthcare sector.

To be sure, the US probably already devotes too many resources to healthcare (including insurance). It is highly likely that implementation of universal "Medicare" for all would reduce the healthcare sector's use of resources—even though it would mean greater access to healthcare. That means that we will find that we do not need to raise taxes but it still would make sense to spread the taxes more fairly across all sources of income rather than targeting wages. It is conceivable that implementation of the single-payer system could reduce the national share of GDP going to healthcare from the current 18% toward the 10% or so that is common in other rich developed countries.

If we got down to 12% of GDP that would be a huge reduction of aggregate demand that would require a big tax cut. Imagine that: healthcare for all plus a tax cut! However, as discussed earlier, the United States seems to have specific health challenges that might prevent such big savings. Still it is likely that the health services sector (again, including insurance) would shrink by a few percentage points of GDP. If some other sector did not grow, we might find we need more spending or a tax cut even as we phase in Medicare for all simply because we will release a few percentage points worth of resources from the healthcare sector.

Of course, this high-level aggregate analysis is too simple, as the already employed plus unemployed resources may not be appropriate for provision of the extra healthcare services that will be demanded by those who finally have access to decent healthcare—as well as by the growing numbers of seniors who need more healthcare. It will take some time to train and retrain workers, and to invest in healthcare facilities and pharmaceuticals production. The nation will need to rely on a combination of market forces (responding to higher demand for healthcare) as well as government incentives (taxes to reduce spending elsewhere, subsidies to encourage investments in healthcare delivery, and spending on training and infrastructure) to prepare for the tide of baby boomers requiring more healthcare.

Eliminating private insurance premiums would reduce costs for employers. This could allow them to reduce prices of their output, to increase wages, or to reap higher profits. Eliminating the insurance premiums would also increase net take-home pay for the workers. It is possible that these benefits would boost consumption to at least partially compensate for the reduction of aggregate demand caused by elimination of the private health insurance sector. It might also allow workers (and firms) to pay down some debt and increase their savings. It is possible—although I think it is unlikely—that the net impact of all this could be inflationary. If so, we might have to impose some new taxes as we phase-in the single-payer system. This would not be to "pay for" the spending by government but to prevent inflationary pressures from building.

Single-payer systems are much cheaper, more efficient, and simpler to understand and implement (Frank, 2017). While it might seem counterintuitive, eliminating competition in the payments system actually reduces costs. Competition among for-profit insurers works to exclude those who need healthcare the most, while simultaneously boosting paperwork and billing costs even as it leaves people undercovered. If we do not allow insurers to exclude preexisting conditions, and if we could somehow block insurers' ability to deny payments for expensive and chronic illnesses, then each insurer needs young and healthy people in the pool to subsidize the unhealthy. The best way to ensure such diversification is to put the entire nation's population into a single pool. This is essentially what we do with our single-payer Social Security retirement system. Medicare does the same thing, albeit only for those over age 65 years. Medicare for all would provide the truly diversified pool needed to share the risks and distribute the costs across the entire population.

If the "insured" pool includes all Americans, there is no possibility of shunting high-cost patients off to some other insurer. And total costs are much lower because billing is simplified, administrative costs are reduced, and no profits are required for operating the payments system. Medicare is a proven, highly cost-efficient payments system, and it is compatible with the more market-oriented system that Americans seem to prefer over a nationalized healthcare delivery system such as that enjoyed in the United Kingdom.

A single-payer Medicare-style universal program is also compatible with the existence of private health insurance that can be voluntarily purchased to supplement the coverage offered by the single payer. Medicare itself already offers such supplemental coverage, and, of course, Americans have access to a plethora of private supplements to Social Security's retirement program.

Basic healthcare is not an insurable expense. All other rich nations provide universal basic healthcare. The United States stands out because, even with Obamacare, it has huge gaps in coverage while facing the highest healthcare bill in the world (as a percentage of GDP)—by a long shot.

In the 2016 election, few politicians aside from Senator Bernie Sanders were willing to stand up for single-payer healthcare. However, the debate over "repeal and replace" as well as problems that linger (and are growing) after enactment of Obamacare has made it clear that if we are serious about providing universal healthcare to Americans, the only sensible option is single payer. A new wave of activists is pushing for universal care under a single payer as part of their Green New Deal. This time, we might actually get healthcare included in our Social Security package.

III. Conclusion

Unsurprisingly, when it comes to pensions and retirement savings we reached a conclusion similar to what we conclude here with respect to our healthcare system that relies largely on private for-profit health insurance: it is best to keep Wall Street out of it. A universal single-payer "Medicare-for-all" style system would be cheaper and more efficient and would improve the provision of healthcare. A universal single-payer Social Security system would also be a cheaper and more efficient way to deliver a decent retirement for all, and would improve life in retirement if benefits were increased.

References

Aaron, H.J., 1990−1991. Comment: can the social security trust fund contribute to savings? Journal of Post Keynesian Economics 13 (2), 171.

Aaron, H., Bosworth, B.P., Burtless, G., 1989. Can America Afford to Grow Old?: Paying for Social Security. Brookings Institution.

American Society of Civil Engineers, 2017. Infrastructure Report Card. https://www.infrastructurereportcard.org/the-impact/economic-impact/.

Anderson, J., September 5, 2009. Wall street pursues profit in bundles of life insurance. The New York Times.

Das, S., 2006. Traders, Guns & Money: Knowns and Unknowns in the Dazzling World of Derivatives. FT Press, p. 32.

Ehrlich, P., 1968. The Population Bomb. Ballantine Books, New York.

Frank, R.H., July 7, 2017. Why single-payer health care saves money. The New York Times.

Ghilarducci, T., 2008. When I'm Sixty-Four: The Plot Against Pensions and the Plan to Save Them. Princeton University Press.

Greenspan, 2015, http://www.mygovcost.org/2015/06/02/what-social-security-trust-fund/ (Last accessed 8 nov 19).

KKF Report 2019. https://www.kff.org/uninsured/report/the-uninsured-and-the-aca-a-primer-key-facts-about-health-insurance-and-the-uninsured-amidst-changes-to-the-affordable-care-act/.

Kotlikoff, L.J., Burns, S., 2005. The Coming Generational Storm: What You Need to Know About America's Economic Future. The MIT Press, Cambridge, MA.

Krugman, P., May 2, 2005. A gut punch to the middle. New York Times.

Langer, D., 2000. Cooking social security's deficit. Christian Science Monitor. https://www.csmonitor.com/2000/0104/p9s2.html. last accessed Nov 19, 2019.

Mauldin, J., 2017. www.forbes.com/sites/johnmauldin/2017/10/10/your-pension-is-a-lie-theres-210-trillion-of-liabilities-our-government-cant-fulfill/#4b96102065b1.

Papadimitriou, D.B., Wray, L.R., 1999a. Can Social Security Be Saved? Jerome Levy Economics Institute Working Paper No. 270.

Papadimitriou, D.B., Wray, L.R., 1999b. Does Social Security Need Saving? Providing for Retirees Throughout the Twenty-First Century. Public Policy Brief No. 55. The Levy Economics Institute.

Papadimitriou, D.B., Wray, L.R., 1999c. More Pain, No Gain: The Breaux Plan Slashes Social Security Benefits Unnecessarily. Policy Note 8. The Levy Economics Institute, Annandale-on-Hudson, N.Y.

Pigeon, M.-A., Wray, L.R., 1999. Demand Constraints and Economic Growth. Economics Working Paper Archive Working Paper 269. Levy Economics Institute.

Pollan, M., 2008. In Defense of Food. Penguin Press.

Reid, T.R., 2010. The Healing of America: A Global Quest for Better, Cheaper, and Fairer Health Care. Penguin, New York, NY.

Roosevelt, D.F., 1941. The Four Freedoms Speech. https://www.fdrlibrary.org/four-freedoms.

Sanders, B., 2019. https://www.vox.com/2019/6/12/18663217/bernie-sanders-democratic-socialism-speech-transcript.

SIERRA, January/February 2007. Sierra Club Magazine, p. 25.

Skidmore, M.J., 1999. Social Security and Its Enemies. The Case for America's Most Efficient Insurance Program. Boulder, CO.

Skidmore, M., 2001. What happened to the social security surplus? an examination of the trustees' projections. In: Paper Presented at "The Social Security 'Crisis': Critical Analysis and Solutions" Conference at the University of Missouri—Kansas City.

The Hill, 2018. https://thehill.com/homenews/house/419349-ocasio-cortez-says-death-panels-now-exist-in-health-care.

Uncle John's Bathroom Reader, 2006. Bathroom Readers' Hysterical Society. Portable Press, p. 115.

Woolhandler, S., July 31, 2007. Interviewed by Bybee Roger "more than a prayer for single payer". The American Prospect. http://www.prospect.org/cs/articles?article=more_than_a_prayer_for_single_payer.

Woolhandler, S., 2017. Interview by Amy Goodman. Democracy Now!. https://www.democracynow.org/2017/6/23/support_grows_for_single_payer_medicare.

Wray, L.R., 1990—1991. A review of can Americans afford to grow old?: paying for social security, by Aaron, Bosworth, and Burtless. Journal of Economic Issues 24 (4), 1175—1179.

Wray, L.R., 1999. Surplus Mania: A Reality Check. Policy Note 1999/3. The Levy Economics Institute.

Wray, L.R., 2001. Killing Social Security Softly with Faux Kindness: The Draft Report by the President's Commission on Social Security Reform. Policy Note 2001/6. The Levy Economics Institute.

Wray, L.R., 2005. Manufacturing a Crisis: The Neocon Attack on Social Security. Policy Note 2005/2. The Levy Economics Institute, Annandale-on-Hudson, NY.

Wray, L.R., 2006. Global Demographic Trends and Provisioning for the Future. Working Paper No. 468. Levy Economics Institute of Bard College.

Wray, L.R., 2008. The Commodities Market Bubble: Money Manager Capitalism and the Financialization of Commodities. Economics Public Policy Brief Archive ppb_96. Levy Economics Institute.

Wray, L.R., 2009/8. Healthcare Diversions: The Elephant in the Room. New Economic Perspectives.

Tackling poverty and inequality. The road to full employment and price stability

In this Part we continue our analysis of policy to enhance social and economic security, in line with the vision laid out by President Roosevelt in 1941. Here we tackle the problems that contributed to rising inequality, joblessness, and poverty. As we noted in Part B, FDR's third freedom—freedom from want—is inextricably linked to the other recognized freedoms. Unfortunately, we have not made substantial progress in this area—outside improvement for older Americans who now have much better access to healthcare and retirement income through the New Deal's Social Security program and President Johnson's Medicare. But we are left with millions of unemployed people, and with inequality as extreme as it was on the eve of the Great Depression. In this part we will address these twin, related, problems, which have been exacerbated by the rise of Neoliberalism since the mid-1970s. It is hard to see the plague of unemployment and rising inequality as anything but the result of policy choices made over the past half century. It is, indeed, tempting to see them as the desired result of those choices.

I. Poverty and the trickle-down economy

a. One percenters

Back in the Summer of 2005 I wrote a piece, *"The Ownership Society: Social Security Is Only The Beginning"* that examined President Bush's promise to create a new society of owners. During the 2004 campaign, he had proclaimed: "The more ownership there is in America, the more vitality there is in America, and the more people have a vital stake in the future of this country". The centerpiece of his "Agenda" was the belief that "every American should have the right to own his or her home, to build his or her own future, and to have the flexibility to make the decisions about their own health care and retirement." In addition, his "ownership" manifesto included the promise to "fix Social Security," expand saving and investment through tax-free savings accounts, reform pension rules and streamline retirement accounts, endorse health savings accounts, repeal "death taxes," promote "affordable, reliable" energy, and "reduce the lawsuit burden." Taken together, the policy changes would encourage ownership and individual responsibility.

While supporters held out the promise that access to wealth would be broadened by the president's agenda, I argued at the time that such policies actually would increase inequality, a point that undermines an important justification for proposed ownership-society programs. And inequality did boom! But hindsight is twenty-twenty. What did I say in 2005?

First, I showed that except for the rich, the only significant wealth held by the average American is the family home. As I said in 2005, "therefore, the case for the existence of an ownership society rests on home ownership, since owner-occupied homes represent the only significant asset held by families across all income and wealth percentiles …. [F]amilies that do not own a home have insignificant amounts of other forms of wealth, with median family net worth equal to $4,800, median retirement accounts valued at only $6,800, and financial assets equal to just $3,900 …. By contrast, families that own their home have a median value of asset holdings equal to $240,100—about 18 times greater than the median holdings of renters who had any assets. Home ownership does seem to open the path to wealth."

However, I warned that all was not hunky-dory even for homeowners because it is rather misleading to count homes as wealth. First, mortgage debt was rising rapidly, from 40% of personal disposable debt in 1984 to 80% by 2005, and it continued to rise rapidly until the Global Financial Crisis as many homeowners used their houses as "ATM machines", borrowing against them to pay for consumption. Second, families have to live somewhere, "so liquidating the family home means purchase of another, or moving into a rental unit that is not usually of comparable quality, and that commits the family to rents in perpetuity …. "

Other debt was rising, too, and in an inverse manner so that those at the bottom of the income pyramid were taking on relatively more debt (Wray, 2005):

> *American families* have *taken on a lot of debt. About 75 percent of all families have some kind of debt. This varies—mostly inversely—by net worth, with 69 percent of the poorest quartile having some kind of debt, and 80 percent of families in the second-lowest quartile having debt … Nearly half of families at the very bottom of the wealth distribution had installment loan and credit card debt. Interestingly, while over 55 percent of all families in the top decile of net worth had home-secured debt, only a quarter had installment loan debt, and only 22 percent had credit card debt … Hence, installment debt and credit card balances entail a burden that varies inversely with wealth and income.*

The appearance that we were achieving Bush's promised ownership society was deceiving—because wealth of all kinds but especially financial wealth was concentrated in the hands of the few. I calculated that the top decile enjoyed median family net worth that was 1184 times greater, financial assets that were 544 times greater, and nonfinancial assets worth 166 times more than those held by the lowest quartile. While 95% of the wealthiest decile of households owned a primary residence, and 42% also owned other residential property; only 14% of the bottom quartile owned a home. While homeownership was concentrated among higher wealth households, debt was more "democratically" shared, with the poorest households facing much higher debt burdens: nearly 14 times more families in the lowest income quintile carried debt greater than 40% of their incomes. Low wealth families were 60 times more likely to have debt in arrears when compared with the wealthiest families. So while the richest households enjoyed financial assets and net worth, the bottom half of the wealth distribution "enjoyed" relatively more debt.

Folks, that was back in the good old days before the Global Financial Crisis destroyed millions of jobs and trillions of dollars of wealth.

Finally, I warned of the precarious nature of home finance in the midst of a real estate bubble (Wray, 2005):

> There is a sort of inexorably perverse ownership-society logic in all this. In recent years, banks have promoted "100 percent" (typically "80/20") mortgages in which home buyers borrow a "down payment" (for example, 20 percent of the home value) at a high-interest rate. According to one report, nearly half of new mortgages are no-money-down deals, and 36 percent of homes are bought with adjustable-rate mortgages …. With little or no equity cushion on many of these new mortgages, even a slight downturn in real estate prices—or a decline in household income—could lead to foreclosures. Moreover, the Fed continues to raise rates; although this has not yet had much impact on household mortgage rates, it will eventually succeed in raising them, causing variable rates to spike.

And, indeed, it was the "hybrid" subprime loan with floating rates that triggered the crisis in 2007.[1]

I went on:

> All of this comes at the peak of what appears to be a real estate bubble, [Greenspan] even invented a new term for the phenomenon, calling it housing market "froth," fueled by speculation that has caused residential real estate prices to climb at double-digit rates for the last several years in many cities. One recent study found that 818,000 of the two million new jobs created since the end of 2001 can be linked to housing: construction, home-furnishing stores, and the real estate services sector. Greenspan tried to downplay the risks, arguing, 'Even if there are declines in prices, the significant run-up to date has so increased equity in homes that only those who have purchased very recently, purchased before prices actually, literally go down, are going to have problems'.

Right, no big problems—homeowners have tons of equity. I did not buy it for several reasons. First, it was clear we were in an unsustainable housing bubble that would crash—and the longer it went on, the bigger the fall. The Fed had begun

---

[1] A hybrid loan has a very low initial interest rate (say, one or 2%) that would reset two to 3 years later at a much higher rate (say 12% or even higher). Borrowers typically could qualify for the mortgage only at the lower interest rate—they would not be able to make payments on the higher rate—meaning default was ensured. Only if they could refinance into a new mortgage on more favorable terms would they be able to avoid foreclosure. By 2006 since house prices had stopped rising, it became impossible to find those favorable terms.

raising interest rates in 2004—and continued until the target rate had risen by about 4% points. By 2006, housing prices stopped rising. Homeowners who had taken out dangerous hybrid mortgages that would reset to double-digit interest rates after a couple of years had been refinancing into better mortgages before the resets. However, that required both rising house prices to build their (fictitious) equity and low rates they could lock-in with a 30-year fixed rate mortgage. That worked for those who had bought before 2005. When prices stopped rising and rates rose, they could no longer refinance—so those who needed to refinance exploding rate hybrid loans after 2006 were unable to do find better mortgages.

Second, with its infinite foresight, Congress had "reformed" bankruptcy law just in time to make it impossible for homeowners to get out of their mortgage debt when the crisis hit. Even if they lost their homes through foreclosure, they would still owe the debt. As I concluded back in 2005, "It is ironic that the 30-year mortgage brought to us by New Deal government guarantees—making home ownership possible for working Americans for the first time—has morphed into a speculation-fueling, debt-pushing juggernaut that is likely to bury homeowners in a mountain of liabilities from which they will not be able to seek bankruptcy protection. Creditors will emerge as owners of the foreclosed houses and with claims on debtors, who will be subject to a form of perpetual debt bondage under Chapter 13 (which, unlike Chapter 7 bankruptcy—that was eliminated for homeowners–requires a repayment plan)."

Well, how did all that work out? Exactly as planned. Wealth flowed to the top few tenths of a percent. That is what the Ownership Society was all about.

In 2013 there was an amazing update by David Dayen on the progress made on that score:

> *Over the past couple of years, hedge funds, private equity firms and the biggest banks have raised massive amounts of capital to buy distressed or foreclosed single-family homes, often in bulk, at bargain prices […] to convert them to rental units for a while before reselling them when prices appreciate.*

An "REO" is real estate owned by banks that have foreclosed on hapless borrowers. Wall Street put up billions of dollars to buy these for pennies on the dollar from the banks, and now rents them back to all the people who lost their homes (but still pay mortgages on the homes seized by predatory lenders). For example, Dayen reports that Blackstone had already purchased $2.7 billion worth of homes and planned to buy another $100 million weekly. Wall Street was using its market power to raise rents. And those rents, themselves, were becoming another asset class: Wall Street was beginning to securitize the rental revenue—pushing risk to buyers in the same way they had securitized mortgages a decade before. (See Part A for discussion of securitization and financialization.)

Here we go again, folks. Rinse and repeat. Step one: financialize homes. Step two: foreclose and concentrate ownership of homes in the hands of Wall Street's finest. Step three: financialize the rents paid by the former homeowners.

The National Low Income Housing Coalition has estimated that a full-time worker in any metro area in the United States would need to earn an average of $22.96 an hour to afford the rent on a modest two-bedroom apartment (HuffPost, 2019). This is in part due to Wall Street driving up rents, but also to the lingering effects of the GFC: the housing crash caused developers to stop building, tightening immigration reduced the supply of construction workers (driving up costs of building), and the triple whammy of foreclosures, loss of jobs and income, and loss of family wealth, all reduced homeownership rates and drove more families into the rental market.

And remember that—meanwhile—we buried households under credit card debt and student loans,[2] as well as auto-related debt (loans and leases, also securitized). Americans are stuck with debt they can barely service (even with currently low interest rates), insufficient wealth to qualify for new mortgages, and unaffordable rents. What role do American families play in this new ownership society? Peasants in perpetual bondage to Wall Street's lords, with their income tapped out to pay rent and interest on debt. Feudalism is back in the garb of the Ownership Society. (See Part D of this book for discussion of rent extraction.)

b. Rising tide

The Global Financial Crisis caused unemployment to rise to a peak of about 10%; it wiped out $8 trillion of US stock market wealth and $9.8 trillion of the value of US housing (The Washington Post, 2018). Household net worth dropped by 18%, up to 30 million workers lost their jobs, and median family incomes declined by about 8% (NCBI, 2018).

In 2009, the United States entered a long and very slow recovery—by far the weakest recovery we had seen since the Great Depression. Even after a decade of recovery, long-term effects remained: at the end of 2017 4.4 million homeowners remained underwater in their mortgages in spite of recovery of house prices to precrash averages. And the Federal Reserve Bank of San Francisco estimated that each American had permanently lost $70,000 in lifetime income (The Washington Post, 2018).

The biggest banks survived—either intact or through merger. They are now considerably bigger than they were before the crisis. In spite of all the frauds they committed, no top executive of any of the biggest banks was prosecuted. Note that the claim of fraud is not conjecture on my part. The banks *admitted* they had committed fraud after fraud, and paid huge fines: Bank of America paid $17 billion in fines and J.P. Morgan paid $13 billion just for fraudulent mortgages they sold (and billions more for a full laundry list of other frauds). It is a sad commentary on the way that our criminal justice system operates—the banks somehow engaged in massive fraud without any individual bearing responsibility. I guess the robots really have taken over. Bonuses paid by the biggest banks have recovered—and are now nearly as high as they were precrisis. And stock prices have resumed their bubblicious ways.

---

[2] Student loan debt now stands at $1.5 trillion, credit card debt at about $1 trillion; Bernie Sanders plans to eliminate the student debt: https://readersupportednews.org/opinion2/277-75/57276-bernie-to-student-loan-sharks-drop-dead.

Still, it is not just the Wall Street bankers that recovered. By 2012 real per capita GDP in the United States had returned to its precrisis level, and by 2016 job growth had improved enough for the Fed to start raising rates in the belief that labor markets were approaching full employment.[3]

In 2014 the work of my colleague (and former student), Pavlina Tcherneva was reported in *The New York Times* in an article titled "The Benefits of Economic Expansions are Increasingly Going to the Richest Americans". Pavlina showed that more than all of the growth of income since the crisis had gone to the top 10% of the income distribution.

You mean that *Rising Tides Don't Lift All Boats*? Who would have thought?[4]

Actually, you have to conclude that economists and policy-makers are an optimistic lot. Going all the way back to the "Camelot" days of the administration of President Kennedy, it has been conventional wisdom that if you can boost economic growth, everyone wins. As I have long argued, that is remarkably naïve and counterfactual. In good times, the rich and powerful grab the spoils. In bad times, they get government bailouts.

Why on earth would you want to be rich and powerful if you could not protect and even enhance your well-being no matter what the economy does?

Why do elites everywhere always clamor for economic growth? Every policy advocated by them is justified on the argument that it will boost growth. Cut taxes on the rich! Eliminate regulations! Free trade! Slash welfare! Balance the budget! Save Wall Street!

By contrast, every policy they hate is said to hinder growth: raising minimum wages; environmental protection; school lunches for poor kids; support for unions; vacations and sick leave for workers. All are said to be Job Destroyers!

Where policies do enhance growth, the rich will get more than their fair share. Where the policies do not boost growth, they will increase the share of the rich. Heads they win and tails they win too.

Who would be surprised by that? Well, just about every economist and policy-maker on the planet. Why? Because they refuse to consider POWER. While our economy is often referred to as "market-driven", it is actually driven by power. P. O. W. E. R.

Anyone who has been paying attention has noticed that the power of the top 1% has risen inexorably over the postwar period. The one-percenters control both "the market" as well government policy. Their ability to shift ever more of the gains from growth in their direction has risen commensurately. As Tcherneva demonstrates, the payoff is obvious. Here is one of her graphs, showing the share of the gains from growth going to the top 10% versus the bottom 90% during recoveries from recession (through 2012).

---

[3] This wasn't true, as we'll discuss later.
[4] See Pigeon and Wray (1998) for a critical analysis of the notion that rising tides raise boats at the bottom.

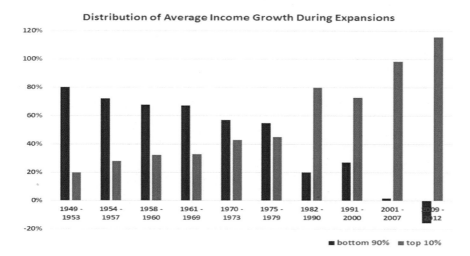

As you can see, with each recovery from a downturn since WWII, the rich capture a larger share of the subsequent growth. She has shown that no matter how you slice up the rich at the top of the income distribution—the top 10%, the top 1%, or the top few tenths of a percent of the top 1%, their share of the spoils from growth has increased in each subsequent recovery.

And when things go bad, Uncle Sam jumps in to rescue them. In the latest calamity, we had tens of trillions of dollars of attention paid to rescuing our top tenth of a percent on Wall Street, and mere peanuts thrown at Main Street. My former students, Andy Felkerson and Nicola Mathews, showed that Uncle Ben (Bernanke) at the Fed originated well over $29 trillion in very low-interest rate loans to rescue Wall Street (Felkerson, 2012; Mathews, 2013).Main Street got a stimulus package spread over 2 years totaling just $800 billion, while the Treasury supplemented the Fed's $29 trillion largess with a fiscal package for Wall Street that was also about $800 billion. Let us see—by simple subtraction that means Wall Street got an extra $29 trillion.

No wonder that when the economy began to recover, our One Percenters captured more than all the gains. They are rich and powerful, and Uncle Sam directed almost all his efforts to them.

As Hyman Minsky argued back in the 1960s, if you want to reduce poverty, you must include job creation as a central component of your War on Poverty. He (correctly) predicted that the Kennedy-Johnson War on Poverty would fail because it did not contain such a program.[5] Further, he argued that once you have provided jobs to all who want to work, you need to gradually shift the distribution of income

---

[5] For an analysis of Minsky's views and an assessment of the War on Poverty's lack of success see Bell and Wray (2004a).

toward the bottom. You do that by holding down income growth at the top while gradually increasing pay at the bottom.

We did neither, of course. Inflation-adjusted minimum wages have plummeted since the 1960s. Joblessness has risen. As documented by many, while labor productivity has continued to rise on trend, inflation-adjusted median wages have stagnated since the early 1970s.

Who got the difference? The rich and powerful. Their take exploded.

Some progressives want to continue the failed policies of the past. They want to use the tried-and-failed twin strategy of economic growth plus welfare dressed in its modern garb, the basic income guarantee (BIG) (see below). As Minsky argued, we certainly need welfare. Our generosity is a measure of our humanity, he said. However, throwing more money at the poor will never solve our unemployment and poverty problems. As he argued (Bell and Wray, 2004b):

The war against poverty is a conservative rebuttal … It can spread poverty more fairly … However, this approach, standing by itself, cannot end poverty … The liberals' War on Poverty was born out of neoclassical theory in which it is the poor—not the economy—that is to blame for poverty. The War on Poverty tried to change the poor, not the economy.

As Stephanie Kelton and I wrote in 2004, 40 years after the War on Poverty began:

'Keynesian' policies to raise aggregate demand in order to stimulate private sector employment have also been adopted on the belief that economic growth would raise the demand for labor and thereby "lift the boats" of the poor. Still, unemployment rates have trended upward, long-term unemployment has become increasingly concentrated among the labor force's disadvantaged, poverty rates have remained stubbornly high, real wages for most workers have declined, and labor markets and residential neighborhoods have become increasingly segregated as the "haves" construct gated communities and the "have-nots" are left behind in the crumbling urban core …

The critical component that was missing in 1964 and remains missing today is a firm government commitment to full employment. Minsky insisted that only a targeted jobs program, paying decent wages, could successfully fight poverty among the nonaged in a politically acceptable manner, and without increasing inflation pressure. He would have used the jobs program to help wages at the bottom—by slowly increasing program wages over time. He would also have imposed constraints on the highest wages and nonwage income in order to compress the distribution from the top. Together, these policies would have provided true full employment and at the same time improved the distribution of income. (Later in this Part we will look at the kind of job creation program Minsky advocated—what is now called the Job Guarantee [JG].)

As Pavlina's work has demonstrated, that was also the position of J.M. Keynes, who favored policies that would directly employ workers over the "pump priming" policies favored by 1960s "Keynesians". As Minsky explained, those policies would favor the "already well-off". Pavlina's work shows convincingly that that was precisely the result. Rising tides do not work as they really rely on "trickle down"—using policy that favors the rich in the hope that something will trickle down. What will work is, instead, "bubble up" policy: target help to the bottom and shared prosperity bubbles up. In the following sections we formulate such a strategy.

II. Addressing inequality

a. Redistribution or preredistribution? Uncle Sam should not play Robin Hood

America has discovered inequality. As Jared Bernstein (Chief Economist and Economic Adviser to Vice President Joseph Biden in the Obama Administration) said, dealing with that will be expensive. He came up with a nice wish list of policies to help the poor, but warned it will be expensive (Bernstein, 2014):

> *All of the above — the expanded earned-income tax credit, universal preschool, job-creating infrastructure — will take more tax revenue, and much of that new revenue will need to come from those at the top of the wealth scale*

He wagged his finger at those who think there is some free lunch that would let us help the poor without soaking the rich. Nope, he claims. Uncle Sam needs those taxes. We have to take from the rich to pay for programs for the poor.

We all love Robin Hood. Would it not be great if Kevin Costner rode his trusty stead through Wall Street, relieving the rapacious thieves of a few trillions of their ill-gotten gains, to be redistributed throughout the lands to all the deserving poor?

You remember Robin Hood from your children's storybooks. Of course, those were well-laundered so as not to cause little kiddies to question the authority of your friendly monarch, the "good" King Richard the Lionheart. Robin was supposed to be a dispossessed aristocrat who helped restore the good king to his rightful throne. Ahh, yes, there are oh so many of those nice aristocrats who want to help plain ordinary folk.

Actually, Robin was a yeoman living in feudal times, fighting the attempt by the lords to enclose the commons. He robbed the rich to give to the poor so that they could pay the rent-collecting sheriffs (who served the lords). Today he would steal from the Banksters and pay the overdue mortgages to forestall foreclosures.

Take from the rich and give to the poor. We love that meme.

Virtually every liberal I know wants to raise taxes on the rich to pay for programs to benefit the poor. They see these taxes as necessary to reduce income inequality.

Me? I would rather send Robin Hood to Wall Street to aim his straight and true arrows at the Black Hearts of the conniving CEOs that President Obama refused to investigate for their crimes. Obama's Attorney General, Eric Holder, argued that the CEOs were running banks that were too big to prosecute—a policy that became known as "too big to jail". What held him back from going after the criminal class was "the fear that bringing criminal charges against a big financial firm might cause it to collapse" (The New Yorker, 2014). He worried that going after criminal top management might hurt the reputation of the firm and hence lead to job losses of innocent employees. David Sirota provided a nice analogy (Salon, 2013):

> *If Breuer applied the very same Too Big to Jail ideology to [drug] cartel leaders, he would be effectively arguing that we shouldn't prosecute Pablo Escobars because that would result in an unacceptable loss of wages for those kingpins' secretaries, messengers and secondary workforces.[6]*

Robin Hood and his Merry Band would have carted them off to the dungeons where they belong. Real punishment would do one heck of a lot more to reduce income inequality than taxes will ever do. Put a thousand of Wall Street's "finest" behind bars. Put fear into our Bankster Class so that before they try to push some new fancy derivative deal on a pension fund, they will imagine what it would be like waking up in a prison cell.

Besides, trying to punish them with taxes or fines is a fool's errand. They will just raise their compensation package, pay for insurance that will cover their indiscretions, and buy tax exemptions from Congress. Besides, Uncle Sam does not need taxes to "pay for" jobs and income and healthcare and decent retirements for the poor.[7] If you have unemployed resources, free lunches abound! Just put the resources to work, and you have got Bernstein's wish list filled.

Forget taxes for redistribution. It will not work. It is a bad meme, especially in America. Once you let the greedy get their riches, trying to take them away is harder than prying guns out of the "cold dead hands" of NRA members. Every time a progressive proposes a tax hike on the rich to pay for welfare, the Koch brothers giggle in gleeful delight. It is the surest way to prevent any policies that would help the poor. Tying tax hikes to sensible policy plays right into the greedy hands of the Conservatives and Regressives. Did you ever hear a One-Percenter ask for a tax hike to bail out Wall Street? Come on, they are not that stupid.

What I have long argued is that we need "predistribution", not "redistribution".

The well-known radical economist Rick Wolff has made the same argument. He has been beating the inequality drum since long before Piketty brought it to the attention of our nation's liberal thought leaders (Piketty, 2013). In his powerful piece, *Better than Redistributing Income*, Rick Wolff argues that history shows that redistribution policies have three negative aspects. First, they rarely last long; second, opposition to the taxes used for redistribution can be extremely socially

---

[6] Lanny Breuer worked under Holder as the Assistant Attorney General for the Criminal Division of the U.S. Department of Justice. Both before and after working in the Obama administration, he defended white collar Wall Street bankers accused of fraud while employed at the Washington law firm of Covington & Burling LLP.

[7] See Part D for a discussion of the "affordability" issue.

divisive; and third, they are inefficient as the taxing, spending, and regulations to undertake redistribution require large, costly bureaucracies (Wolff, 2014b).

Yep, let us see: unsustainable, divisive, and inefficient. That is why he prefers "predistribution". Rick Wolff's "predistribution" plan is to challenge capitalism by creating a system of worker's co-ops, in which workers get to keep the profits. Not bad, but I would add jobs for all.

I do not agree with Rick on this "taxes pay for government services" notion—except for the case of state and local taxes (see the discussion of sovereign money in Part D). But he is absolutely correct that when the public begins to see taxes as payment for services rendered, then they start trying to calculate whether their own payment is "fair". That is a path to hell so far as government services are concerned. Since around 1970 that is exactly what has happened to state and local government finances. In the economics literature it is called "devolution"—moving provision of most government services to the state and local government level, and forcing them to pay for it with taxes, which inevitably leads to tax revolts.

It encouraged the "donut holes" that devastated cities as the more affluent whites ran off to the suburbs to escape city taxes. With new infrastructure and higher income and wealth in the burbs, relatively low tax rates could provide good services. The cities that were left behind had to raise tax rates ever more on an ever-shrinking tax base to try to provide even basic services. Witness Camden, NJ, which has essentially abandoned large swaths of its jurisdiction to "Escape from New York" dystopia. This "stakeholder", "taxes pay for the goodies I get" view has already reduced much of America to third world living standards. No wonder that Regressives pushed the devolution that wiped out cities. The well-do-do get gated communities and the rest are left behind in gutted communities.

Now the Progressives want to do the same at the federal level—by tying progressive policy to unpopular tax hikes.

The notion that you will significantly reduce inequality through taxes on the rich is a pipe dream, anyway. How high would taxes have to be on the top few tenths of a percent? 50%? 75%? Forget it. They would still be filthy rich and you would be poor by comparison. Some Progressives do not get the point, that is economic *and* political at the same time. Like Wolff, I argue for "predistribution"—prevent the growth of excessive income and wealth by controlling payments of high salaries in the first place. And eliminate the practices that lead to inequality—such as huge compensation for top management of public companies.

I do like high taxes on high income and high wealth. I have argued they should be set so high as to be confiscatory. Not at a marginal income tax rate of 70% (as Alexandria Ocasio-Cortez has proposed in January, 2019), but at 99%. Or even 125%. I am not confident that the effective tax rate will ever be that high—due to the exemptions the rich will write into the code—but that does not mean we should not aspire for better. All I am arguing is that (a) we do not need tax money to pay for the programs we want and (b) high tax rates on the rich, alone, will not be sufficient in our struggle to reduce inequality.

We can justify taxes on the rich not for revenue purposes but as sin taxes. Look at it this way. Let us raise sin taxes on the rich to reduce the sin of ill-gotten gains. Take everything: all their income, all their wealth, the house, the car, the dog. Do not let crime pay. But you will not collect the 99% tax anyway. As the great *Philadelphia Inquirer* reporters Donald Barlett and James Steele documented, rich folk do not pay taxes because they purchase tax exemptions from Congress. Leona Helmsley was right: taxes are for little people.[8] Big people escape them, unfortunately.

Bill Clinton has a better idea. At a Pete Peterson "fiscal summit" he argued: you cannot do anything about the top 1% doing better "unless you want to start jailing people." One wonders what the One Percenter Peterson thought as he contemplated President Clinton's recommendation! Why is it that Presidents can only tell the truth once they have left office? Yes, that is the same President Bubba who auctioned off the Lincoln Bedroom to the highest bidder, filled every Administration position higher than toilet cleaner with a Goldman Sachs or CitiBank official, and found novel uses for his favorite cigar. Now he says that if you want to reduce inequality you have got to "start jailing people" at the top.

And give decent jobs to the rest.

b. Basic income: how BIG is big enough? Would the basic income guarantee satisfy the unemployed?

One proposal that has received a lot of attention recently is a plan to reduce inequality by directly providing income to everyone. Andrew Yang[9]—a Presidential Candidate for the 2020 election—has called it a "Freedom Dividend" that would pay $1000 per month to every adult citizen. This approach to poverty reduction has been variously called a Universal Basic Income (UBI) or a BIG. (Van Parijs, 2004) In this section I will use the term BIG and will address two main questions: how big should the BIG be? and is this a good substitute to providing jobs?

I will first lay out the BIG proposal and then I will compare two alternatives: a universal offer of income (no strings attached) for all versus a universal offer of a job to anyone who wants to work. Allan Sheahen provides a good introduction to the case for universal income rather than jobs for all, arguing that "Jobs Are Not the Answer" to America's unemployment problem (Sheahen, 2013). The thesis is based on two propositions. First, labor productivity has grown so we would never be able to find sufficient work for all. Second, we do not need jobs anyway because:

When we say we need more jobs, what we really mean is we need is more money to live on. One answer is to establish a basic income guarantee (BIG), enough at least to get by on—just above the poverty level—for everyone.

---

[8] Leona Hemsley is well known for saying "We don't pay taxes. Only the little people pay taxes." Turned out she was only partially correct. She went to prison for tax evasion. So she served time; I don't know if she ever paid the taxes.

[9] Yang was CEO of Venture for America before quitting.

I think the first proposition is bogus—labor productivity has been rising since a caveman first grabbed a club. Productivity's importance as a cause of unemployment is at best of second-order importance and certainly not new. (See Section IV for discussion of "robotization", said to be the cause of today's job losses.) The real cause is money. To be more specific, it is because we choose to organize a huge part of our social provisioning process through the monetary system, with much of our production controlled by capitalists—and capitalists will not employ labor if they do not believe it will be profitable. (Note that is a statement of fact, not necessarily a criticism.)

The problem is NOT that we cannot find useful things for people to do. Any one of the readers of this book could come up with a list of hundreds of useful things to do that are not being done because no one can think of a way to make profits at doing them. So we can use the JG program to put people to work doing useful things without worrying about profiting off their labor.

And if all else fails, we can share all the work that we can imagine by cutting the workday and the workweek and providing vacations to Americans. Why not the 30-day type of vacation that other rich nations provide? Four-day workweeks? A legal right to 12 months paid paternal and maternal care? Paid sabbaticals for all, one year off out of every seven? (Why should tenured faculty have all the fun of a sabbatical?) All we need is the JG and we will get everyone employed while simultaneously pushing for more time off—no matter how productive we get. I will discuss the JG approach in more detail later.

So what we need to do is to look at the second argument in more detail—why we do not need jobs. To understand that, we need to look at what the BIG is, and what it is supposed to accomplish. The BIG is supposed to be much more than a cash gift handed out by Uncle Sam. It is supposed to provide an attractive alternative to work—providing sufficient income to provide a dignified lifestyle even for those who prefer not to work. The message has become muddled in public discourse, in part because advocates like Andy Yang have been less than forthcoming.

For example, Yang and other BIG proponents often point to Alaska's "Permanent Fund" as an example of a BIG that "works" because it provides income with no strings attached to all qualifying residents of Alaska. Essentially it is a distribution of the state's revenue from taxes on oil. Since oil sales vary from year to year, the income paid to individuals varies too. In 2015 oil prices were high and the fund paid about $2000 for the year to every resident; when oil prices are not booming, it pays in the range of $800–900 annually. In 2012 it was $878—the figure I will use here.

That is why I criticize BIG-gers—including Andrew Yang—for the bait and switch of pointing to Alaska as evidence that "BIG works".[10] Alaska gives a tiny little handout. $878 is not BIG enough. It is a nice Christmas gift from Alaska Claus. But no one can live on it. It is not an alternative to a job. As I will argue, even Yang's

---

[10] Yang argues the Alaskan program is proof that BIG works.

$1000 per adult does not come close to living up to what the BIG is supposed to accomplish, which is to offer an *alternative to a job*.

The BIG goal is to disconnect income from work, to "free" people from the need to work. They see jobs-for-all supporters as holding on to a "work fetish". The BIG program is universal and seeks to provide a decent living standard—just like the JG/ELR (discussed below)—but without any work. So the difference is that BIG checks go out to everyone. And no one needs to work to get them. And everyone gets a dignified, American, living standard no matter whether they want to work or not. That is BIG.

BIG proponents insist that one must be able to live a dignified life on BIG alone. Not a life of dumpster diving and sleeping under cardboard. On that score, Alaska's $878 is a BIG bait and switch. Add some zeros if you are serious about dignity. Yes, we can start smaller than that—say $8780—but eventually we have got to put up or shut up about dignity. Even $8780 is not dignified, let alone $878. Now $87,800—a hundred times Alaska's payment—would be dignified!

I would put an "American" living standard somewhere around $30,000 per year per person.[11] We could quibble a bit about the $30K. If you watch TV, you do not see lifestyles that could be supported on much less than that, at least since the days when *Sanford and Son* dominated the airwaves (indeed, the contrast between their lifestyle and the American lifestyle was the main gag that drove the laughs). I do not see how you could make the argument that one really is "free to choose" not to work if the BIG payment is less than that. How could one live the life of "dignity" BIG proponents talk about on less? Yes, you can survive on less, but most people would feel the economic pressure to search for jobs.

BIG proponents seek to guarantee a BIG sufficient to gain access to no less than "full membership and participation in social life to all members of society". That has got to be more than food, clothing, and shelter. It almost sounds like membership in golf and yacht clubs to me. The BIG should thus be sufficient for "all play, no work", full membership in society, and active participation in all aspects of social life without any compulsion to work.

Remember this. Sheahen's argument is that we do not need any more jobs—the unemployed will get BIG, but no more jobs. So if BIG pays anything less than an American living standard, then BIG is a Big bait and switch—the unemployed

---

[11] Note: in 2012, average US per capita income was $43K; in Alaska it was $47k, or about 54 times greater than the BIG Permanent Fund payment that the BIG-gers get all breathless about. In other words, if the Permanent fund paid out $878 PER WEEK instead of per year, I'd go starry-eyed, too. If you lived in D.C per capita income was $75K—over double my $30k estimate. Go figure. I guess it helps to have high paid lobbyists greasing the wheels of commerce. The JG program I will put forward below would pay $15 per hour (plus generous benefits)—or $30,000 per person. The value of the benefits provided with the job would boost that to a substantially higher value, above $35,000. The JG would provide substantial family benefits, however it must be noted that the JG would employ only those of legal working age, while some advocates of the BIG would provide income to children (Yang's proposal would not, but the Alaska Permanent Fund does include children).

would rather have a job than the life of low-paid "leisure" BIG proponents offer up instead of work.[12]

When you are talking about $30,000 payments going to all Americans, you are talking BIG money—a gross figure that starts to look scary. It raises the inevitable "how you gonna pay for it?" questions—not from me (see Part D), but from almost everyone, including BIG's own supporters. So some say we will give everyone the BIG check, but then we will tax higher-income people to pay for it. This sounds a lot like Milton Friedman's negative income tax. But that defeats one of the main arguments for BIG: it should be universal. That eliminates any stigma because everyone gets it. It will enjoy universal support—who would be against a Big BIG check from Uncle Sam? Giving an upper middle-income household a Big BIG check, and then taxing it all back would not generate universal support. It would stigmatize the program immediately. Everyone must benefit from the program to garner the support.

If you tax half the population to "pay for" BIG, you will have to take twice as much from them through taxes as you provide to them through the BIG in order to "afford" the Big BIG paid to the untaxed half. In that case you are not giving a universal BIG—you have got a BIG for half and a tax for the other half.

Further, even if the BIG is universal, it does not necessarily benefit society. I can take my BIG check and blow it all on booze, burgers, coke, and guns—consumption that probably does not advance society's interests. So to garner universal (or nearly so) support, everyone must get a BIG check that cannot be taxed away. Otherwise, it is bait and switch. If you get your Big BIG check taxed away, you must work to support yourself and if you watch me lounging about guzzling booze and shooting the local wildlife and traffic signs, whilst supported by my Big BIG check and paying no taxes, you are not going to be a happy camper.

So, we have got several potential bait and switch traps that have muddied the water in discussions about BIG:

1. Some advocate a BIG tax. But BIG is a Universal program, which guarantees universal support, but if you work for a living we are going to tax away your BIG. To avoid a bait and switch, everyone needs to get a Big BIG. And they get to keep it. Otherwise we have just got welfare.
2. Some advocate low BIG payments. But BIG payments are supposed to allow individuals the freedom to choose to live a life of dignity—whether they work or not. If the BIG payment is too low, then if you choose not to work, you will need to dumpster dive. That is not dignified. To avoid a bait and switch, BIG needs to be Big.

---

[12] I do realize that some advocates have admitted that it will be necessary to start somewhat smaller, then scale up the BIG payments. That is fine—the JG proponents have sometimes suggested the same thing with regard to the program wage. Maybe start at the minimum wage then scale it up to a living wage. But no one should get all hot and bothered about $878 a year. BIG has got to start at $15,000 a year, or so, and work toward $30k in order to deliver on its promises.

3. Some BIG proponents argue we do not need jobs because BIG payments allow all to choose not to work. If the BIG payments are too low, then most will choose to work anyway—in jobs *that may not exist*. So BIG must be Big to replace the jobs that would have been supplied by a JG so that the unemployed are happy not to work. Otherwise, it is a bait and switch.

4. Some claim most people will continue to work even if they get a BIG—the claim is that a universal BIG will not affect the supply of labor. But BIG is said to provide an alternative to the "work fetish", allowing all to explore their full potential, living a life of freedom so people can abandon the work ethic in favor of something more elevating. If this is not just bait and switch, BIG must be Big. And since working is oh-so-20th century, we need for lots of people to choose NOT to work (since BIG is replacing work, not encouraging more of it). If after implementation of BIG, most do continue to work (as some BIG proponents have predicted), then BIG was a Big bait and switch after all. We could have just raised wages and did not need the BIG at all since it turns out that work is not a "fetish" but rather something people actually want to do.

That would mean, of course that Sheahen is wrong: we do need more jobs, not a BIG. So why not advocate a Jobs Program rather than a BIG?

c. What is wrong with a big BIG, as viewed from the JG perspective?

I have been involved with BIG for a very long time. One of its main proponents worked with me at the Levy Institute in the 1990s; I have been invited to present on BIG panels; and I have published comparisons of BIG and ELR, including one for the BIG website.[13] So in the rest of this subsection, I will show that I have not misrepresented what BIG advocates and explain what I see is wrong with it.

But before delving into the details let me stress the position that the jobs-for-all supporters hold: ***BIG is compatible with the JG***. We can have both. What we object to is the BIG claim that "we don't need no stinking jobs" or that BIG makes work somehow obsolete. Our position is this: once the JG program is in place, we can add a *targeted* form of BIG.

Let me summarize the reason BIG cannot be universal: Sending a BIG check to everyone would be inflationary and would devalue the currency as prices rise. In effect, the BIG payment essentially becomes the entry price to the marketplace as prices rise to keep aggregate purchasing power essentially constant. So we will need to target the BIG to those who do not (or cannot) work. Yes there is some stigma involved in a targeted social support program. But, first we implement the JG so that anyone who is ready and willing to work has a job in the JG. Then we provide BIG (or whatever you want to call it) to those who cannot, should not, or will not work.

---

[13] Go here for a list of BIG publications, including articles by me and PavlinaTcherneva as well as by Phillip Harvey (all JG supporters): http://www.usbig.net/papers.php.

Even Americans do not mind so much that old people and kids mostly do not work. Most of the rest of Americans want to work—including large portions of those who now do not have jobs: the officially unemployed, but also many who are now classified as out of the labor force. Americans generally support providing aid to those who cannot work, or should not work—such as those with disabilities or newborns. But even most Americans with disabilities want to work but cannot find jobs. And even many mothers with young babies do want to work but need child-friendly workplace policies. The JG option eliminates involuntary joblessness.

We will still need help for those who cannot work or do not want to work—so let us target the BIG to them. Yes there will still be some who are stigmatized by accepting a BIG over taking a job. But at least all who want to work would be able to work if jobs were made available. The number on BIG will be very much smaller once we have got the JG option available. This approach to social welfare spending would be far less inflationary—and that is why social welfare spending has generally been targeted to those who need it.

Sorry, folks, but we need an anchor to the currency. It is only worth what you need to do to obtain it. As your wise mom told you long ago: if money grew on trees, it would be worthless. A BIG payment to everyone is essentially the same thing as letting people rake a pile of leaves off the lawn to go buy Beemers. Will the price of a BMW rise? You betcha. Just sufficiently so that the post-BIG price of a BMW exhausts the BIG income received by Beemer Buyers. Ditto everything else consumers will buy.

Some years ago, PavlinaTcherneva and I laid out our objections to the BIG in our paper, *Common Goals—Different Solutions: Can Basic Income and Job Guarantees Deliver Their Own Promises* (Tcherneva and Wray, 2005), which analyzes BIG and contrasts it with the JG approach. I will summarize here some of the main points.

1. What are the shared goals of BIG and JG?

Proponents of income and JG schemes agree on two things. The first is that both the market economy and the modern welfare state have failed many members of society by increasing the precariousness of the labor market, reducing safety nets, and leaving many without the basic resources for a decent living. Poverty, income inequality, and unemployment are pervasive features of capitalism and modern welfare often takes the form of punitive measures aiming to discipline the "undeserving" poor and the unemployed. The second is that to begin addressing these problems, public policy needs to provide some form of universal guarantees to all citizens—to promote FDR's four freedoms.

It is the nature of these guarantees that represents the sharp division in policy recommendations made by BIG and the JG approaches.

Income guarantee supporters champion the provision of an adequate standard of living to all members of society. They argue that this objective can be achieved by guaranteeing a minimum income to all. Job creation proponents want to guarantee access to a job that could provide a decent income to the economically active population (and their dependents). They believe that adequate resources can be provided by guaranteeing a job to all. The key distinction between the two is that basic income advocates want to decouple the income-work relationship on the basis that economic justice and freedom require that resources are provided to individuals without the compulsion to work. JG supporters, on the other hand, want to directly address the unemployment problem, arguing that there are many people who want to work but cannot find employment. Once that problem is resolved, then JG supporters would provide income support to those who cannot or do not want to work.

By contrast, BIG seeks to provide an income sufficiently high that no one needs to work. The belief is that if everyone gets this income, those who choose not to work will not be stigmatized because anyone who does not want to work does not have to work. JG counters that such a system will continue to produce sufficient output only if most people do not choose to stop working. Further, prices are likely to rise, reducing the purchasing power of the BIG income to the point that maintaining a decent living standard will require paid work.

Note that JG supporters agree with the argument that programs that target only the poor stigmatize them. That is why the JG is universal. There is no means testing. All can work in the program. Bill Gates can send his kids to the JG if they want to do something useful with their lives. And we will not tax Bill Gates to "pay for" the wages his kids get in the program. Heck, if Bill gets tired of running Microsoft and wants to take a couple of years off, doing some Meals on Wheels in the JG, he could take a real job, too, actually helping people rather than trying to monopolize the software universe. While JG supporters do recognize that targeting income support to those who cannot or do not want to participate in the JG program will stigmatize some people, they argue that with the JG available the number of people in social welfare programs will be dramatically reduced. This would help to reduce opposition to such programs and perhaps would increase compassion for participants in them. And the JG undertakes projects that have widely shared benefits—essential to build wide support for the program, so that even those who never work in a JG job still see benefits.

2. Rights to income and work contrasted

a. *The Right to Income.* Philippe Van Parijs (1995) is one of the main developers of the BIG approach. He champions a profound reform in policy based on the ethical imperative of securing freedom, equality, and justice for all. He advances the libertarian concept of real freedom that rests on two pillars. The first is that individuals are formally free within a well-enforced structure of property rights and personal liberties. The second is the concern with the worth of that individual liberty. According to Van Parijs "the worth or real value of a person's liberty depends on the resources the person has at her command to make use of her liberty (Van Parijs, 2001, p. 14)." Our object of concern, Parijs continues, must be: "the distribution of opportunity—understood as access to the means that people need for doing what they might want to do—[which is] designed to offer the greatest possible real opportunity to those with fewest opportunities, subject to everyone else's formal freedom." (Van Parijs, 2001, p. 14) Thus, real freedom is not only a matter of rights but also of means (Van Parijs, 1995, p. 30). The provision of a basic income to all which offers equal access to resources and opportunity is seen as an unalienable human right.

b. *The Right to a Job.* JG supporters see employment not only as an economic condition but also as an inalienable right. (Wray and Forstater, 2004) Some JG supporters such as Harvey (1989) and Burgess and Mitchell (1998) argue for the right to work on the basis that it is a fundamental human (or natural) right, a view supported in modern legal proclamations such as the United Nations Universal Declaration of Human Rights or the Employment Act of 1946 and the Full Employment Act of 1978. Social justice arguments rest on more than the official recognition of the right to work as a fundamental human right. Amartya Sen, for example, supports the right to work on the basis that the economic and social costs of unemployment are staggering with far-reaching consequences beyond the single dimension of a loss of income (Sen, 1999, p. 94). In sum, JG proponents support the right to income and the right to work on the grounds that they are inalienable human rights, consistent with the goals of social justice and freedom. The BIG and JG are therefore not incompatible.

3. Is BIG an efficient way to reduce poverty and inequality?

In essence, BIG offers the freedom to say "no" to undignified forms of employment and to choose the form of activity an individual wishes to pursue The underlying assumption is that the labor market can no longer ensure adequate wages for all to cover their basic needs. Global transformation, high inflation, and protracted periods of unemployment have marginalized those individuals whom the market mechanism has found to be redundant.

According to Van Parijs maximization of individual life chances and opportunities and, therefore, real freedom, requires that BIG be set at the highest sustainable level (Van Parijs, 1992, 1995, 2004). However, BIG proposals vary greatly in size.[14] The size of the basic income is crucial for its ability to accomplish its goals. As discussed above even the relatively generous $12,000 income advocated by Andrew Yang will not do if the goal is to maximize life's chances. My suggestion of $30,000 is closer to the high mark set by Parijs.

A decent BIG is going to be expensive because everyone gets the BIG check. For that reason, government spending on the BIG will be much bigger than spending for

---

[14] Among the relatively modest proposals is Atkinson's revenue neutral participation income for the UK for 1992, which ranges from £17.75 to £39/per week (or approximately £925 to £2034 annually) (Atkinson, 1996, pp. 69—70). One of the most generous is Schutz's $30,000 per year for 1996—obviously significantly higher for today. (Schutz, 1996, pp. 14—15). Generally, however, proposals hover around the official poverty line (see Herbert Simon's pitch for $8000 (2001) and Clark's proposed $9359 minimum (2004)). Brian Barry defends a subsistence level basic income (Van Parijs, 2001, p. 64), while Ronald Dore (Van Parijs, 2001, p. 80) and Van Parijs see subsistence-level incomes as the first step toward the highest sustainable income guarantee.

a JG that pays the same amount. Perhaps a big JG would on average employ 5% or 8% of the working age population; by contrast, the BIG pays 100% of the working-age population as well as the retired population (and maybe it pays children, too). It will cost at least 10 times more—and maybe much more than that—to give the same living standard to the lowest income levels (i.e., to those most likely to be in the JG). The JG is in a sense targeted—to those who take a JG job. It puts wage income directly into the hands of those who did not find higher-paying jobs outside the program (or, at least, who did not want those higher paying jobs if they did find them). Estimates of total spending on a JG program run between 1% and 3% of GDP (see estimates for our proposal below). The main reason that total spending is low is because it is a relatively small program.

The American Institute for Economic Research released an evaluation of a UBI for the United States in 2019. The author notes that the US government now spends about $1 trillion on aid to low-income Americans—equivalent to about $20,000 per year for each of the estimated 40 million living in poverty. Note that most BIG proponents envision elimination of this spending as the BIG replaces means-tested "welfare" that is said to be degrading. Using Yang's proposal of $12,000 per year to all 325.7 million Americans would total $3.9 trillion—or nearly equal to the entire 2018 Federal budget ($4.1 trillion). If we subtract the presumably eliminated welfare spending, the net cost of Yang's UBI is $2.9 trillion (three-fourths of the current budget).

What is most interesting about the report is its estimate that of the $3.9 trillion total spending on UBI only $500 billion would go to those living in poverty. Assuming that they are the ones who suffer most of the lost spending as welfare is phased out, they would end up with only half of what they now receive. However, this is an overstatement of their loss because only a portion of welfare spending actually reaches the poor. Still, it is interesting that the vast majority—$3.4 trillion—of UBI spending would go to the nonpoor. AIER estimates that $1.2 trillion UBI (30%) would go to Americans living in households with incomes greater than $100,000.

As an inequality-fighting tool, the UBI is extremely inefficient. While it might raise the income of poor and near-poor people to something approaching a living income, 87% of its spending goes to those living above the poverty line. In terms of sheer dollars, the poor move no closer to the incomes of the nonpoor—as everyone gets the same income added. And whether the poor will actually be better off in real terms depends on how much they are affected by the cuts to welfare—which will not have much impact on those households living with income above $100,000 now. The well-off see only benefits, not costs of replacing welfare with BIG.

Note, also, that we have used Yang's relatively meager BIG. A truly sufficient BIG would cost perhaps two or three times as much—maybe $8 trillion to $12 trillion—far more than the total federal budget today. That is a Big BIG.

There is one issue that could change the net impacts, however: how do you "pay for" it? If the net cost of Yang's small BIG is almost $3 trillion and if new taxes were targeted at those with incomes above $100,000, the net impact of the program could be progressive. To "pay for" the benefits paid to those with incomes less than $100,000 would require that those above $100,000 pay in taxes more than three times what they receive through the BIG. This undermines one of the main goals of the program—which is to provide benefits to all in order to maintain support. It would amount to a sort of "means testing" even though all receive benefits—since those of "means" would pay more in taxes. It is, as AIER says, "a sort of arithmetic shell game".

4. BIG can be highly inflationary

The value of the dollar is determined on the margin by what must be done to obtain it. If money "grew on trees", its value would be determined by the amount of labor required to harvest money from trees. In a JG program, the value of the dollar is determined on the margin by the number of minutes required to earn a dollar working in the JG job. If a JG job paid $15 per hour for working, on the margin a dollar is worth 4 minutes of labor. The $30,000 annual wage ($15 times 2000 hours) is worth 2000 hours of labor.

Assuming that BIG provides a payment of $30,000 per year to all citizens, the value of the dollar on the margin would be the amount of labor involved in retrieving and opening the envelopes containing the weekly checks from the treasury, divided into $30,000. For a couple of minutes of labor effort each week (say it totals 10 hours of "work" a year), you get $30,000. Obviously, the purchasing power of the dollar in terms of labor units required on the margin would be small—$3000 for each hour of effort. Remember that everyone gets this check—that first $30,000 of annual income requires only 10 hours of work annually. To earn more, you have got to take a "real job"—probably at a lower pay than $3000 per hour. But as prices adjust to the "basic income" of $30,000 (that totals about $10 trillion of extra income to be spent on output) all wages will rise.

As BIG sets off inflation, it erodes the purchasing power of the BIG check. In order to maintain its policy goals (i.e., pulling people out of poverty, maintaining a decent standard of living, and offering an appealing alternative to the drudgery of work), the basic income payment must necessarily increase to compensate for the inflationary pressures. If the payment is not increased, we will have a "one-off" inflation when the recipients receive their check; but this check will not be able to buy the (now) more expensive goods necessary to maintain the desirable standard of living. If policy keeps the basic income at the original level, the benefit would be deficient—inconsistent with the professed goals of the BIG—so it would have to grow (rapidly) over time. From $30,000 in year one perhaps to $40,000 in year two. That in turn boosts prices and wages so the BIG payment will rise each year chasing up inflation. We are caught in a vicious cycle, which creates "an inflationary trap".

What must be recognized here is that in a modern monetary economy, unconditional provision of monetary income does not offer the means to a good standard of living, rather it erodes these means; i.e., it redefines that standard of living (or the poverty line, if that is the desired benchmark) in monetary terms.

Note that if people do what BIG supposes they should do—choose not to work so that they might enjoy a life full of adventure, self-actualization, contemplation, and freedom—then the supply of output goes down. That means your BIG check will be competing with everyone else's BIG checks for a declining amount of things to buy. Inflationary pressures are made worse—unless the BIG presumptions are wrong and everyone actually prefers work over paid leisure. Also note that the BIG is not countercyclical—as the JG is. You get the $10 trillion in Big BIG checks in recession and even in runaway economic booms.

5. How JG addresses some of BIG's goals without introducing its disadvantages

While the primary objective of a JG is somewhat narrower than that of BIG—it only aims to eliminate unemployment while maintaining stable prices—it accomplishes a number of goals that are important to BIG advocates as well but avoids some of BIG's disadvantages.

Most importantly, JG does not introduce inflationary pressures. The JG wage unit maintains a relatively constant purchasing power of the dollar—the dollar will be worth the amount of labor it can hire out of the JG labor pool. This is a major advantage over basic income. JG does not introduce inflationary pressures for several reasons. The most important one is that it fixes the value of the currency to the labor buffer stock wage.

JG does not suffer from the inflation trap characteristic to BIG and if the wage is set at the living wage level (something most JG supporters favor), neither does it have the unemployment or poverty trap that BIG proponents fear since anyone who is willing to work[15] can get a job at a living (nonpoverty) wage. Note that JG is strongly countercyclical, rising when the private sector downsizes. In an expansion, workers are pulled out of the JG program to work in the rebounding private sector. The JG helps to stabilize the economy in both the upswing and the downturn; BIG does not.

Like BIG, the JG is universal and purely voluntary. JG supporters strongly object to punitive conditionality criteria or demeaning means tests—as do BIG proponents. Furthermore JG jobs provide not only an income but also socially valuable goods and services.

The JG offers a way to achieve many of the goals that democratic society determines are worth pursuing. If the goal is the adequate provision of care for the young, sick, and elderly, then JG can explicitly incorporate these services in its institutional structure. If it is deemed that communities require environmental cleanup, then JG jobs can be targeted specifically to solving these problems. In other words JG can be designed as an open and flexible program that can serve many societal needs. JG can also broaden the meaning of work by recognizing certain activities as socially useful and by compensating for them—such as caregiving. By extension then, through the

---

[15] As discussed, above, the JG does not solve the problem of low income among those who cannot or do not want to work. We will still need income support for them.

many forms of community involvement which become recognized as legitimate JG jobs, we foster advanced citizenship, reciprocity, and social cohesion.

Finally, JG increases efficiency. By training and educating workers and maintaining them as gainfully employed, JG also enhances human capital, thus the detrimental effects of idleness and unemployment are avoided. JG increases efficiency because it increases production, maintains human capital, and protects the environment.

In conclusion, BIG and JG share many of the same goals and objectives. Some BIG proponents oppose JG because they believe it promotes the "fetish" of work. JG proponents advocate providing jobs to those who want to work, recognizing the individual and social value of work that contributes to general welfare. In their view, JG is compatible with BIG, and so they do not oppose it. However, JG proponents prefer to target a basic income to those who do not want to or cannot work.

JG supporters do agree that we need decent incomes for all. Most people can achieve decent income through work so long as their wage is high enough. Others will need income not related to work—some form of BIG. Hence, JG supporters are not opposed on principle to BIG. They just want to get the horse (jobs) before the cart (decent incomes for all).

A JOB FOR ALL. Dignity, income, and social production for shared prosperity

a. A plan for all Detroits out there

In 2013 the city of Detroit declared bankruptcy, an ignoble ending to the downfall of one of America's greatest cities. It had been the center of global automobile production, with a well-to-do middle class built on the good wages of its unionized workforce. It was a beacon of hope for the wave of African Americans who migrated from the south in search of good jobs. By 1920 it was the nation's fourth largest city and its population peaked at almost 2 million in 1950. It was a cultural center, with internationally recognized architecture and the home of Motown. But even as early as the 1950s it began its long march down the wrong fork in the road—a march followed by many of America's other industrial and population centers.

The auto culture that made Detroit great also helped to destroy it. Its 534 miles of streetcar lines were torn up to make room for the auto's monoculture. Modern highways were built through African American neighborhoods, helping to break up and isolate them. Racism and discrimination promoted segregation and fueled white flight to suburbs and the creation of the "donut hole" city center with inadequate public and private services. Manufacturing downsized as factories moved to the nonunionized south and as foreign competition increased. Robots replaced workers. The power of unions there (and everywhere) fell—the best they could do was to fight a rearguard battle to retain wages and benefits for the remaining legacy workers. The suburbs grew; the city shrank. Faced with higher costs and lower tax revenues, the city fell deeply in debt—until it finally defaulted. All of this is a story that can be told about many of America's cities, but Detroit stands out not only for the depths of its fall but also because many of the others had somehow managed to eke out some semblance of a Renaissance in recent years.

At the time of Detroit's bankruptcy, President Obama saw the solution as one of providing the proper incentives to the business community. Like Johnson's War on Poverty, which had focused on retraining the unemployed for jobs that did not exist, Obama's proposal focused on incentivizing the businesses community to hire workers to produce for customers that do not exist. At one point the city considered simply bulldozing a significant portion of the city and turning it back to farmland. Notably missing from proposals was a plan to permanently eliminate unemployment with jobs at good wages. In any event, Obama's plan amounted to little and Democrats lost the rust belt to President Trump.

In the Washington Post, Josh Pacewicz wrote: *"Rust Belt populism is rooted in the region's loss of locally owned industry—not simply because of economics but because of how that loss hollowed out the community structure that once connected people to politics, leaving residents alienated and resentful."* Yes, people want jobs connected to the community. Participation against alienation.

Also, a careful examination of Trump's voters showed that they viewed themselves as left behind—in regions devastated by job loss, slow growth, low income, high poverty rates, and declining living standards. But their perceptions turned out to be largely false—at least in a relative sense. Pundits pointed out that they typically live in regions with above-average incomes, and lower than average rates of unemployment and poverty; in comparison with the urban core of cities like Detroit and Chicago, or the ghost towns of the farm belt, the average Trump voter had it pretty damned good.

But what the pundits do not understand is that voters are not comparing their situation to the devastation found across America. Their reference is both to where they thought America would be in the 21st century, as well as to how it has been pictured in movies and on television since the mid-1980s when John Hughes forever altered expectations of American living standards.[16]

For an unexpurgated look at the views of the underclass held by our white-collar elite, we need to look no further than the comments made by their unelected representatives in Washington, the FOMC.[17] As transcripts from the Fed's meetings reveal, FOMC members enjoy poking fun at those left behind by America's neoliberal policies. In 2011, when the unemployment rate was still a shocking 9%, the FOMC focused on drug addiction as the major cause:

---

[16] John Hughes was a writer, director and producer known for funny movies, especially for featuring young characters in upscale neighborhoods with the problems facing white affluent teens—such as Sixteen Candles (1984), The Breakfast Club (1985), Weird Science (1985), and Pretty in Pink (1986).
[17] Federal Open Market Committee—the decision-making body of the Fed, see references for the meeting transcript link.

Dennis P. Lockhart (Atlanta Fed President): I frequently hear of jobs going un-filled because a large number of applicants have difficulty passing basic require-ments like drug tests or simply demonstrating the requisite work ethic. As an example, one contact in the staffing industry told us that during their pretesting process, a majority—actually, 60% of applicants—failed to answer "0" to the question of how many days a week it's acceptable to miss work. (pp. 138–139)

The transcripts note that, at that point, the room of central bankers broke into laughter.

Charles Plosser (Philadelphia Fed President): Contacts with directors and the business community echoed many of President Lockhart's comments about jobs and challenges. It's not just mismatch; it's also the problems that—whether it be drug testing, which is a very common theme I hear. The other common theme I heard is work ethic. An employer in the Third District who owns, I think, 60-some-odd McDonald's restaurants in southeastern Pennsylvania and New Jersey says passing drug tests, passing literacy tests, and work ethic are the primary problems he has in hiring people, as far as he's concerned. (p. 165)

In other words, the "deplorable"[18] unemployed—particularly those in inner cities and rural areas—have no one to blame but themselves for their failure to obtain jobs in fast food joints, euphemistically referred to as "restaurants".

It probably should not be surprising that our elite cannot understand that it is the poor prospect for the average American worker that is contributing to their "deplorable" behavior, including drug use and weak "attachment" to the labor force. In truth, the low official unemployment rate achieved in the long recovery from the GFC is in good measure due to declining labor force participation rates—and not to a well-performing economy that is creating lots of new jobs. Until the GFC, the overall labor force participation rate was held up by women, in spite of a long-term declining participation rate by men.[19] It is significant that prime-age women now have experienced a reversal—even in the "recovery" from the GFC, their participation remains depressed. Adding that to continuing declines in male participation rates and we have got overall participation rates falling. The only "bright spot" is that after the GFC, older workers had to forgo retirement—so that the only demographic actually working more is the group that would be retired if they had not lost their financial wealth in the crash.

---

[18] Candidate Hillary Clinton is credited for coming up with the disparaging term "deplorables" as applied to what she claimed to be "half of Trump's supporters"—presumably the lower income, lowly educated, uncouth whites who abandoned the Democratic party because it had abandoned them. https://www.bbc.com/news/av/election-us-2016-37329812/clinton-half-of-trump-supporters-basket-of-deplorables. In truth, as argued here, Trump's voters were above average by important measures, but felt ignored by the country's elite.

[19] The overall labor force participation rate reached its peak in 2000 and has been falling ever since; it has now fallen back to its 1977 level. This is not simply due to aging, as it has been falling since 2000 even for prime age and younger workers. See Dantas and Wray (2017).

Ironically, the usual explanation for the falling participation rate of men is that it is due to demographic changes (mostly, aging of the population). Clearly that does not hold water as participation rates of the elderly are rising—while rates of prime-age men continue to fall. And even taking account of the demographic changes, we find that most of the decline of male participation is not due to aging—but rather to prime-age labor force dropouts. On any given day, just about one out of every six men of prime working age has no paid job of any kind.

Those that do find jobs are increasingly trapped in contingent, often part-time work at pay that does not offer an American living standard. Trump's voters can beat the averages because the average is not that great. Too many "average" Americans have little job security, too much debt, mandated health insurance they cannot afford (even with Obamacare subsidies), and no savings for rainy days or retirement. They are only a couple of paychecks away from losing their homes to foreclosure fraud, their kids attend schools facing budget problems, and they see no light at the end of the tunnel.

As Rick Wolff has documented, real median wages have been stagnant since the early 1970s in spite of steadily rising productivity (Wolff, 2014a). This opens a tremendous demand gap—wages are not even close to sufficient to buy the output our workers produce. And because we run an overall trade deficit, foreigners are not buying them, either.

Wall Street found the solution: fill the gap with loans to the working class so that the capitalists can sell the output and our rentier class can collect interest on the loans. Workers spend more than their incomes to keep the system afloat. As a result, the dire strait of America's workers was long hidden behind a growing mountain of debt, and by a plethora of amazing gadgets (smartphones and flat-screen TVs) kept cheap by outsourcing to foreign labor and purchased on credit. This was revealed in the GFC that began in 2007. Is it any wonder that they no longer feel middle class, even if their incomes are above average? Is it really so puzzling that they chose Trump, who promised to throw a wrecking ball into the machinery that destroyed America's middle class? He would punish firms moving jobs overseas, tear up "free trade" agreements, go after Wall Street, drain the swamp, build a wall to block undocumented immigrants, fund infrastructure and create jobs, and Make America Great Again. He had the answers to the questions most Americans were asking, while Hillary Clinton was busy creating technocratic policies to address questions most Americans had never thought to ask.

However, as I foresaw in an analysis written soon after the election "*he will not be able to implement his agenda. He might cave to the mainstream Republicans and sign-off on some policy-making around the edges, but he will not successfully shepherd through any of his big ideas. […]It would take a powerful and trusted president to overturn nearly four decades of deficit hysteria, whipped up by both parties*". (Wray, 2017) After 3 years of Trump, the promise of jobs is still unfulfilled and the Rust Belt could make the difference at the 2020 elections once again.

So what should be done?

Well, I and others have long advocated a longer-term solution to deal with all of the Detroits that are out there: The government could serve as the "employer of last resort" under a JG program (Wray and Kelton, 2011; Wray et al., 2018). As I argue in the remainder of this Part, the program would offer a job to any American who was ready and willing to work at the program wage, plus legislated benefits. No time limits. No means testing. No minimum education or skill requirements.

The program would take workers as they are and where they are, with jobs designed so that they could be performed by workers with the education and training they already have, but it would strive to improve the education and skills of all workers as they participate in the program. The program should include provisions for part-time work and other flexible arrangements for workers who need them, including but not restricted to flexible arrangements for parents of young children.

That is the approach we would take on behalf of all of the Detroits out there.

b. How to eliminate the scourge of unemployment: jobs now at a living wage

It is amazing no one has thought of this before. A dozen years after the GFC began, we have still got up to 15 million people who want jobs but cannot find them. Of course, that is far more than the official unemployment numbers—which do not count anyone who worked just an hour or so, or who gave up looking altogether.

I wonder how on earth we can find a solution to joblessness, or to low pay? It is all so complicated. How can we stroke the business class in just the right manner to get them to create a job or two? How can we prevent our corporations from taking jobs abroad? How can we add a few more jobs without stoking the fires of inflation?

Should we slash government regulations to raise the spirits of our business undertakers? Maybe we should just eliminate minimum wages so that they can afford "expensive" American labor? Then we could compete with Viet Nam's low-wage labor.

Or slash taxes to boost the supply side?

Or maybe we should just throw in the towel and admit that we will never solve the problem of unemployment? Just toss more welfare handouts at the jobless? Expand the dependent classes to include more of the able-bodied. Admit that our Captains of Industry, as well as our Public Stewards, have failed us. That we have created a dysfunctional social system that cannot provide jobs to those who want to work.

As Hyman Minsky put it 6 decades ago, providing welfare rather than jobs is "a conservative rebuttal to an ancient challenge of the radicals, that capitalism necessarily generates 'poverty in the midst of plenty'".

Rather than paying people not to work, Minsky proclaimed we must pursue an alternative: "We have to reverse the thrust of the policy of the past 40 years and move towards a system in which labor force attachment is encouraged. But to do that we must make jobs available; any policy strategy which does not take job creation as its first and primary objective is but a continuation of the impoverishing strategy of the past decade."(Minsky, 1975).

Here is Minsky's idea: why not create jobs with decent pay? Now, why didn't anyone ever think of that before?

Put people to work doing socially useful things. Take workers as they are, design jobs that they are able to do. Offer a high enough wage with good, supportive working conditions so that no one would take the demeaning and low-paying jobs that the private sector creates. If the private sector wants to compete, it will have to pay more and provide more interesting and fulfilling work.

We must change the system, not the people.

Moreover, a JG program is not just jobs creation, it will act as an automatic stabilizer as employment in the program grows in recession and shrinks in economic expansion, counteracting private sector employment fluctuations. Further, a JG program with a uniform basic wage will also help to promote economic and price stability.

The mainstream view has long been that "full employment" and "price stability" are incompatible goals. They claim that you must have substantial unemployment to keep prices in check. You can call it NAIRU, you can call it the "natural rate" or you can call it the "reserve army of the unemployed".[20] It is a view shared by virtually all economists outside the MMT camp. According to all of them, the unemployed serve as a price anchor; the suffering of the unemployed does the duty of keeping the currency scarce and valuable. Unemployment is the "cost" to achieve the "benefit" of low inflation.

We reject that view as unnecessarily defeatist.

However. And here is the *Big However*. We do agree with the mainstream that the economy needs a price anchor, or otherwise pursuit of true, full employment probably *would*, at least much of the time, cause inflation. So, we, too, want a price anchor. We object to the (usually implicit) claim of just about everyone outside the MMT camp that unemployment is the *only* possible price anchor. Other economists do not have the imagination to come up with any alternative price anchor for a fiat currency.

In our view, that is wrong.

Here is Warren Mosler's response, in what is almost a *Haiku* in its simplicity:

---

[20] The NAIRU is the "non accelerating inflation rate of unemployment"—a mainstream notion that there exists some unemployment rate that policy-makers ought to pursue because it is consistent with a constant rate of inflation (usually somewhere around a 6% official unemployment rate). The "natural rate" is the unemployment rate that is supposed to be "naturally" produced by a "free market" capitalist system in the absence of government intervention. The "reserve army of the unemployed" was Marx's term for the necessity of keeping a large number of unemployed workers, desperate for work in order to keep pressure on the employed—who would fear that if they did not work hard enough at low enough wages, employers would replace them with the unemployed. Note, Marx was not in favor of this—he was simply arguing that from the perspective of capitalist this reserve army is necessary to maintain high profits.

It comes down to this:
With 'state currency'
There necessarily is,
Always has been,
Always will be,
A buffer stock policy.
Call that the MMT insight if you wish.
So it comes down to 'pick one'-
1. Gold
2. Foreign Exchange
3. Unemployment
4. Employed/JG/ELR
5. Wheat
Whatever!
I pick employed/JG/ELR
As it works best as a buffer stock based on any/all criteria for buffer stock.
So yes, it's an option.
You are free to pick one of the others.

So …. You can have full employment but you have got to choose a price anchor. Some want a commodity buffer stock (usually gold). Others want to tie the domestic currency to a foreign currency. Most want unemployment. By contrast, MMTers follow Warren Mosler in choosing an employed buffer stock—the JG (also called the Employer of Last Resort—ELR—program, Tymoigne and Wray, 2013).

We can analyze the JG as a program that uses labor as its buffer stock. Labor goes into all output. It is a domestic resource that can be found in every nation—and it is virtually always in excess, that is, not fully employed. Providing jobs to those who want to work but cannot otherwise find paid work is consistent with an internationally recognized human right. It has many individual, familial, and social benefits that go far beyond earning an income. Keeping the labor buffer stock employed maintains that buffer stock in good working condition. Enforcing idleness on those who want to work is like letting the rats invade your buffer stock of corn—that reduces the value and effectiveness of the buffer stock in controlling the price or wage. A reserve army of the employed is much better than a reserve army of the unemployed as the unemployed are perceived by employers to deteriorate in quality at a rapid pace. In consequence, they prefer to bid already employed workers away from other employers over recruiting the unemployed.

The JG program is quite explicitly a targeted spending program in which government spending is directed precisely to those who want to work but cannot find a job. This places no direct pressure on wages and prices because the workers in the program were part of the "surplus" or "redundant" labor force. And even when they are employed in the JG program, they are still available for private employers (at a small mark-up over the JG program wage—which becomes the effective minimum wage).

For that reason, employing workers in the JG program is no more inflationary than leaving them unemployed. Indeed, the JG lowers recruiting and hiring costs as employers would have an employed pool of workers demonstrating readiness and willingness to work, which should reduce inflation pressures. The JG program will have a work history for each of its participants that can be used for placement purposes. It will be relatively easy for an employer to search through the JG pool of workers to recruit those most suitable to the openings.

Turning to effects on aggregate demand, many critics worry that if, say, 10 million people obtain jobs in the JG and thereby increase their incomes above their pre-employment levels, consumption would increase and drive up inflation. This seems to be a major concern of JG critics. By logical extension, they would also worry about a private sector—led expansion that created minimum wage jobs in, say, the fast food sector. In other words, they should be opposed to *any* increase of employment on the argument that the employed will spend more. We find such a position to be overly defeatist—a "let the poor eat cake" response to unemployment and poverty.

This criticism is also often combined with the claim that workers in the JG would just "dig holes", adding nothing to national output. Again, we see that as overly pessimistic—since a jobs program can be designed to produce desirable output, as the New Deal's jobs programs did.

Note also that if the newly employed private workers produced goods for export, the extra wages would increase consumption without producing more domestic goods to absorb the demand. So this would be at least as inflationary as employing workers in a JG. And yet virtually all economists would celebrate increased employment in the nation's export sectors, while most oppose employing more workers in the government sector!

Let us imagine that the JG program is extremely successful at creating jobs and income, so much so that the economy moves from slack to full employment of all productive capacity, resulting in rising prices. The presumed problem is that while JG workers get wages (and thus consume) they do not contribute any production that is sold (hence, does not absorb wages). The "excess" wages from newly employed workers induces spending to rise and beyond some point the producers raise prices rather than increase output. (As noted, increasing employment in the export sector would create the same problem.)

What could government do in that case? It would have at its disposal the usual macroeconomic policy tools: raise taxes, lower government spending on programs other than the JG, and tighten monetary policy. It could also do what the United States did in WWII when the economy operated beyond full employment: wage and price controls, rationing of some key resources, patriot saving (selling war bonds to encourage saving and reduce consumption), and postponed consumption (workers were offered good pensions instead of wage increases). (We will not get into an argument here about the relative effectiveness of these—but they kept inflation manageable during the war when government spending absorbed half the nation's output and a significant portion of the labor force was in the armed forces.)

Indeed, this is what the government would do in the absence of the JG if the private sector achieved full employment through creation of 10 million new minimum wage jobs in the private sector. The only difference is that the government would not be able to fight inflation by increasing unemployment—because the macro policies used to fight inflation would dampen demand but any worker losing a job could turn to the JG program for work.

What this means is that with a JG in place, the inflation-fighting adjustments to spending will occur among the employed rather than by causing unemployment and poverty. In other words, the costs of fighting inflation can be made to be borne at higher income levels. We are surprised that our critics appear to prefer to use unemployment and poverty to fight inflation, which forces the least able to bear more of the costs. With the JG in place, these policies put at least some of the burden of fighting inflation on those who are well-off.

Our position is similar to Keynes's: "No one has a legitimate vested interest in being able to buy at prices which are only low because output is low." (Keynes, 1964, p. 318) So while those who like an unemployed buffer stock ("reserve army of unemployed") argue against creating jobs on the argument that those with jobs would have more income, and this could cause inflation, that is not a morally defensible position.

It must be recognized that increasing the number of private sector workers in the fast food industry (or in the export sector) will cause the same sort of inflation, raising prices in the same sectors that consumption by new workers in the JG program would affect. It does no good to argue that hamburger flippers are "productive" (they flip burgers) while JG workers are not (they provide, for example, public services to the aged), because the "semi-inflation" will occur in all sectors where increased spending faces anything less than what economists call perfect "output elasticity" (that is, where output can rise on a one-for-one basis as demand rises, so that prices do not rise at all).

Hence, if our critics were consistent, they would *always* fight against job creation if *any* sectors that would experience increased sales to workers had less than perfect output elasticity. Their argument against the JG is a red herring. An employed buffer stock is more effective at constraining wages and prices than is an unemployed reserve army because employment keeps labor in better shape.

Employment also has substantial benefits for the individual, the family, and society as a whole. Unemployment has few (questionable at best) benefits and lots of horrendous costs to individuals, families, and societies, including divorce, deteriorating physical and mental health, abuse of children and spouses, gang activity, and crime. Keeping humans employed avoids tremendous social and individual costs.

c. Workers will do nothing useful and the JG will not be manageable: a response

Whenever you talk about a JG, that promises to hire anyone ready and willing to work, the critics pop up proclaiming that JG workers will never do anything useful. They will all be hired to dig holes, and then will be rehired to bury those holes. It is not desirable or feasible to run a JG program for the "obvious" reason that we will not find anything useful for them to do. Much better, it is claimed, to leave them jobless.

The bleeding hearts who take this position are willing to throw the jobless a few scraps. Maybe some welfare or food stamps, or maybe even a small BIG. The heartless want to throw the jobless to the wolves, to preserve incentives. Better you than me, they think!

MMTers think all of this is not only far too pessimistic, but also disastrously wrong. There are lots of people who want to work but cannot find paying jobs. And lots of stuff that needs to be done. We have got a serendipitous problem here, and the solution is to bring the two together (Wray, 2000).

The main issues examined in this subsection concern the desirability and feasibility of a JG program. The JG program is *desired* because (a) a more-or-less free market system *does not*, and perhaps cannot, continuously generate true full employment; (b) no civilized, and wealthy, society can allow a portion of its population to go without adequate food, clothing, and shelter; and (c) our society places a high value on work as the means through which most individuals should obtain a livelihood.

The JG is feasible because we can design it to ensure that it can be managed; corruption will be kept within acceptable bounds (way below what we accept in private firms!) and we can ensure workers do things that are socially valuable and that develop skills of the workers.

JG policy cannot resolve all social problems; it cannot even replace all transfer spending. Some individuals will not be *able* to work—even in a JG program. Some individuals will not be *willing* to work. However, a JG will ensure that all of those willing and able to work at the JG wage will be able to obtain a job by selling their time to the government at the JG wage.

Indeed, "ableness" should be defined as broadly as possible to include virtually all those who are willing to work. There is no reason to impose a narrow "efficiency" standard to ensure "productivity" above the program wage. *Any* production will normally be better than *no* production; if one begins with the belief that even the relatively unproductive must be supported, then the government will have to provide income whether or not one works. Generally, it will be better to have someone working and producing something of use.

But that sets too low a bar for most workers. We want them to produce up to their ability, so we must "take workers as they are" and provide the conditions that allow them to do so.

In many individual cases, the "net product" may well be negative from a narrow economic standpoint because supervision, capital investments, and personal services required to put some people to work (for example, to employ those with severe disabilities) could exceed the economic value of output. However, a rich society can afford inefficiencies, and the noneconomic benefits of work can offset the economic costs. And most workers will provide substantial net benefits, so we as a society can "afford" to provide jobs even to those who cannot produce economic net benefits because the social benefits of doing so are positive.

JG intervention is *feasible*. The modern government does not face the narrow "financial constraints" under which households and firms must operate. The national government can afford to employ anyone who wants a job—a topic we will take up in Part D below. In any case, however, the increase of government spending associated with operation of a JG program will be relatively small—and JG could even "pay for itself" in society-wide savings—as shown in the final section of this Part. (To be clear, the sovereign government faces no affordability constraints, so could always afford both JG and as well all other demands. What really matters is the "real" resources. However, many are concerned about "exploding" deficits, but the fact is that a JG can be implemented with little, or even no, net expansion of total government spending if that is desired.)

Once the primary issues have been resolved, there remain many issues, problems, objections, and extensions that must be analyzed. I will merely list a few objections that immediately come to mind, and will provide a sentence or two to indicate the direction that might be taken to resolve the problems.

i. It will be impossible to administer the program due to incompetence, corruption, racism, and opposition. Clearly, this is a significant problem. Although Roosevelt's New Deal jobs programs were less than ideal—especially with regard to treatment of African Americans—the leadership was competent and the programs were relatively free from corruption. We might ponder whether there are administrators today as capable as those who administered the New Deal.

Supporters of the JG have suggested several methods to ease administrative problems. First, the existing unemployment benefits program administration might be used to administer a JG program. Alternatively, administration could "devolve" to the state and local government level and to not-for-profits. The federal government would simply provide as much funding as necessary to let every state and local government as well as qualifying not-for-profit community service organizations hire as many new employees as they desired, with the condition that these jobs could not replace current employment. These agencies would expand existing operations with the federal government paying the wage and benefit package. The program would include groups such as AmeriCorps, VISTA, the Student Community Service Program, the National Senior Service Corps, the Peace Corps, the National Health Service Corps, school districts, and Meals on Wheels. The agencies would be held accountable and would lose access to JG workers if their projects were not successful.

ii. JG employment will consist of nothing but "make-work" jobs, like the WPA before it.

As we move farther from the 1930s, people seem to have forgotten the contributions made by Works Progress Administration (WPA; of the New Deal). WPA workers *not only built or reconstructed 617,000 miles of roads, 124,000 bridges and viaducts, and 120,000 public buildings; they also left the nation with thousands of new parks, playgrounds, and athletic fields. Moreover, they drained malarial swamps, exterminated rats in slums, organized nursery schools, and taught illiterate adults to read and write. Unemployed actors set up theaters throughout the land, often performing in remote towns and backwoods areas. WPA orchestras gave 6000 live concerts. WPA artists produced murals, sculptures, and paintings that still adorn our public buildings.*

Ginsburg (1983, p. 11).

Indeed, it is rather easy to make the case that the WPA played *the* major role of bringing the United States out of its 19th-century position as a mostly lesser developed country and finally into the 20th century as a developed country that could (successfully) rival the developed European countries. (see more below). We do not believe it requires much imagination to come up with a list of useful tasks for JG workers. Possible JG jobs include:

- *Companion* for the elderly, bed-ridden, orphans, and those with mental and physical disabilities
- *Public school classroom assistant*
- *Safety monitor* for public school grounds, areas surrounding schools, playgrounds, subway stations, street intersections, and shopping centers
- *Neighborhood cleanup/Highway cleanup engineers*
- *Low-income housing restoration engineers*
- *Day care assistants for children of JG workers and others*
- *Environmental safety monitors*
- *JG artist or musician*
- *Community or cultural historian*

    Obviously, this list is not meant to be definitive but is only to suggest that there are many jobs that could be done by JG workers. We have not listed the more "obvious" jobs, such as restoration of public infrastructure (patching holes in city streets, repairing dangerous bridges), provision of new infrastructure (highway construction, new sewage treatment plants), and expansion of public services (new recycling programs) that should be carefully considered because they might reduce private costs and increase private profitability; further many of these jobs are unionized or subject to federal and state and local government laws regarding "prevailing" wages (they must pay the equivalent of union wages) so should not be done by JG workers. Further, some of these are types of social spending that should be done even without a JG program, and that might be better accomplished by non-JG (including unionized) workers. However, it should be noted that WPA employees did indeed engage in this sort of work. (see below)

iii. What can be done with belligerent/antisocial/lazy JG workers? JG will require that one show up for work on time; beyond that, requirements would have to be made almost on a case-by-case arrangement by project managers. Discipline would be maintained *primarily* by the promise of promotion to more desirable JG jobs, and, eventually, to private sector employment. JG workers could be fired from their jobs for just cause; there could be conditions placed on rehiring (for example, the fired worker might have to wait for 3 days—without pay— before rehiring; the penalty could be increased for subsequent firings), and grievance procedures would be enforced to protect workers from arbitrary firing. In extreme cases, some individuals may not be allowed to work in a JG job; JG cannot provide income for all the needy. It cannot replace all other social programs.

iv. What effect will JG have on unions? On one hand, JG removes the fear or threat of unemployment, which is often said to be an important disciplinary method used by firms against workers. It also establishes a true, universal minimum wage—below which wages will not fall. It still permits unions to negotiate benefits with employers. JG could include a package of benefits, including healthcare. This would then set the lowest standard (and could, for example, lead to universal healthcare). On the other hand, the JG pool will also dampen wage (and benefit) demands of non-JG workers as employers will have the alternative of hiring from the JG pool. JG projects would go through an approval process and it is important that unions (especially public employee unions) sit on the boards that approve the projects. This helps ensure that employers do not replace existing workers with JG workers. Thus, it is not clear that JG is biased in favor of workers or employers—each side will experience some benefits.

v. Will participation in JG lead to stigmatization? If JG takes only those workers the private sector "does not want", will participation in JG be seen as a negative indication of character, education, or skill level, much as participation in "welfare" stigmatizes a person? This danger can be reduced through creative action. For example, JG can be promoted as a universal "AmeriCorps" service, open to all who would like to perform community service (unlike the current AmeriCorp program, which limits the number of participants). JG might even provide for part-time positions (perhaps even unpaid) for volunteers who would like to perform community service without giving up other employment. It is possible that JG service could come to be seen as an advantage on the resume, rather than as a stigma. In any case, those who are jobless are already stigmatized; providing a job to those who want to work will provide a better path to employment. Even if there remains some stigma, it will be less than the stigma attached to being out of work.

vi. What about program manageability? Some critics have argued that the program could become so large that it would be unmanageable. The central government would have difficulty keeping track of all the program participants and ensuring that they are kept busy working on useful projects. Worse, corruption could become a problem, with project managers embezzling funds. We will briefly look at some methods that can be used to enhance manageability.

First, it is not necessary for the national government to formulate and run the program. It can be highly decentralized—to local government, local not-for-profit community service organization, parks and recreation agencies, school districts, and worker cooperatives. Local communities could propose projects, with local agencies or governments running them. National government involvement might be limited to providing funding and final project approval and review.

In order to reduce the likelihood that funds are embezzled, the national government could pay wages directly to program participants. This can be facilitated by using the social security number—and paying directly into a bank account much as social security programs pay retirement pensions. If project managers never get their hands on government funds, it will be difficult to embezzle them. To be sure, there will be some cases of fraud, such as paying to a social security number of someone who is not working, or who is dead. Transparency is one way to fight corruption—public recording of all participants and all payments, through use of the internet, for example, with rewards for whistle-blowers.

(Privacy is a concern. However, note that even in the United States the wages of public sector employees are commonly made available. As JG workers would have wages paid by the public sector, there already is a precedent for transparency for public programs.)

To cover management and materials costs, the national government might provide some nonwage funding to projects. For such kinds of job creation programs an amount equal to 25% of the wage bill has been common. The greater the payment, the greater the adverse incentive for project managers—who might create projects simply to get this funding. For this reason, nonwage funding should be kept small, and the national government should require matching funds from projects to cover nonwage expenses.

While it is tempting to include private for-profit employers in such a program, adverse incentives are even greater where production is for profit. A private employer might replace employees with JG employees to reduce the wage bill. Worker cooperatives might work better. A group of workers could propose a project designed to produce output for sale in markets. The JG program could pay a portion of their wages for a specific period of time (say, for 1 year) after which time the cooperative would have to become self-supporting. If it could not stand on its own, the workers would have to move into regular JG projects. (Argentina's *Jefes* program—a limited, targeted JG scheme—experimented with worker's coops, see Tcherneva and Wray, 2007.)

vii. What can we learn from historical examples?

Obviously, there are many more management issues that must be explored but we can look to the past for lessons. There are many real-world examples of direct job creation programs funded by government. Programs must be adapted to the specific conditions of each nation. There will be many trial-and-error experiments. Some projects will not be successful—in terms of providing useful jobs that produce socially useful output. But what must always be kept in mind is that the alternative—unemployment—is more socially wasteful. There have been many job creation programs implemented around the world, some of which were narrowly targeted while others were broad-based. The American New Deal included several moderately inclusive programs such as the Civilian Conservation Corp and the WPA. Sweden developed broad-based employment programs that virtually guaranteed access to jobs (Ginsburg, 1983). From WWII until the 1970s a number of countries, including Australia, maintained a close approximation to full employment (measured unemployment below 2%) through a combination of high aggregate demand plus loosely coordinated direct job creation. (Often there would be an informal "employer of last resort", such as the national railroads, that would hire just about anyone.) As Mitchell and Muysken (2008) argued, a national commitment to full employment spurred the government to implement policies that created jobs—even if it did not explicitly embrace a national and universal JG program. During the Great Depression of the 1930s, like many other nations, the United States adopted several jobs programs. Again, these were not part of a universal JG program, but the New Deal programs were huge, and had lasting effects, in the form of public buildings, dams, roads, national parks, and trails that still serve America. For example, workers in the WPA:

shouldered the tasks that began to transform the physical face of America. They built roads and schools and bridges and dams. The Cow Palace in San Francisco, La Guardia Airport in New York City and National (now Reagan) Airport in Washington, D.C., the Timberline Lodge in Oregon, the Outer Drive Bridge on Chicago's Lake Shore Drive, the River Walk in San Antonio .... Its workers sewed clothes and stuffed mattresses and repaired toys; served hot lunches to schoolchildren; ministered to the sick; delivered library books to remote hamlets by horseback; rescued flood victims; painted giant murals on the walls of hospitals, high schools, courthouses, and city halls; performed plays and played music before eager audiences; and wrote guides to the forty-eight states that even today remain models for what such books should be. And when the clouds of an oncoming world war loomed over the United States, it was the WPA's workers who modernized the army and air bases and trained in vast numbers to supply the nation's military needs.

Taylor (2008).

The New Deal jobs programs employed 13 million people; the WPA was the biggest program, employing 8.5 million, lasting 8 years, and spending about $10.5 billion (Taylor, 2008, p. 3). It took a broken country and in many important respects helped to not only revive it but to bring it into the 20th century. The WPA built 650,000 miles of roads, 78,000 bridges, 125,000 civilian and military buildings, 700 miles of airport runways; fed 900 million hot lunches to kids, operated 1500 nursery schools, gave concerts before audiences of 150 million, and created 475,000 works of art. It transformed and modernized America (Taylor, 2008, pp. 523–524).

Dimitri Papadimitriou summarizes a number of real-world experiences with direct job creation by government—several of them in developing countries:

Direct job creation programs are not limited to those implemented in the United States in response to the Great Depression; the international experience of such programs is extensive … The program in Sweden (1938–70) was the "right to work"; the Maharashtra State Employment Guarantee program in India was the "right to food," while their national program (NREGA) enacted in 2005 is an entitlement or a "right to employment" program. Other prominent examples of emergency public works programs were implemented in Indonesia and South Korea responding to the East Asian financial crisis, and Argentina's Heads of Households (Jefes) Plan in response to that country's crisis in 2001. Similarly, the social funds programs were set up to ameliorate the effects of structural adjustment as those in Bolivia (1986), Chile (1975–1987), Peru (1991), and the Expanded Public Works Programme in South Africa in 2004. Another motivation for such strategy was the ILO's extensive employment-based intensive public works programs throughout Africa. (Papadimitriou, 2008)

viii What about high turnover in the JG program? Many wonder how the JG projects could handle high turnover with its workforce of relatively low education and training. Workers would flow in during recession and flow out in a recovery. Could the JG projects operate on a continuing basis with such turnover?

It must be remembered that low wage employers across the nation regularly recruit, employ, and train from a pool of potential workers similar to those who will go into the JG workforce. Those workers cook your food, clean your hotel rooms, care for your children, and take care of your elderly grandparents. These firms are under constant pressure to increase the workload, depress wages, and harden the working conditions of those workers as they engage in ruthless competition at the bottom of the wage pool. A JG program will not be run for profit; it will set the minimum wage and working conditions tolerated in the United States. We can choose to enforce humanitarian conditions and livable wages in the JG.

Furthermore, the economic fluctuations would be attenuated with the JG in place—since the JG moderates the business cycle. In a recession, incomes do not fall as much as they do now since workers released by the private sector continue to work (in the JG); and in expansion there may be less upward pressure on wages since employers can recruit from the JG program. In past recessions in the United States, the swing of employment has been around 4 million between peak and trough (it was much larger than this in the global financial crisis). If (as we project) the JG begins with about 15 million workers a swing of 4 million over the course of the cycle is relatively small—and it could be smaller if the JG does indeed moderate the business cycle. The JG will need to have some kinds of work "on the shelf" that can be done as the program swells in recession, and then be curtailed as the economy recovers.

The JG program will focus on those areas of production that are not currently undertaken by private undertakers,[21] either domestic or foreign. It will offer socially productive work for our unemployed. It will raise the bar for our domestic undertakers. It will offer real opportunities for workers that our undertakers neglect—whether because the demand for the undertaker's output is too low or because our undertakers discriminate against groups of workers by race, class, and gender.

d. A consensus strategy for a universal job guarantee program

The idea of a JG policy has been vaulted to prominence in the context of several endorsements of the idea (or variants thereof) by a number of likely contenders for the 2020 Democratic presidential nomination (including Senators Elizabeth Warren, Kirsten Gillibrand, Bernie Sanders, and Cory Booker). In that context, I coauthored a report that presented a JG proposal along with estimates of the economic impact of the program over a 10-year horizon (Wray et al., 2018). However, several other variants have been proposed and/or endorsed. Here I seek to establish some common ground among the major JG plans by laying out the most important principles to which an effective JG should adhere.

Our approach to the JG would provide new jobs in a Public Service Employment (PSE) program for approximately 15 million workers at $15 per hour, while creating an additional 4.2 million private sector jobs because of the program's boost to aggregate demand. It would include a package of benefits worth 25% of the wage bill and cover additional costs (administration, equipment, and raw materials) at 20% of the wage bill. The generous wage and benefit package would become standard across the country, as all private and government sector employers would need to match it to retain workers. In other words, once the program is in place, the effective minimum wage would be $15 per hour (plus benefits)—raising all wages at the bottom to at least that level—and 19 million more workers would be employed.

We used a well-respected economic model to simulate the economic outcomes of the program for the United States.[22] This was, so far as we know, the first time an economic model has been used to project the effects of a universal JG program. According to the simulation, it would boost real GDP by about $560 billion per year, while inflation would peak at just 0.74 percentage points above baseline projections

---

[21] Recall that "undertaker" was Adam Smith's term for "capitalist"; a commonly used alternative, *entrepreneur*, comes from French, and was derived from the Old French word *entreprendre* that meant "to undertake". The term "undertaker" began to be used in reference to the funeral business in the 18th century, although it continued in use as a general term for "undertaking" business. It was apparently originally used as a term to refer to the English expropriators of Irish lands in the 16th century, probably evolving from the term meaning "to entrap".

[22] The simulation used the Fair Model—see Wray et al. (2018).

(falling to just 0.09 percentage points above the baseline by the end of the program's first decade).

The federal government's budget deficit would rise by a maximum of 1.5% of GDP over the baseline, falling to an average of 1.13% of GDP (over the baseline) by the second half of the decade. State budgets would improve by $53 billion per year—even after raising the wages and benefits of all government employees to the PSE program's standards.

These estimates do not take account of many of the cost savings that would be enjoyed by all levels of government, firms, and households as a result of the increase in wages and reduction in unemployment and poverty rates. The federal government would pay the wages, benefits, and other program costs, but implementation would be highly decentralized—with qualifying not-for-profits, state and local governments, and school districts, as well as the federal government creating the jobs. An important feature of our proposal is that, other than establishing a minimum wage and benefit package, projects would not compete with the private sector. We have focused our program on PSE because we expect most of the jobs to involve provision of care services: care for the environment, care for people, and care for communities.

We think this reflects the best match of the potential program labor force with the needs of their communities.

In the early weeks of the 2020 presidential campaign, there were several other proposals that adopted similar features ($15 per hour wage minimum, universal availability, generous benefits), with some prominent differences. These include tiered wages (some employees would receive much more than $15 per hour), subsidized private for-profit employment, guaranteed income whether one works or not, a focus on construction of infrastructure, and centralized program administration (with the federal government actually employing the workers).

To clarify the positions we have taken in our report (Wray et al., 2018), and in an effort to see where supporters of the idea of a JG might be able to come to a common agreement in what follows I briefly summarize what I think are essential components of a JG proposal, and indicate where I think compromises can be made.

1 **The JG should pay a living wage with good benefits.** In line with other progressive proposals, the JG wage should establish a national minimum wage at $15 per hour, with free Medicare-style healthcare. It should also provide free childcare to enable parents to participate in the program. The JG program itself can greatly expand childcare provisioning, as many JG workers can be employed to provide childcare to underserved communities and to JG workers.

2 **Congress will appropriate the necessary funds to pay program expenses.** No additional taxes will be levied. Advocates of the JG should not play the "how you gonna pay for it" game. (The topic of sovereign government financing of such a program will be discussed in Part D.)

3 **The JG should be universal—providing paid work to anyone ready and willing to work.** It should also be universal in the sense that it serves every

community, offering jobs where people live and providing real benefits to their communities. The JG's wage and benefits will set the minimum standard nationwide. This will provide a boost to communities across the nation, with relatively greater benefits where they are needed most: where jobs are scarce, where pay is lowest, and where markets suffer the most from lack of income to support buying power.

4 **The JG should not devolve to either workfare or welfare.** The social safety net should not be dismantled; no existing social services should be eliminated. Individuals should be able to continue to receive existing benefits if they do not want to work in the JG program. At the same time, the JG should not provide income support to those that do not work in the program. The JG should be seen as an employment program in which workers are paid for work. The program should have visible benefits to communities so that the workers in the program are recognized as making positive contributions in return for their wages. Workers can be fired for cause—with grievance procedures established to protect their rights, and with conditions on rehiring into the program.

5 **However, there should be room in the JG for time-limited training and education.** While on-the-job training should be a part of every project, proposals can be solicited for specific training and basic education programs that will prepare workers for jobs in the JG—and, eventually, for work outside the JG. It is important that these are time limited and that the training is for jobs that actually exist.

6 **Project implementation and management will be decentralized.** There should be diversity in the types of employments and employers—to help ensure there are projects that appeal to workers and their communities. Projects should go through several layers of approval before implementation (local, state or regional, federal) and be evaluated at these levels once in progress. Decentralization helps to protect the program from whatever political winds emanate from the *du jour* occupant of the White House.

7 **Where possible, proposals should scale up existing projects with proven track records and with adequate administrative capacity to add JG workers.** Making use of existing capacity will minimize additional overhead. Program funds should be focused on paying wages and benefits to JG employees. Federal spending should not unduly subsidize administrative expenses.

8 **The JG should not be used to subsidize wages of workers employed by for-profit firms.** This distorts markets and is not likely to generate substantial new employment. Private business is already heavily subsidized by all levels of government. The JG should not be used as yet another corporate welfare program. However, private firms will benefit indirectly (and greatly) from the program as it provides a pool of hirable labor and as it contributes to economic growth that improves markets for firms.

9 **Direct employment by the federal government for the JG should not dominate the program.** Most employment should be administered at the local

level—where the workers are, in the communities where they will work. The JG program will probably need to create 15 million new jobs—six times greater than the number of federal employees today. If all 15 million were to join the federal workforce, supervision of all these new workers would, alone, require hiring a large number of additional federal employees. This would be politically difficult even if the massive scaling up of the federal workforce were administratively possible. The federal government's role in the direct provision of jobs should be focused on providing projects to underserved communities and workers—after not-for-profits and state and local governments have employed as many as they can.

10 **Inclusivity and experimentation should be encouraged.** The federal government should solicit proposals for novel approaches to job creation. For example, workers' co-ops could be formed to propose projects in which wages, benefits, and limited materials costs would be covered by the federal government for a specified time period.

11 **Consistent with point 10, project proposals put forth should not be summarily dismissed simply due to political bias.** The JG program should welcome diversity. We should entertain the notion that even those at opposite ends of the political spectrum might have good ideas for projects. Determination of an organization's eligibility to submit projects would be similar to the process the IRS uses for designation of tax-exempt status, although the standards for keeping politics and religion out of the projects should be higher, since federal government money will be spent directly for employment in the program.

12 **With decentralization, the types of projects permitted would take account of local laws and rules, including prevailing wage laws and union wage rates.** With the JG paying $15 per hour, this means that in many states and localities, rules and laws will prohibit various types of work, including construction. In those areas, JG workers will not build infrastructure, for example. It is possible that limited-term training or apprentice projects could be funded in those areas instead. However, in many states construction by JG workers paid $15 per hour would be permissible. Decentralization helps to ensure conformity with local laws and rules, while maintaining a uniform JG wage.

13 **Exceptions to the uniform wage should be considered, but this should not become the norm.** For example, state or local governments might want to subsidize (at their own costs) the federally paid wage of $15 per hour in order to increase wages to some higher level. This might be because of high living costs locally. Or some JG employers might want to offer additional benefits (at their own cost) to workers, including housing allowances for high rent areas.

In conclusion, a JG program cannot be expected to solve all social and economic problems. It is not a substitute for other social and economic programs. We will still need various labor force programs, including retraining of and compensation for skilled workers who lose their jobs to imports or robots. We will still need a major public infrastructure program to bring the country into the 21st century. We will still need a safety net for those who cannot, should not, or do not want to work. We will still need a major reform of the healthcare system—although extension of coverage to all JG workers will make that much easier to do. We will still need to downsize and constrain the runaway financial sector. We still have a long legacy of neoliberalism and the destruction that it has caused to our society and economy. And we still have excessive inequality, although the JG will go a long way toward reducing inequality at the bottom by providing paid work at a living wage.

IV. Robotization: a not so scary tale

Amazon's Jeff Bezos has announced that drones will sooner or later be delivering packages to your home. Predictably, this has generated two types of buzz—about the inevitable mishaps, and about the displaced UPS workers.

For me, the first is a wee bit scary. Of course, you now have the prospect of being run over by a UPS driver whose workload has already been increased so much that she or he does not have the time to drive carefully. With the coming of drones we will have to constantly scan the sky for incoming errant flights and packages hurtling to earth. I suppose the drones are more scary than the trucks.

However, it is the second worry that is getting most of the attention: What are we going to do as robots increasingly replace human workers? That sort of apocalypse has been featured in science fiction from time immemorial. Not only do we have the worry of rising unemployment of humans, but also the growing intelligence of robots as they realize they do not need no damn humans any more. Ahhhnold Is Baaaack! Open the pod-bay Doors, Hal!

And the big reason that Silicon Valley execs (like Andrew Yang) have been promoting the BIG is to protect their technology. You see, they fear that as robots become smarter and take more of our jobs, this will inevitably spur a "Luddite"-type reaction.

An interesting piece in Salon addresses these fears. Indeed, the title tells it all: "Amazon, Applebee's and Google's job-crushing drones and robot armies: They're coming for your job next". Andrew Leonard lays out the issues nicely:

> *The sense of increasing momentum toward a more robot-infested future is undeniable. […] Whether this transition is driven because it delivers true convenience for consumers, or whether it simply makes economic sense for the masters of capital, the logic of this technological evolution is inexorable ….*

He goes on to describe the "Panglossian" view: this is great because robots will take over all the drudgery leaving humans free to do all the fun and creative stuff. But can we really create enough of those types of jobs? And what about humans who are not all that creative? What do we do with them?

Well, BIG. That is the Silicon Valley view, discussed above.

Most economists are not too concerned, however. The typical economist's take on all this is that by filling the lower-skilled jobs with robots, we will be able to move human workers into the higher-skilled work. Of course, as robots get smarter (or as we continually reduce complex processes to a series of simple steps—which has been the basis of automation since the days of Adam Smith), humans will be funneled into ever-higher-order tasks. Not to worry, say the economists, because we will need more and more robots, too. Hence, the final refuge for human workers will be to make the robots that do everything else.

Economist Joan Robinson (who should have been the first woman to win the Nobel for Economics—but was disqualified for taking the winning side of the "Capital Controversy" debate, while all the losers did get a Nobel as a consolation prize for losing to Robinson!) saw all this coming long ago when she wondered "But what do we do when robots make the robots?"

Back in 1991 I wrote about all this in a journal article: *"Saving, Profits, and Speculation in Capitalist Economies", Journal of Economic Issues, vol. 25, no. 4, December 1991, pp. 951−975.* I just took a look at it and still consider it to be the best article I have published. I wrote it in one sitting, mailed it off to the journal's editor, Marc Tool, who accepted it on sight. Directly from pen to publication—the fastest and easiest publication I ever had. Let me quote myself from two relevant sections. I know, it is a bad habit, but I cannot improve on it:

Profits from Production, Paper Profits, and Instability

There has been a long-running debate over "productive" versus "unproductive" spending, which has been renewed in a recent concern with the transformation of the US economy to a "casino" society in which speculative behavior has replaced "productive" investment …

As Keynes argued, the sole goal of capitalist production from the perspective of capitalists is "to end up with more money than it started with". When there are alternatives to production for earning profit, capitalists need not engage in production. Profits can be generated by capitalist purchases of producibles or nonproducibles—capitalist spending on anything other than the wage bill in the consumption goods sector necessarily returns to capitalists as profit. {note this follows from the Kalecki equation—I won't go into that in detail here.} *Capitalist purchases of Rembrandts, real estate, or paper must also generate gross profits, and if these purchases represent net deficit spending they will increase aggregate profits. I will call profits resulting from purchases of nonproducibles "paper profits".*

Net deficits used to finance purchases of nonproducibles will lead to growth of capitalist income. There is nothing within the workings of the capitalist system that guarantees that credit is created only to finance production …. [F]inancial innovations have continually expanded the types of activity that are deemed acceptable. Thus, in the current period, credit is freely extended to finance speculative booms in the prices of everything from real estate to stocks to foreign exchange futures.

Credit created to finance purchases of nonproducibles can lead to a speculative boom of the prices of such assets. As long as new flows of spending are continuously entering the market for paper, prices of assets will continue to rise and reward speculation. As long as the boom continues, speculation generates income. However, given that the boom can continue only as long as new spending on nonproducibles generates new income (rewarding the speculation by creating paper profit), it will come to an end as soon as spending stops rising. Every speculative boom will end, although the timing of the end is unpredictable. As soon as spending falls, prices and income fall.

Although there are no automatic mechanisms to ensure that capitalist activity is directed toward production, the inherent instability of speculation drives capitalists back to the productive sphere in search of profits. The productive sphere is made more stable by the spending habits of workers. Workers must spend most of their income to acquire the necessities of life—through the purchase, primarily, of producibles. Advertising and the propensities of conspicuous consumption and pecuniary emulation help to ensure that even if wages are in excess of the income required to satisfy biological necessities, workers still spend most wages on producibles. It is this consumption behavior of workers that "grounds" capitalist economies by imparting stability to the production of consumer goods …

Note that as the wage share of national income has fallen on trend since the 1970s, the stabilizing force of worker consumption has been diminished. Indeed, workers had to make up for stagnant wages by borrowing, which added another dimension to the instability. All this is now well known, and is part of the secular stagnation argument recently brought into the limelight by Larry Summers.

Joan Robinson once asked what would happen if robots replaced labor. When the wage bill falls to zero, all capitalist spending will represent profit since costs of production will fall to zero. {Note that this is because robots don't earn wages.} Capitalist spending on consumer goods would represent the only spending on consumption, and would generate an equivalent amount of profit income. Additional profit income would be generated by capitalist purchases of investment goods and by capitalist purchases of nonproducibles. Given the small scale of production of consumption goods, profits from capitalist consumption and capitalist purchases of investment goods would have to be small. Thus most profits would come from nonproducibles, and would fluctuate widely as a result of speculative activity. Without the stabilizing influence of worker consumption, this society would cycle between boom and bust due to "whirlwinds of optimism and pessimism". There is no reason to believe that capitalists would be better off if the wage bill could be reduced to zero, for their profits would have to come largely from speculation in a "casino" society.

Well, there you go. This was 1991, folks. In the paper I go on to talk about the real-world events of the 1980s that created our casino society, in which "saving and speculation became the favored activities, while productive activity was scorned", where even "retirees became adept players in financial markets, shifting their liquid wealth in search of the highest possible returns" and "professional money managers took control of pension funds, and computer-program-generated decisions could instantly cause a boom or bust in the price of an asset".

Of course, all of this is related to our most recent Global Financial Collapse and as well to the newly found recognition by Very Important People such as Summers, Krugman, and Robert Gordon that we are in a phase of secular stagnation.

Back in the early 1990s I used to joke that the solution to our problems would be to encourage speculation in Martian Oceanfront Condo Futures. We could bubble up condo prices on Mars without screwing up our own economy. In hindsight, that looks like it would have been a far better policy than that pursued by Larry Summers (at the Treasury in the Clinton administration)—deregulating Wall Street, which bubbled up our food and home prices, with the disastrous results we are still living through.

But is there a better solution? Certainly!

I will be brief as we will build on the arguments made in the last two sections. We need to recognize that our workers of the future will be in the service sector, with far less than 1% of the workforce in manufacturing and perhaps a few percent in construction. Agricultural employment will remain low (1% or 2%), although it could rise a little if the "slow food" movement continues to gain speed (so to speak). The rest of the workforce must be in the service sector. Many of those will be in personal care: care of the young, the aged, and the sick. There will also be jobs caring for the environment and caring for communities. The entertainment sector will be much bigger—we will need a lot more clowns to keep up our spirits. I am hopeful that we will downsize the FIRE sector, but who knows. Lifelong education will preserve jobs in the education sector, even though the internet and teaching robots will take a lot of jobs.

I used to joke that all the jobs of the future will be in the three "P" sectors: Professorial, Prostitution, and Politics. Some might object that that is at most two distinct sectors.

To ensure full employment we will need the JG. To ensure decent wages and sufficient demand for consumer goods produced by all those robots we will need a generous wage and benefit package in the JG program (which of course forces all other employers to be generous, too, or they lose their disgruntled workers).

We will need to reduce the work week. That brings on lots of problems—how will we keep people occupied in their nonwork, nonsleep hours? If we are to have anything approaching a good, democratic society, we cannot let them spend those extra hours in front of the TV or on social media, which has made many in today's generations far too stupid, selfish, and reactionary to self-govern. You need proof? Look at the 2016 Presidential election which led to a sitting President who governs by tweet.

All of this was foreseen by John Maynard Keynes, of course, in his ruminations on the economic possibilities for his grandkids—written in 1930—that provided an optimistic antidote to both the pessimistic outlook that gripped the world in the onset of the Great Depression and as well to the current prognostications made by peddlers of the secular stagnation thesis. He foresaw resumption of economic growth so that living standards would increase tremendously over the century after 1930—allowing work weeks to be radically shortened so that workers could live in what he characterized as a future "age of leisure and of abundance".

I see us free, therefore, to return to some of the most sure and certain principles of religion and traditional virtue-that avarice is a vice, that the exaction of usury is a misdemeanour, and the love of money is detestable, that those walk most truly in the paths of virtue and sane wisdom who take least thought for the morrow. We shall once more value ends above means and prefer the good to the useful. We shall honour those who can teach us how to pluck the hour and the day virtuously and well, the delightful people who are capable of taking direct enjoyment in things, the lilies of the field who toil not, neither do they spin.

(Keynes, 1932, pp. 372–373).

He did warn that this was not foreordained. And living standards have been falling while work weeks have lengthened for most American workers over the past half century. Still, there is a sliver of hope that he will be proven correct, eventually. For more on that future, read *How Much is Enough? Money and the Good Life* by Robert and Edward Skidelsky.

In the meantime, let us create good-paying and useful jobs for all, including those displaced by robots. In the long run of time, those robots are our friends—just as machinery has been in the past—as they will allow us to continue to increase the economy's productivity, enabling (but not guaranteeing) rising living standards. There are two barriers. The first is that wages do not rise with productivity (which is what has happened over the past half century) as rapacious employers broke labor unions and held real wages constant. All the gains to productivity since 1974 have gone to the employing half—and none to the workers.

The second danger is that workers displaced by robots cannot find jobs.

The JG approach resolves both of these issues, first by establishing a living wage that will rise overtime as worker productivity rises (in part due to increased use of machines and robots), and second by providing good-paying jobs, primarily in the services sector, and largely in the care services (care for people, community, and the environment). These are also the types of activities that Keynes thought would dominate in the future he foresaw.

As we saw above, proponents of the BIG see the solution as universal access to income. This would, indeed, help to resolve the problem of displaced labor (paying the unemployed not to work), and would allow capitalists to sell consumer goods and services to BIG recipients. The problem, however, is that BIG delinks work and income (this is a feature, not a bug, in their view)—and it provides this income universally. Even if it did not have a huge impact on the work incentive, it would add so much income, supplementing the wage bill paid for the production of the consumer goods and services, that spending on the output would outstrip supplies. As discussed, inflation is the likely result.

The JG is the better solution for several reasons. First it is targeted and hence provides a much smaller boost to aggregate income. Second, it does not diminish the value of work—payment is made for working. Third, it can provide useful output that helps to raise living standards. Fourth, it is countercyclical. And fifth, it grows overtime as displacement of workers by robots occurs—unlike the BIG, which immediately begins paying workers (and all others) who have not suffered displacement.

As we will discuss in Part D, the JG is only part of the answer—it will help to put us on to the path Keynes had envisioned. But we will need other policies so that we might live "virtuously and well", as he put it.

References

American Institute for Economic Research, 2019. https://www.aier.org/article/universal-basic-income-little-more-smoke-and-mirrors.

Atkinson, A.B., 1996. The case for participation income. The Political Quarterly 67 (3), 67–70.

Bell, S., Wray, L.R., 2004a. The "War on Poverty" After 40 Years: A Minskyan Assessment. Economics Working Paper Archive wp_404. Levy Economics Institute.

Bell, S., Wray, L.R., 2004b. The War on Poverty After 40 Years. PPN 78. The Levy Economics Institute.

Bernstein, J., May 2014. To lift the poor, you can't avoid taxing the rich. The New York Times.

Burgess, J., Mitchell, W.F., 1998. Unemployment human rights and full employment policy in Australia. In: Jones, M., Kriesler, P. (Eds.), Globalization, Human Rights and Civil Society. Prospect Press, Sydney, Australia.

President George W. Bush, June 17, 2004. https://georgewbush-whitehouse.archives.gov/news/releases/2004/08/20040809-9.html.

Cassidy, J., September 2014. The New Yorker. https://www.newyorker.com/news/john-cassidy/didnt-eric-holder-go-bankers.

Dantas, F., Wray, L.R., 2017. Falling Labor Force Participation: Demographics or Lack of Jobs? Economics One-Pager Archive op_53 Levy Economics Institute.

Dayen, D., 2013. Your New Landlord Works on Wall Street: hedge funds are snatching up rental homes at an alarming rate. The New Republic.

Felkerson, J.A., 2012. A Detailed Look at the Fed's Bailout by Funding Facility and Recipient. PPB 123. The Levy Economics Institute.

FOMC, 2011. https://www.federalreserve.gov/monetarypolicy/files/FOMC20111102meeting.pdf.

Ginsburg, H., 1983. Full Employment and Public Policy: The United States and Sweden. Lexington Books.

Harvey, P., 1989. Securing the Right to Employment: Social Welfare Policy and the Unemployed in the United States. Princeton University Press, Princeton, NJ.

Kalleberg, A.L., Von Wachter, T.M., 2018. The U.S. Labor market during and after the great recession: continuities and transformations. RSF 3. NCBI. https://www.ncbi.nlm.nih.gov/pmc/articles/PMC5959048/.

Keynes, J.M., 1964. The General Theory of Employment, Interest, and Money. Harcourt Brace Jovanovich, New York and London.

Keynes, J.M., 1930. Economic possibilities for our grandchildren. In: Essays in Persuasion. Harcourt Brace, 1932, New York, pp. 358−373.

Mathews, N., 2013. The FED Rate that Resuscitated Wall Street. http://www.levyinstitute.org/pubs/op_40.pdf.

Merle, R., September 10, 2018. A guide to the financial crisis—10 years later. The Washington Post. https://www.washingtonpost.com/business/economy/a-guide-to-the-financial-crisis−10-years-later/2018/09/10/114b76ba-af10-11e8-a20b-5f4f84429666_story.html?utm_term=.246b2eaa768d.

Minsky, H. The poverty of economic policy. In: Presented at the Graduate Institute of Cooperative Leadership, New York, July 14, 1975.

Mitchell, W., Muysken, J., 2008. Full Employment Abandoned: Shifting Sands and Policy Failures. Edward Elgar Publishing.

Ocasio Cortez, A., January 2019. https://www.vox.com/policy-and-politics/2019/1/4/18168431/alexandria-ocasio-cortez-70-percent.

Papadimitriou, B.D., 2008. Promoting Equality Through an Employment of Last Resort Policy. WP 545. The Levy Economics Institute.

Pigeon, M.-A., Wray, L.R., 1998. Did the Clinton Rising Tide Raise All Boats? PPN 45 The Levy Institute. http://www.levyinstitute.org/publications/did-the-clinton-rising-tide-raise-all-boats (for a critical analysis of the notion that rising tides raise boats at the bottom).

Piketty, T., 2013. Capital in the Twenty-First Century. Harvard University Press.

Sen, A., 1999. Development as Freedom. Alfred A. Knopf, New York, NY.

Schutz, R.R., 1996. The $30,000 Solution: A Guaranteed Annual Income for Every American. Fithian Press, Santa Barbara, CA.

Sheahen, A., June 2013. Jobs are not the answer. The Gilmer Mirror.

Sirota, D., January 2013. To big to jail? Salon. https://www.salon.com/2013/01/23/are_banks_too_big_to_jail/.

Smith, C., June 2019. 3 reasons why your rent is so high. HuffPost. https://www.huffpost.com/entry/high-rent-reasons_n_5d03d65ae4b0304a120f25e4?ncid=newsltushpmgnews__TheMorningEmail__062719.

Taylor, N., 2008. American-made: the enduring legacy of the WPA: when FDR put the nation to work. Tantor Media 2.

Tcherneva, P., Wray, L.R., 2005. Can Basic Income and Job Guarantees Deliver on Their Promises? University of Missouri-Kansas City. Working Paper No. 42. For more on the JG versus BIG, You can read our paper (#112) as well as many others at the BIG net: http://www.usbig.net/papers.php.

Tcherneva, P., Wray, L.R., 2007. Public Employment and Women. WP 519. http://www.levyinstitute.org/publications/public-employment-and-women.

Tcherneva, P., September 2014. NYT. https://www.nytimes.com/2014/09/27/upshot/the-benefits-of-economic-expansions-are-increasingly-going-to-the-richest-americans.html.

Tymoigne, E., Wray, L.R., 2013. Modern Money Theory 101: A Reply to Critics. Economics Working Paper Archive wp_778. Levy Economics Institute for a detailed exposition.

Van Parijs, P., 1992. Arguing for Basic Income. Verso, New York, NY.

Van Parijs, P., 1995. Real Freedom for All. Oxford University Press, Oxford, UK.

Van Parijs, P., 2001. A basic income for all. In: Cohen, J., Rogers, J. (Eds.), What's Wrong with a Free Lunch? Beacon Press, Boston, MA.

Van Parijs, P., 2004. Basic income: a simple and powerful idea for the twenty-first century. Politics & Society 32 (1), 7—39.

Wolff, R., December 2014a. https://truthout.org/articles/the-wages-of-global-capitalism/.

Wolff, R., May 2014b. Better than redistributing income. Truthout.

Wray, L.R., Forstater, M., 2004. Full employment and economic justice. In: Champlin, D., Knoedler, J. (Eds.), The Institutionalist Tradition in Labor Economics.

Wray, L.R., Kelton, S., September 2011. What the country needs is a new new deal. Truthdig.

Wray, L.R., Kelton, S., Tcherneva, P., Fullwiler, S., Dantas, F., 2018. Guaranteed Jobs Through a Public Service Employment Program. Economics Policy Note 18-2. Levy Economics Institute.

Wray, L.R., 1991. Saving, profits, and speculation in capitalist economies. Journal of Economic Issues 25 (4), 951—975.

Wray, L.R., 2000. Public Service Employment: Full Employment without Inflation. CFEPS Working Paper No. 3.

Wray, L.R., 2005. The Ownership Society: Social Security Is Only the Beginning. Economics Public Policy Brief Archive ppb_82. Levy Economics Institute.

Wray, L.R., March 22, 2017. Trumponomics: causes and prospects. Real-World Economics Review (78).

Further reading

Alaska Basic Income. https://www.vox.com/policy-and-politics/2018/2/13/16997188/alaska-basic-income-permanent-fund-oil-revenue-study.

Barlett, D.L., Steele, J.B., April 10, 1988. A rich Texas widow could save $4 million. The Philadelphia Inquirer A15.

Clark, C.M.A., 2002. The Basic Income Guarantee: Ensuring Progress and Prosperity in the 21st Century. The Liffey Press, Dublin, Ireland.

Clinton Bill, on the rise of the 1 percent: "I don't think there's much you can do about that unless you want to start jailing people"; 8:14 AM—May 14, 2014. https://twitter.com/josephlawler/status/466597333749497857. From https://www.pgpf.org/what-we-are-doing/fiscal-summit/2014-fiscal-summit-our-economic-future, approximately 6:30 minutes into his talk.

Fitzpatrick, T., 2003. After the New Social Democracy. Manchester University Press, Manchester, UK.

Leonard, A., 2013. Amazon, Applebee's and Google's job-crushing drones and robot armies: they're coming for your job next. Salon. http://www.salon.com/2013/12/06/triumph_of_the_drones/.

McElwee, S., McAuliffe, C., Green, J., March 20, 2018. Why democrats should embrace a federal jobs guarantee. The Nation.

Meyerson, H., April 25, 2018. Why the cause of full employment is back from the dead. The American Prospect.

Minsky, H.P., 1965. The role of employment policy. In: Gordon, M.S. (Ed.), Poverty in America. Chandler Publishing Company, San Francisco, CA.

Mosler, W. http://moslereconomics.com/2019/06/28/reposting-a-prior-comment/.

Offe, C., 1992. A non-productivist design for social policies. In: Van Parijs, P. (Ed.), Arguing for Basic Income. Verso, New York, NY.

As a result, in most developed economies around the world, the real sector is very weak. The crisis is not over—especially in Euroland.

While it might appear that the United States, United Kingdom, and some other developed non-European countries have recovered, their real sectors are weak and their financial institutions have resumed risky practices. The global economic system is fragile and a full-blown crisis could return. The United States, Europe, and the United Kingdom focused on propping up their financial systems while letting their real sectors fall into deep recessions. Only growth led by the government sector will allow these nations to fully recover while reducing private debt ratios. It is not happening.

Finance should always serve the economy. It should be of an appropriate size. When finance is freed of constraints and allowed to become "globalized" it begins to dominate the economy. It is fairly crazy for developing nations to open their economies to globalized finance. Finance is not a scarce resource. Any nation can have as much as it wants, within its own borders. It does not need global financial institutions. What they do is to "financialize" the economies—to run the economies in the interests of global finance.

What is the solution? Finance needs to be downsized, eliminating the dangerous "too big to fail" institutions that operate with impunity in the knowledge that Uncle Sam will always bail them out no matter what risks they take. We need to take bank charters away from institutions that refuse to shed their riskier arms that do not serve a legitimate public purpose—instead engaging in activities such as speculative trading in assets, creating derivatives that shift risk, operating off-balance-sheet entities to hide risk, and packaging and selling asset-backed securities. Institutions with bank charters ought to do good underwriting, hold assets to maturity, and bear all interest rate, exchange rate, and default risks. This would simplify our system and make it much less risky.

We discussed many of the risky and fraudulent practices that crashed the global economy in 2007 above in Part A. Most of them are still in practice. Some of them are illegal; many more should become so. Most importantly, however, even if we allow risky practices, we need to restrict their use. First, we need to keep a portion of the financial system safe and directed toward the capital development of the economy. The chartered commercial banking system (that is, banks with charters) is the prime example. These have historically offered deposits and made commercial, consumer, and real estate loans. Their activities should be greatly restrained in order to get them back on track. Big banks that do not wish to do so should be stripped of their charters—meaning they would also lose access to FDIC insurance as well as access to the Fed.

Once we carve out a safe part of the system, there will remain a risky part. That is fine. If they make mistakes (and they will), we let them fail. But that means that we cannot let that risky part have access to households of moderate means, to state and local governments, to pension funds, or to any other entities that serve a clear public purpose (other retirement savings, not-for-profits, incorporated business, etc). This makes it more politically feasible to let them fail. The Vampire Squids of Wall Street should only be allowed to play with truly rich people's money. And if they fail, rich folks lose. That sounds pretty good to me.

We have long been told that we needed to "free" financial markets to increase the supply of finance—as if finance is a scarce resource. That is false. We do not need more private finance. We need less. However, we do need the government to play a bigger role in financing the development of the economy. To understand the government's proper role, we need to understand government money—a topic we now turn to.

II. The role of the government in the monetary system
a. The basics of money creation

Let us begin to build an understanding of what money really is.

The dominant narrative is that money "greases" the wheels of commerce. Sure, you could run the commercial machine without money, but it runs better with lubricant. In that story, money was created as a medium of exchange: instead of trading your banana for her fish, you agree to use cowry shells to intermediate trade. Over time, money's evolution increased efficiency by selecting in succession unworked precious metals, stamped precious metal coins, precious metal-backed paper money, and, finally, fiat money comprised of base metal coins, paper notes, and electronic entries.

In this view, money is a "veil" that obscures the simple reality of exchange; in the conventional lexicon, money can be ignored as "neutral". (That means it does not affect any decisions.) We only worry about money when there is too much of it: Friedman's famous claim is that "inflation is always and everywhere a monetary phenomenon"—too much money causes prices to rise (Friedman, 1991). Hence, all the worry about the Fed's Quantitative Easing, which has quadrupled the "Fed's money" (reserves) and by all rights should have caused massive inflation. (It did not.)

In this section we will examine a different narrative, drawing on Joseph Schumpeter's notion that the banker is the ephor of capitalism as well on the alternative view of government's money developed by Modern Money Theory (MMT)—a new approach to money that I helped to develop over the past quarter of a century.

Looking at money from the perspective of exchange is highly misleading for developing an understanding of capitalism. In the Robinson Crusoe story, I have got a banana and you have got a fish. But how did we get them? In the real world, bananas and fish have to be produced—production that has to be financed. Production begins with money to purchase inputs (labor, capital, intermediate goods), which creates monetary income used to buy outputs.

As mom insisted, "money doesn't grow on trees". How did producers get money in the first place? Maybe by selling output? Logically, that is an infinite regress argument—a chicken and egg problem. The first dollar spent (by producer or consumer) had to come from somewhere. It could not have come from another's spending.

There is another problem. Even if we could imagine that humanity inherited "manna from heaven" (Friedman said we can just assume money is dropped into the economy by helicopters) to get the monetary economy going—say, an initial endowment of a million dollars—how do we explain profits, interest, and growth? If I am a producer who inherited $1000 of manna, spending it on inputs, I am not going to be happy if sales are only $1000. I want a return—maybe 20%, so I need $1200. If I am a money lender, I lend $1000 but want $1200, too. And all of us want a growing pie. How can that initial million dollars of manna do double and triple duty so that we all can end up with more of it than we started with? After all, that is what capitalism is all about: start with some quantity of money and end up with more of it. (Marx put it this way: M-C-M': start with money [M], buy commodities and labor to produce a commodity as output [C], and sell it for more money [M'].)

Here is where Schumpeter's "ephor" comes in. An ephor is "one who oversees", and Schumpeter applied this term to the banker. We do not need to imagine money as manna, but rather as the creation of purchasing power controlled by the banker. A producer wanting to hire resources submits a prospectus to the banker. While the banker looks at past performance as well as wealth pledged as collateral, most important is the likelihood that the producer's prospects are good—this is called "underwriting". If so, the ephor advances a loan that allows the production process to get underway. Where did the money come from that the ephor lends? The ephor created it.

More technically, the banker accepts the IOU of the producer and makes payments to resource suppliers (including labor) by crediting their deposit accounts. The producer's IOU is the banker's asset (a loan); the bank's deposits are its liabilities but are the assets of the deposit holders (resource suppliers).This is how "money" really gets into the economy—not via manna from heaven nor Friedman's "helicopter drops" by central bankers.

When depositors spend (perhaps on consumption goods, perhaps to purchase inputs for their own production processes), their accounts are debited, and the accounts of recipients are credited. This goes on until the loans are repaid—in which case the deposits originally created are debited (disappearing from balance sheets). That is, when a bank loan is repaid, the bank's asset (a loan) and its liability (a deposit) are both debited (crossed off the balance sheet). That means a depositor's asset (the deposit) and a borrower's liability (the loan) are also debited. These four keystrokes occur simultaneously, wiping out the money that was created in the initial loan.

Today, most "money" consists of keystroked electronic entries on bank balance sheets. It is created when banks make loans.

Because we live in an economy with many banks, payments often involve at least two banks. Banks clear accounts by debiting claims against one another (if Bank of America has a $100 check drawn on Citibank and Citibank has a $100 check drawn on Bank of America, they can "clear" by cancelling both checks). However, net clearing among banks is usually done on the central bank's balance sheet. Let us see how this works.

In the following diagram, Bank 1 lends to the firm to start the production process. The bank accepts the firm's IOU and credits the firm's deposit account. The firm writes a check to the household to pay wages. The household deposits the check at its bank, Bank 2.

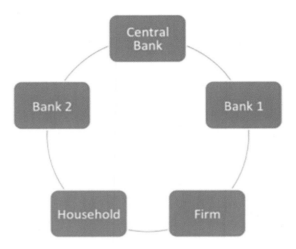

Bank 2 sends the check on to the central bank, which debits Bank 1's reserves and credits Bank 2's reserves. When the household buys output from the firm, it writes a check on its account at Bank 2. The firm deposits the check into its account at Bank 1. Bank 1 sends the check to the central bank, which debits Bank 2's account and credits Bank 1's account. The firm can now use its deposit credit to repay its loan to Bank 1. The deposit created in step one is "destroyed"—wiped clean from the balance sheets—and the firm's loan is simultaneously debited.

This is called a monetary circuit and is based on Schumpeter's view. The initial loan starts the production process, and the bank money created circulates output. The money is "destroyed" at the end of the circuit when the loan is repaid. Note that the bank cannot "run out of money" since it is simply created as a deposit liability as the bank makes a loan. Banks clear with each other using central bank "money" (called reserves). The central bank cannot run out of reserves either because these are simply central bank deposit liabilities—created to allow banks to clear accounts. They are created today by a "keystroke" either when the central bank lends or buys an asset.

Like any banker, the Fed or the Bank of England "keystrokes" money into existence. Central bank money takes the form of reserves or notes, created to make payments for customers (banks or the national treasury) or to make purchases for its own account (typically, buying treasury securities or mortgage-backed securities).

Bank and central bank money creation is limited by rules of thumb, underwriting standards, capital ratios, and other imposed constraints. After abandoning the gold standard, there are no physical limits to money creation. We cannot run out of keystroke entries on bank balance sheets.

This recognition is fundamental to issues surrounding finance. It is also scary for most people—who worry that central banks and private banks would go crazy creating money without limit, causing hyperinflation as in Zimbabwe and the Weimar Republic. However, this really is the way modern money is created in all modern economies—and hyperinflations are exceedingly rare occurrences. In other words, 99.999% of the time, banks and central banks do not create hyperinflations. In truth, our biggest problem has been with private banks financing too much speculation in asset markets, causing bubbles—and not with too much money causing inflation.

So there is some danger involved, but the good thing about Schumpeter's banker ephor is that sufficient finance can always be supplied to fully utilize all available resources to support the capital development of the economy. We can keystroke our way to full employment and rising living standards.

The bad thing about Schumpeter's ephor is that we can create more funding than we can reasonably use. Further, our ephors might make bad choices about which activities ought to get keystroked finance.

It is difficult to find real-world examples of excessive money creation to finance productive uses. Rather, the main problem is that much or even most finance has been created to fuel asset price bubbles. And that includes finance created both by our private banking ephors and in recent years by our central banking ephors.

The biggest challenge facing us today is *not* the lack of finance, but rather how to push finance to promote both the private and the public interest—through the capital development of our country.

It is also important to understand that from the beginning of their creation, central banks have always been involved in government finance. Today, all spending by the national treasury is handled by the national central bank. And all tax payments are received by the national central bank. In short, the Fed makes and receives all payments on behalf of the US Treasury.

And remember this: the Fed cannot run out of money. This has implications for government spending that will be important when we turn to our analysis of financing the progressive agenda.

b. Taxes drive the sovereign's currency

MMT has emphasized that there is a close relation between sovereign power to issue a currency and its power to impose tax liabilities. For shorthand, we say "Taxes Drive Money." Let us see why.

First let us describe what we mean by currency sovereignty. As you probably know, the US Constitution gives to Congress the sole power to issue a currency. Throughout history and around the world today, most countries issue their own currency. However, MMT distinguishes between countries that promise to convert their currencies on demand at fixed exchange rates to either precious metals or foreign currencies versus those that do not. The United States—like most developed nations—does not make such a promise, although there was a period in which the dollar was convertible to gold. Some countries today—such as Ecuador—promise to convert their currencies to US dollars. These are often said to have "dollarized". MMT argues that this can make a big difference and categorizes these "convertible" currencies as not fully sovereign. Nonconvertible currencies are sovereign currencies.

In what follows, when I say "sovereign currency", "sovereign currency issuer", or "sovereign government", I am implicitly speaking only of countries that issue their own "nonconvertible" currencies. We must add caveats for other countries as a convertible currency *can constrain* fiscal and monetary policy space.

So let us describe how the sovereign currency issuer creates money. The sovereign government chooses a money of account (dollar in the United States), imposes tax liabilities in the money of account, issues currency in the money of account, and accepts its own currency in tax payments. People will accept the currency because they need it to pay taxes. Logically, if they have to have currency to pay taxes, the government must issue the currency before taxes can be paid.

The upshot is that sovereign governments do not "need" tax revenue in order to spend. As Beardsley Ruml put it, once we abandoned gold, federal taxes became "obsolete" for revenue purposes. This does not mean that taxes are unnecessary for they are critical to creating a demand for the currency. But logically it follows that sovereigns spend first, then collect taxes.

Note that any obligation to pay currency will drive it: it could be fees, fines, tithes, or tribute. If the government imposes these obligations and enforces payment, any of them can "drive" demand for the currency. Further if the government monopolizes an essential commodity—say, the water supply—and will sell it only for its own currency, that can also drive demand for the currency. When you get thirsty enough, you will work for the government's currency to buy the precious water.

MMT argues that it has always been this way—all the way back to the earliest money that we know of, that created in Babylonia.

The fundamental question is this: does the issuer of a money-denominated liability need to obtain some of those liabilities before spending or lending them? I will examine three analogous questions (each of which has the same answer):

1. Does the government need to receive tax revenue before it can spend?
2. Does the central bank need to receive reserve deposits before it can lend?
3. Do private banks need to receive demand deposits before they can lend?

If you have already answered "Of course not!", you are probably up to speed on this topic. If you answered yes (to one or more) or if you do not have a clue, read on.

As we will see, these are reducible to the question: which comes first, Creation or Redemption?

1. The nature of money

What is money? Many think money is a thing—sea shells in the distant past, gold a 100 years ago, or base metal coins or paper today. Some say that we are moving to a "virtual reality" money—with bitcoin as a new innovation. But actually most money today already is "virtual" in the sense that it is an electronic credit to a balance sheet that is kept on a computer hard drive. And even all the way back to Babylonian times, most money took the form of a written record—chalk on a slate, cuniform writing on a clay tablet, hash marks cut across a wooden tally stick, or penned numbers on a passbook record of a savings account. (When I was a kid, we would take our "passbooks" to the bank and a teller would enter the amount of a deposit and write her initials to verify the updated balance. That was "money"—an initialized entry in my passbook.)

What is the nature of the institution that we call money? What do the things that many people call money have in common? Most economists identify money as something we use in exchange. That might move our understanding forward a bit, but it simply tells us "money is what money does".

In the *Treatise*, Keynes[2] began with the money of account, the unit in which we denominate debts and credits, and, yes, prices. He also says something about the nature of the money of account: he argues that for the past 4000 years, at least, the money of account has been chosen by the state authorities.[3] Units of measurement are necessarily social constructions. I can choose my own idiosyncratic measuring units for time, space, and value, but they must be socially sanctioned to become widely adopted. "Money" is a much more difficult concept than "inch" or "meter". Units to measure length, width, volume, weight are relatively simple and have probably existed for tens of thousands of years.

Money, of course, measures something much more abstract—nominal value—to compare a wide variety of things that share no obvious characteristics. While we will never know for sure, substantial evidence indicates that the creation of money as a measuring unit originated in Babylonian temples for accounting purposes. Only later was this accounting unit applied to measure prices, including obligations to be paid to the authorities (taxes, fees, fines, tribute, tithes), wages to be paid to workers, and prices to be paid in markets.

So, one commonality is that all monies are measured in a money of account. All those things economists declare to be money are denominated in the money of account. What is the nature of those money things? The most obvious shared characteristic of some of them is that they are evidence of debt: coins and treasury or central bank notes are government debts; bank notes or deposits are bank debts;

---

[2] Keynes's *Treatise on Money* was published in 1930. It consisted of two volumes examining money in excruciating detail. Six years later he published *The General Theory*, his most famous book that created the discipline that we call macroeconomics. To understand his approach to money, however, it is better to look at the earlier book.

[3] He explicitly follows G.F. Knapp's *State Theory of Money* in the Treatise, but he was also influenced by his earlier reading of A.M. Innes's work. See Wray (1998).

and we can expand our definition of money things to include shares of money market mutual funds, and so on, which are also debts of their issuers.

If we go back through time, we find wooden tally sticks issued by European monarchs and others as evidence of debt (notches recorded money amounts). We find early American Colonial paper notes denominated in, for example, Virginia pounds. And we find "virtual" electronic entries on bank balance sheets. Clearly it does not matter what material substance is used to record the debt—the tally sticks or paper notes are just tokens, records of the relation between creditor and debtor.

We can call these "monies" (coins, notes, tally sticks, electronic entries) money records. While the technology changes, each of these is a record of a money-denominated debt. Each issuer promises to accept back his/her own money-denominated debt in payment. This has been called "redemption"—a term that likely derives from religious obligations.

The monarch or modern democratic government promises to redeem the tally IOU or paper note IOU, following prescriptions that govern redemption. Let us see what that means.

2. Modern money

What we have, then, is a socially created and generally accepted money of account, with debts that are denominated in that money of account. Within a modern nation, socially sanctioned debts are typically denominated in the nation's money of account. In the United States it is the dollar. Some kinds of money-denominated debts "circulate", used in exchange and other payments (i.e., paying down one's own debts).The best examples are currency (debt of treasury and central bank) and demand deposits (debt of banks). Why do we accept these in payment?

It has long been believed that we accept currency because it is either made of precious metal or redeemable for the same—we accept it for its "thing-ness" either because we can exchange the coin or paper money for precious metal or melt it down to extract the precious metal it is made of. In truth, coined precious metal almost always circulated well beyond the value of embodied metal (at least domestically); and redeemability of currency for gold at a fixed rate has been the exception not the rule throughout history. Hence, most economists recognize that currency is today (and most often was in the past) "fiat"—with little to no intrinsic value and not redeemable for precious metal.

Further, and importantly, law going back to Roman times has typically adopted a "nominalist" perspective: the legal value of coins was determined by nominal value. For example, if one deposited coins with a bank one could expect only to receive on withdrawal currency of the same nominal value. In other words, even if the currency consisted of stamped gold coins, they were still "fiat" in the sense that their legal value would be set nominally—with nominal value of the coins determined by the rulers rather than by the embodied gold. (Old coins did not have a nominal value stamped on them—unlike today's coins—making it easy to "cry down" the value of coins. All it took was an announcement—by the town crier, publicly "crying" down the coin—that a coin's value was being reduced from a shilling to half a shilling. This was an effective way of raising taxes as taxpayers would have to deliver twice as many coins.) Ultimately, the value of the sovereign's money (coins, notes, or sticks) would be determined at the public pay office (where obligations to the authorities would be paid)—a coin's worth is equal to the amount of taxes it pays.

The argument of MMT is that currency will be accepted if there is an enforceable obligation to make payments to its issuer in that same currency. Hence, MMT has adopted the phrase "taxes drive money" in the sense that the state can impose tax liabilities and issue the means of paying those liabilities in the form of its own liabilities.

There is an institution, or a set of institutions, that we can identify as "sovereignty". As Keynes said, the sovereign has the power to declare what will be the unit of account—the Dollar, the Lira, the Pound, the Yen. The sovereign also has the power to impose fees, fines, and taxes, and to name what it will accept in payment. When the fees, fines, and taxes are paid, the currency is "redeemed"—accepted by the sovereign.

While sovereigns also sometimes agree to "redeem" their currency for precious metal or for foreign currency, that is not necessary. (And, as argued above, a promise to redeem a currency for foreign currency or gold reduces sovereign power by potentially constraining monetary and fiscal policy space.) The agreement to "redeem" currency in payment of taxes, fees, tithes, and fines is sufficient to "drive" the currency—that is, to create a demand for it.

When pondering why anyone would accept a fiat one dollar paper note, many people will conclude "I accept it because I believe someone else will accept it." I call this the greater fool theory of money: I know the paper money has no intrinsic value and I know I cannot redeem it for gold, but I think there are other people who will accept it. The value of money relies on an infinite regress: Billy Bob takes it because he thinks Buffy Sue will take it.

But in the case of currency, we do not need an infinite regress argument. While it could be true that I am willing to accept the state's IOUs if I know I can dupe some dope, I will definitely accept it if I have a tax liability and know I must pay that liability with the state's currency. This is the sense in which MMT claims "taxes are sufficient to create a demand for the currency". It is not necessary for everyone to have such an obligation—so long as the tax base is broad, the currency will be widely accepted.

There are other reasons to accept a currency—maybe I can exchange it for gold or foreign currency, maybe I can spend it at the store, maybe I can hold it as a store of value. These supplement taxes—or, better, derive from the obligations that need to be settled using currency (such as taxes, fees, tithes, and fines).

3. The fundamental "law" of credit: redeemability

A century ago A. Mitchell Innes posed a fundamental "law" of credit: the issuer of an IOU must accept it back for payment. We can call this the principle of redeemability: the holder of an IOU can present it to the issuer for payment for any debt the holder owes to the IOU's issuer. Note that the holder need not be the person who originally received the IOU—it can be a third party. If that third party owes the issuer, the IOU can be returned to cancel the third party's debt; indeed, the clearing cancels both debts (the issuer's debt and the third party's debt).

If one reasonably expects that she will need to make payments to some entity, she will want to obtain the IOUs of that entity. This goes partway to explaining why the IOUs of nonsovereign issuers can be widely accepted: as Minsky said, part of the reason that bank demand deposits are accepted is because we—at least, a lot of us—have liabilities to the banks, payable in bank deposits.

We repay our loans from banks by writing checks against bank deposits. In modern banking systems that have a central bank to clear accounts among banks at par, one can deliver any bank's deposit IOU to cancel a debt with any other bank. Anyone with a loan from any bank can accept a check drawn on any other bank to "redeem" himself (make a payment on the loan).

Acceptability can be increased by promising to convert on demand one's IOUs to more widely accepted IOUs. The most widely accepted IOUs within a society are those issued by the sovereign (or, at least, by some sovereign—perhaps by a foreign sovereign of a more economically important nation[4]). In that case, the issuer must either hold or have easy access to the sovereign's IOUs to ensure conversion. Bank "demand" deposits can be converted "on demand" to the government's currency. The central bank stands ready to ensure banks can make this conversion on demand.

We can use the metaphor of a pyramid of liabilities to visualize how liabilities lower in the pyramid leverage those higher in the pyramid, and with the sovereign's liabilities at the apex. Monetary contracts for future delivery of "money" typically designate whose liabilities are acceptable, usually either commercial bank demand deposits or the sovereign's liabilities. As the government's backstop of chartered banks includes both the central bank (lender of last resort) and the treasury (deposit insurance), bank deposits are generally as acceptable as cash. Hence, the need to use sovereign liabilities for settlement has been reduced to clearing among banks, to foreign exchanges, and to illegal activities. For the most part, we use bank liabilities as our primary medium of exchange (to make payments). Liabilities of nonbank financial institutions are lower in the pyramid and may need to be converted to bank liabilities before payments can be made.

In any event, whatever final payment courts of law enforce can be used as final payment. From Roman times, courts have interpreted money contracts in nominal terms as requiring payment in "lawful money" which is always in the form of designated liabilities denominated in an identified money of account.

---

[4] In some countries, US dollar—denominated deposits might be in demand alongside deposits denominated in the nation's own currency.

4. Redemptionism or creationism?

We can ponder again the three analogous questions:

1. Does the government need to receive tax revenue before it can spend?
2. Does the central bank need to receive reserve deposits before it can lend?
3. Do private banks need to receive demand deposits before they can lend?

It should be clear now that the answer to each is "No!". Indeed, the logic must run from CREATION to REDEMPTION. One cannot redeem oneself from sin or debt unless that sin or debt has been created.[5]

The King issues his tally stick or his stamped coin in payment for your wagon or horse or labor. That puts him in the position of a "sinful" debtor. He redeems himself when he accepts back his own IOU in payment of your tax liability.

The central bank issues its reserve deposit as its debt—normally when it makes a loan to private banks, or when it purchases treasury debts in the open market. (These reserve deposits can always be exchanged on demand for central bank notes—which keeps the central bank indebted.) The central bank redeems itself when it accepts its notes and reserve deposits in payment.

The private bank issues its demand deposit as its debt—normally when it makes a loan to a private firm or household. The bank redeems itself when it accepts a check written on its demand deposit in payment.

Note that we have looked at two sides of one balance sheet (the "money issuer") in each of these cases, but there is another sinful debtor in every case:

> Before the sovereign can issue tallies or coins, he must put taxpayers in debt by imposing a tax obligation payable in his tally stick or coin. This creates a demand for his tally or coin.
> When the central bank lends reserves to a private bank, it puts that bank in debt, crediting its account at the central bank with reserves, but the bank simultaneously issues a liability to the central bank.
> When the private bank lends demand deposits to the borrower, it credits the deposit account but the borrower becomes a debtor to the bank.

So each "redemption" simultaneously wipes out the sinful debt of both parties. The slate is wiped clean. Hallelujah!

You see, folks, it is all debits and credits. Keystrokes. That record bonds of indebtedness, with both parties united in the awful sinfulness. Until Redemption Day, when the IOUs find their ways back to the issuers.

- Those who think a sovereign must first get tax revenue before spending;
- Those who believe a central bank must first obtain reserves before lending them;

---

[5] See Margaret Atwood's great book (*Payback: Debt and the Shadow Side of Wealth*, House of Anansi Press, 2008) that makes the connection among sin, debt, and redemption. It is not a coincidence that many of our words having to do with debt and repayment are related to words that also have religious connotations.

- And those who believe a private bank must first obtain deposits before lending them;

Have all confused redemption with creation.

Receipt of taxes, receipt of reserve deposits, and receipt of demand deposits are all Acts of Redemption.

Creation must precede Redemption. Debts must exist before they can be redeemed.

c. Taxes and the public purpose

We have established that "taxes drive money". What we mean is that the sovereign government chooses a money of account (dollar in the United States), imposes obligations in that unit (taxes, fees, fines, tithes, tolls, or tribute), and issues the currency that can be used to "redeem" oneself in payments to the government. Currency is like the "Get Out of Jail Free" card in the game of Monopoly—you pay your taxes, fees, or fines using currency.

Taxes create a demand for "that which is necessary to pay taxes" (and other obligations to the state), which allows the government to purchase resources to pursue the public purpose by spending the currency.

In addition to creating a demand for currency, the tax also frees resources from private use so that the government can employ them in public use.

To greatly simplify, money is a measuring unit, originally created by rulers to value the fees, fines, and taxes owed. By putting the subjects or citizens into debt, real resources could be moved to serve the public purpose. Taxes drive money. Viewed from this perspective, money was created to give government command over socially created resources. This is why money is linked to sovereign power— the power to command resources. That power is rarely absolute. It is contested, with other sovereigns and also with domestic creditors.

As discussed, we also know that money's earliest origins are closely linked to debts and recordkeeping, and that many of the words associated with money and debt have religious significance: debt, sin, repayment, redemption, "wiping the slate clean," and Year of Jubilee. Early records of credits and debits were more akin to modern electronic entries—etched in clay rather than on computer tapes—than to what is erroneously called "commodity money" such as stamped gold coins. And all known early money units had names derived from measures of the principal grain foodstuff—how many bushels of barley equivalent were owed, owned, and paid. All of this is more consistent with the view of money as a unit of account, a representation of social value, and an IOU rather than as a commodity used for exchange (as in the Robinson Crusoe/Friday seashell money story).

For most of humanity today the original sin/debt is to the tax collector because as they say, the only things in life you cannot escape are death and taxes. You can redeem your tax debts by delivering the sovereign's own IOUs in payment. Widespread debts to the sovereign ensure widespread acceptance of the sovereign's own IOUs. This means that many will work for the sovereign or work to produce what the sovereign wants to buy. Even those without tax debts will work for the sovereign's IOUs knowing that others need them.

This is now the most common way that the sovereign government moves resources to the public sector: in recent centuries through taxes, although as we go back in time, other liabilities such as fines, fees, tithes, and tribute were more important.

From this vantage point, taxes do not "pay for" government spending. Indeed, no taxes can be collected until the government has spent. Taxes create a demand for the government's spending and logically precede that spending. The purpose of the tax is to free up resources to pursue the public purpose. But our tax system is already doing a heckuva job creating unemployed resources. If Congress ever got hold of its senses, it would increase spending (or reduce taxes) to employ idle resources. At some point (probably later rather than sooner) we could come up against resource constraints. At that point, we might need to curtail spending and/or raise taxes. This is a topic we will pursue below. But until that point is reached, government can spend more without increasing taxes.

A broad-based tax makes sense if the goal is simply to move resources to the public sector—a head tax or income tax that hits everyone will reduce resource use, freeing resources for government purchase. However, we need to also look at issues of fairness and incentives.

For that reason, MMT prefers to tax "bads", not "goods" where possible. We should not tax low-income families—we want them to have as much net income as possible to finance their purchases of necessities. Nor should we tax consumption of necessities. We should not tax work—work is generally good because it provides society with useful output. Where possible, tax bads, not goods. But if we need to free up resources, tax the incomes or the consumption of those most able to bear the burden of reduction of living standards.

We can use taxes to discourage "sins" (smoking, drinking, gambling, and polluting)—in which case the purpose of the tax is to eliminate "sin" so the optimal sizing of the tax would eliminate sin and hence raise no revenue at all. Even as it raises no revenue, it reduces the "externalities" of sins like pollution and can free up resources formerly devoted to promoting sinful behavior like gambling in fancy casinos.

We can view excessive riches as a sort of "sin" that we want to tax away. Some have argued that high tax rates on high incomes in the early postwar period "worked" by discouraging corporations from paying high incomes to top executives. Exactly! That is how sin taxes are supposed to work. This helped to keep inequality in check. But you do not tax the rich to provide Uncle Sam with revenue—he does not need revenue as he cannot run out of his own money to spend.

I am always surprised when my progressive friends see the "Tobin tax" (financial transactions tax) as a potentially great source of tax revenue to "pay for" all the goodies they would like the government to provide.

No, the purpose of a Tobin tax is to reduce financial turnover and it would have achieved complete success in eliminating the sin of high-speed turnover even as it raised no revenue at all. Ditto the cigarette tax. Ditto the carbon tax. Ditto the wealth tax. Sin taxes should reduce or even eliminate sin, and the more successful they are, the less revenue they raise.

Another aim of taxes is to allocate the costs of specific public programs to the beneficiaries. For example, it is common to tax gasoline so that those who use the nation's highways will pay for their use (tolls on throughways are another way to do this). Note that while many would see these taxes as a means to "pay for" government spending, the real purpose of such a tax is to make those who will use highways think twice about their support for building them. Alternatively, tolls can be used to impose costs directly on drivers. Again, this rations use as those unwilling to pay either find alternative routes or rideshare. For a national government, tolls should not be seen as a revenue source but rather as a way to allocate resources to those willing to pay—if people do not want to pay the tolls, do not devote resources to building new toll roads. (State and local governments are in a different situation, of course. They really do need the revenue as they are not the currency issuer.)

Likewise, the government does not need the revenue from a cigarette tax, but rather wants to raise the cost to those who will commit the "sin" of smoking. Many would say that it is only fair that those who smoke will "pay for" the costs their smoking imposes on society (in terms of hospitalizations for lung cancer, for example). This is not far from the truth—the hope is that the high cost of tobacco will convince more people never to smoke, which thereby reduces the cost to society. The point is to reduce the "waste" of real resources that must be devoted to caring for those who smoke (and those who suffer the effects of secondhand smoke).

In sum, the MMT alternative view is that taxes may serve several purposes, but "raising money" is not one of them. The national government does not need tax revenue to finance spending.

d. The sectoral balance approach

Credit and debt are two sides of the same coin. Both creditor and debtor are sinful. They balance. Exactly. The balance is ensured by double-entry bookkeeping. Redemption frees both creditor and debtor. It results in a different balance—one without sin. Bankruptcy also results in balance, but one that maintains the power of creditor over debtor—at least within the limits of law. But the point is, debts and credits are always in balance.

Within the private sector for every private creditor there is a private debtor. We call these "inside debts" because they are "inside" the private sector that includes both households and firms. Generally households taken as a whole are net creditors, although there are obviously many households that are net debtors. The business sector as a whole can be either a net creditor or debtor. But when we add up all private sector units, the debts net to zero. There is balance.

When we include a government sector, its IOUs are balanced by credits held by the nongovernment sector. The nongovernment sector includes the private sector plus the "external" sector—which is the rest of the world. (The external sector includes foreign governments, households, and firms.) The nongovernment sector's net credits are claims on government.

Those balances had to do with debts and credits or financial wealth. These are stocks that can be measured at a point in time. There also is a balance between flows over time—spending and income over the course of a year, for example. If I spend more than my income this year, I am running a deficit—let us say it amounts to $1000 for the year. This means I must have issued debt equal to $1000. Every year that I run another deficit, it adds to my debt. If next year I ran a surplus (spent less than my income—what is normally called saving)—say, equal to $600—then it would reduce my debt by that amount so that it would fall by $600 to just $400. Surpluses reduce debt (or increase net assets).

At the aggregate level, just as credits (assets) and debts (liabilities) must balance so too must deficits and surpluses. If the government sector runs a surplus (tax revenue is greater than spending), then the nongovernment sector must have run a deficit (income less than spending). If government runs a deficit, then the nongovernment sector has a surplus. It balances.

Let me repeat that. The government's deficit means a nongovernment surplus. It balances. There is always financial balance. Imbalance can arise only due to arithmetic errors.

Take a look at the US case. The following graph displays the three sectoral balances[6]: government (includes federal, state, and local government), domestic private (US households and firms), and capital account (this is the external balance and is positive if the rest of the world taken as a whole spends less than its income).[7] If a sector is running a surplus, it is above zero; if it runs a deficit, it is below zero.

Let us take a look at US Sectoral Balances for the government sector (all levels of government), the domestic private sector (households and firms), and the foreign sector (rest of the world combined).[8]

---

[6] Note that the economy as a whole can be divided among sectors in various ways, for example into two sectors, three sectors, four or more sectors: government and nongovernment; government, domestic private, and rest of world; federal government, state plus local government, domestic household, domestic business, and rest of world. Which divisions we choose depends on the questions we are asking—in other words, we use the division that is useful. Here we will stick to three sectors.

[7] This may be a bit difficult to understand. What is plotted is the US capital account (normally in surplus) which is the same as the US current account (normally in deficit) but with the sign reversed (which is why it is above zero). The implication is that the United States buys more from the rest of the world than the rest of the world buys from the United States. A big component of the current account is trade in goods and services—and it is no secret that the United States runs a trade deficit. From the point of view of the rest of the world, it has a trade surplus—so it is not surprising that its overall balance is in positive territory in the graph.

[8] I thank Scott T. Fullwiler for the elaboration of this graph.

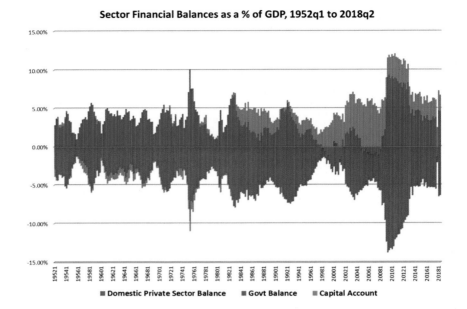

What do you see? Balance. A mirror image. In normal times, the private sector surplus (blue) plus the current account deficit (green) equals the government deficit (red). In the abnormal times of private sector deficits (in the mid- to late 1990s), we still saw balance—the government even ran budget surpluses for a few years to maintain the balance.

You will also note that since the administration of Ronald Reagan, the United States has run a current account deficit (capital account surplus) mostly due to a trade deficit in goods. This means that our government budget must run a larger deficit in order for our private sector to run a surplus: the private sector surplus equals the budget deficit minus the current account deficit. Given the current account deficit it is literally impossible for the private sector to avoid a deficit unless the government runs a (relatively large) deficit.[9]

Take a look at Euroland; what do you see?

---

[9] I thank Eric Tymoigne for the elaboration of this graph.

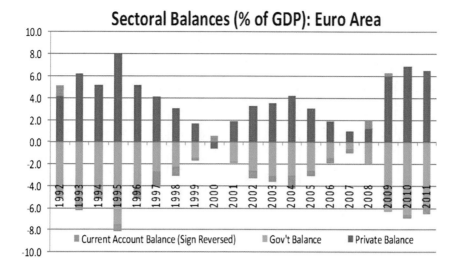

Sectoral Balances (% of GDP): Euro Area

Balance. Is it not amazing? Whenever the private sector surplus rises (red), the budget deficit rises (green)—that is, goes more negative; the correlation is near 100%, with the current account acting as the balancing item.

Financial balances balance.

If you take the world as a whole, there is no external sector since we do not trade with Martians (yet). And so the sum of the global government deficits equals the sum of the global private sector surpluses. It balances.

Keep that in mind later when we discuss government finance. The government's deficit is our surplus. The government's debt is our net financial wealth. If you are against government deficits, you are necessarily opposed to private sector surpluses and financial wealth.

III. Financing government: money and the public interest

In the previous section, we (mostly) looked at private money—money created by private financial institutions. However, as we discussed, even that money is closely related to government because the government chooses the money of account and also backs up in various ways the private institutions. Further, as we discovered in the last section, it all must balance at the aggregate level. In this section we provide a more detailed analysis of what we might call government money—financing government spending.

a. What is the right size for government?

How big should government be? Obviously, it depends on the size of the economy so we usually scale the government's budget, its deficit, and its debt by stating it as a ratio of GDP. In this section and the next we will tackle the question: how big should these ratios be? Even if we focus only on rich developed nations, we find a very large range of ratios: government spending-to-GDP ratios run from about a quarter up to about a half. Government debt ratios run from low double digits to more than 200%. Government deficit ratios swing widely for individual nations and vary considerably among countries—say from near balance (and even occasionally some surpluses) to deficit ratios above 10% of GDP. So, what are the *correct* ratios—or, perhaps better, what ratios should countries strive for?

Let us see what the US federal government actually spends.[10] In 2010 the total was $3.5 trillion, which was 24% of GDP that reached $14.66 trillion. Obviously, government spending grows over time, more or less on pace with GDP. At about a quarter of GDP, US federal government spending is on the low end of the ranking—in spite of the belief of many Americans that ours is an unusually Big Government.

Let us take 24% of GDP as a rough approximation of the size of our "Big Government". Note I am not including state and local governments—these are users, not issuers of the currency. Their spending is "paid for" by taxes, fees, fines, and some funding from Washington. I can see arguments either way for including them in our measure of the size of "Big Government" but I think that from the MMT perspective it makes more sense to leave them to the side because we want to focus on the currency issuer.

I have added in parentheses the components of spending as a percent of GDP for the biggest items in the federal budget: Defense (5%), Education and related spending (1%), Health (2.5%), Medicare (3%), Income Security (4%), and Social Security (5%). Together, these approach nearly 21% of GDP. Nothing else really matters much individually. Note there are well-known problems with the defense number—the reported figure significantly understates actual spending because a lot of "defense" activities are secret; some of the spending is hidden in other categories. Some is probably not reported anywhere.

For our conservative and Austrian Austerians,[11] a government that is almost 25% of our economy is far too big. For our progressive friends it is far too small. Maybe our centrists believe it is like Goldilocks—just about right. Let us focus on the big things to see what our government does.

At least a fifth of all government spending goes to "defense"—and the actual figure is probably double that (say, 10% of GDP). Judging from libertarian support for Ron Paul and from the traditional progressive opposition to US imperialism

---

[10] I am using 2010 data, from the 2012 Economic Report of the President.
[11] By Austrian I am referring to the "free market" libertarian school of economics; by Austerian I mean those who promote the notion of a balanced budget as "sound finance".

abroad, I suspect we can agree that "defense" spending is far too big—at least for libertarians and progressives. Personally, I have opposed all US invasions of other nations with the exception of our participation in WWII. I would bring all troops home, close all foreign bases, and prohibit further military adventures abroad. As our Republican friends say, "starve the beast" by cutting all military spending down to what is necessary to maintain a purely defensive force within our borders. The only foreign intervention I would support would be to airdrop food and medical supplies wherever they are needed.

I know I will not get my way. I would not call this a Big Government or Small Government preference—it is antiwar. But let us presume we scale back "defense" spending to a scale that makes it hard to mount sustained invasions abroad—to, say, 2% of GDP. We have thereby reduced the reported size of government by 3% of GDP (and perhaps actual size by 8% of GDP—but we will ignore that in calculations below). So, let us say we get a 3% reduction of Big Government bringing total spending down to 21%.

MMTers want a universal Job Guarantee program at a living wage. Various calculations have put that at about 1% of GDP, with net cost close to zero (due to savings on antipoverty programs, unemployment compensation, and so on).[12] Let us say that it is too optimistic and the true cost turns out to be 2% of GDP. That offsets some of the reduction of defense spending, getting us up to 22% of GDP.

Now it is unreasonable to presume there is absolutely no reduction of "welfare" spending—in the form of "income security" that is currently 4% of GDP. We will offer a job to all who want to work, creating somewhere between 10 million and 20 million new jobs at a living wage (note that not all of the new jobs will be in the JG program—that depends on "multiplier" job creation in the private sector, but those jobs will also pay living wages or otherwise workers cannot be recruited out of the JG). Unemployment compensation, food stamps, and even some "tax expenditures" on the earned income tax credit will all decline.

Stephanie Kelton and I have replicated earlier work done by Hyman Minsky showing that a JG program will eliminate most poverty (defined as those below the official poverty line) just by providing one minimum wage job per household (Bell and Wray, 2004). At a higher wage, and by offering more than one job to households that want more work, the JG would raise most families well above the poverty line. Let us say that income security spending falls by a couple of percentage points (2% reduction—from the current 4%−2%). That gets us down to 20%.

Note also there will be a bit of saving in the "education, training, employment, and social services" category that currently prepares workers for jobs that do not

---

[12] Scholars at the Levy Economics Institute have estimated that a universal Job Guarantee paying $15 per hour with benefits would run a bit over 1% of GDP after full phase-in. While some cost savings are included, many are not. So if we could take account of all possible reductions of other types of government spending that would result from full implementation, the JG's net spending would probably be substantially less than a percent of GDP.

exist. But let us keep the 1% devoted to that spending but instead prepare workers for jobs that will exist. So I will not count any reduction here.

So we remain at 20% of GDP. Now let us replace our failing US healthcare system with a universal and free, federally paid-for program that offers the range of services that are provided in the average rich nation. That will run about 9%−10% of GDP if the experience of other rich nations (all of which have universal healthcare systems) is any guide. By contrast, in the United States we are nearing 20% of GDP—as discussed earlier. Moving from the current 5.5% (health + Medicare) to 10% adds 4.5% of GDP to the government's budget. Of course, households, firms, and state and local governments would get a tremendous windfall if we shift all costs to the federal government. So we can cut total spending by 9 or 10% of GDP if we ramped up federal spending by 4.5% of GDP.

Let us leave the savings to the nongovernment sector spending to the side and focus on the government's portion: we go from 5.5% of GDP to, say, 10% of GDP for an increase of federal spending equal to 4.5% of GDP bringing it up to 24.5% of GDP.

The remaining big category is Social Security—about three-quarters of which goes to retirees. That is the main income support for the majority of our seniors. Progressives believe benefits are too small—especially for retirees who had low earnings, and also for many who receive payments for disabilities as well as for dependents and spouses of workers who die. Let us ramp that up by 2% of GDP. Our Big Government is now 26.5% of GDP.

But we are not done yet. Let us look to our progressive wish list for more. Public infrastructure is deficient—a point made by President Obama, and by our society of engineers that finds a deficit in our public infrastructure amounting to trillions of dollars. Yes, we need bullet trains, cleaner water, better airports, bridges, and highways, and more dependable sewage treatment. And we need to join the developed world in getting our darned electrical wires safely underground so that power is not knocked out in every ice storm.

How much? Let us look to the estimates provided by the American Society of Civil Engineers, which puts out an Infrastructure Report Card every 4 years. In 2017 it gave our nation's infrastructure a grade of a D+ overall. According to the report, "To close the $2.0 trillion 10-year investment gap, meet future need, and restore our global competitive advantage, we must increase investment from all levels of government and the private sector from 2.5% to 3.5% of U.S. Gross Domestic Product (GDP) by 2025." (ASCE Report Card, 2016). They presume the spending would come from all levels of government plus the private sector. But our state and local governments are not sovereign currency issuers, and they are worse than broke. Only the federal government can afford this boost. Further, their estimate is what I would consider a bare minimum—we need to go beyond this not only to "catch up" to our competitors but to deal with the challenge of climate change. We not only need to update but to completely transform our infrastructure. And we cannot rely on the private sector to do that—the federal government must take the lead (see discussion below of the Green New Deal [GND]). So let us put the full 1% of GDP boost into the Federal Budget.

So we add another percentage point to our Big Government's spending.

Our Big Government is now 27.5% of GDP. We have got true full employment at a living wage. We have got universal and free healthcare. We have got a more generous retirement system and better care for survivors and those with disabilities. We have got bullet trains and bridges that do not fall into rivers. And we are reducing our foreign entanglements.

All for 3.5% of GDP additional spending.

And note that we have mostly avoided "dynamic budgeting"—we have not counted many potential savings in terms of reduced incarceration for the young jobless males who turn to a life of crime. We have not counted many health benefits that result from access to care, lower poverty rates, and enhanced dignity that comes from working. We did not count multiplier effects on private sector spending—that would reduce government spending in some other areas. And so on.

All of us, progressives and Austrians alike, know we can "afford it" because a sovereign government cannot run out of its own currency. Three point five percent.

I do not know if that will comfort our Austerians, who think 24% is already far too big. Nor do I know if it will comfort our Progressives, many of whom are scared by MMT.

To be sure, I can add some more items to the list above: more federal funding for education, federal support for sustainable agriculture (but less support for corporate farming—so that probably balances), more foreign aid, money to tackle climate change. And good wine flowing from every water fountain in America.

All that might add another two or three more percent—and get us to a 30% government. Will that horrify our Austrians, and still dissatisfy our Progressives?

Probably. Both.

What should the government do?

I think reasonable people can disagree when it comes to what the government ought to do. I think it is worth discussing. Lay it out on the table. Forget the silly arguments about deficits and hyperinflations and taxation by dictatorships and bankrupting our grandkids. And about arbitrary government-to-GDP ratios. We do not need to argue about whose is bigger. What matters is what you do with the government.

What should the government do? It is a mostly political question. A 24% government (US) can do most of what most people seem to want the government to do. And more than what others want. And so can a 50% government (France). The jury is still out on a 15% government (Mexico)—but it would be hard to point to Mexico as either a case of a successful government doing what people want it to do or as an Austrian Austerian utopian Small Government.

What do *you* want the government to do?

b. The right size versus the right side of deficit and debt ratio: the Wray curve

In recent months the international policy-making elite has tried to distance itself from MMT, often going to hysterical extremes to dismiss the approach as crazy. No one does this better than the Japanese.

As MMT gathered momentum in 2019, its developers began to receive a flood of calls from reporters around the world enquiring whether Japan serves as the premier example of a country that follows MMT policy recommendations.

My answer is always the same: **No**. Japan is the perfect case demonstrating that all of mainstream theory and policy is wrong. And it is the best example of a country that always chooses the anti-MMT policy response to every ill that ails the country. Reporters find that shocking.

Biggest government fiscal deficits in the developed country world over the past 2 decades? Check. Highest government debt ratios in the developed country world? Check. Is that not what MMT advises? **No**.

Nay, it is the perfect demonstration that all the mainstream bogeymen are false: big deficits cause inflation? No. Japan's inflation runs just above zero. Big debts cause high interest rates? No. Japan's policy rate is about −0.10 (negative rates). Big debts cause bond vigilante strikes? No. Japan's government debt is hoovered up as fast as it can be issued. (All the more true with the Bank of Japan [BOJ] running QE and creating a "scarcity" in spite of the quadrillions of yen bond debt available.)

Critics of MMT counter that Japan is "proof" that big deficits kill investment and growth. Well, it is true that Japan has been growing at just 1% per year—certainly nothing to write home about. However, investment grows at about a 2% pace, but is pulled down by lack of consumption growth—which has averaged just about zero over the past few years. Yet, unemployment clocks in at only 3%—in spite of slow growth—as the labor force shrinks due to an aging population. Per capita GDP has been stuck at about $38,000 for years (not so bad, but not growing). And Japan's current account surplus has surged from under 1% to 4% of GDP over the past few years (considered to be good by most commentators). Unfortunately Trump's trade war seems to have already hurt Japan's exports and the prognosis for growth over the near future is rather dismal. The April 2019 survey of consumer confidence showed it collapsing to the lowest level in 3 years (Focus Economics, 2019).

From the MMT perspective, what Japan needs is a good fiscal stimulus, albeit one that is targeted. Japan has three "injections" into the economy: the fiscal deficit (which has fallen from 7% of GDP to about 5% over the past few years—still a substantial injection), the current account surplus (falling but still large), and private investment. But what it needs is stronger growth of domestic consumer demand—which would also stimulate investment directed to home consumption. Household saving is a drag on the economy—a leakage that reduces growth and discourages investment.

MMT says the obvious solution is to ramp up fiscal policy and target it to spending that would increase economic security of Japanese households to the point that they would increase consumer spending. In spite of low measured unemployment a Job Guarantee would still help—especially for middle-aged workers who have been forced into early retirement because of downsizing. And a more generous government-funded pension for the rapidly aging population. This would encourage younger workers to spend more, rather than saving in fear that they will not have sufficient income in their golden years. What is necessary is to restore confidence to boost spending. And, finally, Japan needs a GND—while Japan commendably became more energy efficient after the OPEC oil price shocks of the 1970s, she, like all other nations, still must do much more. That will require more government spending.

So what is Prime Minister Abe's announced plan? To raise the sales tax to squelch consumption and reduce economic growth on the argument that he will get the budget deficit under control.

You cannot make this up.

This has been Japan's policy for a whole generation. Any time it looks like the economy might break out of its long-term stagnation, policy-makers impose austerity in an attempt to reduce the fiscal deficit—and thereby throw the economy back into its permanent recession. Clearly, this is the precise opposite of the MMT recommendation.

And yet pundits proclaim Japan has been following MMT policy all these years. Why? Because Japan has run big fiscal deficits. As if MMT's policy goal is big government deficits and debt ratios.

No.

We see the budget as a tool used to pursue the public interest—things like full employment and inclusive and sustainable growth. To be sure, by many reasonable measures Japan does OK in spite of policy mistakes. Certainly in comparison to the United States, Japan looks pretty good: good and accessible healthcare, low infant mortality, long lifespans, low measured unemployment, and much less inequality and poverty. But Japan could do better if it actually did adopt the MMT view that the budgetary outcome by itself is not an important issue.

Instead Japanese officials are falling all over themselves to make it clear that they will never adopt MMT. Finance Minister Taro Aso called MMT "an extreme idea and dangerous as it would weaken fiscal discipline" (Reuters, 2019). Japan's "fiscal discipline" would be threatened by MMT? The debt ratio is already approaching 250%! By conventional measures, Japan has the worst fiscal discipline the world has ever seen!

But, wait, it gets even funnier. "BOJ policy board member Yutaka Harada kept up the attack on MMT. The approach proposed by MMT will 'cause [runaway] inflation for sure'(Nikkei Asian Review, 2019)." The BOJ has done everything it could think of for the past quarter century to get the inflation rate up to 2%. Quadrillions of QE. Negative interest rates. And Japan still has deflation (prices falling, not rising). But the BOJ thinks MMT could produce runaway inflation? How? I doubt that even Weimar's Reichsbank could cause high inflation in Japan.

What they do not understand is that there are two ways to produce a high deficit (and debt) ratio: the ugly way and the good way. MMT has been arguing this for a long time, but with little progress in promoting understanding. Perhaps the following will help.

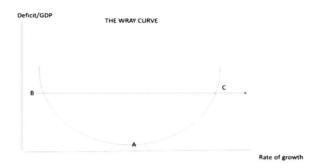

It plots the deficit ratio against the rate of growth. Yes, I gave it a name. There is the Laffer Curve, the Phillips Curve, and now the Wray Curve. I did not draw it on a cocktail napkin at a bar (like Laffer), but, rather, jotted it down on a notepad before bed.

Assume the economy is at Point A—for Japan this would represent a 5% deficit ratio and a 1% rate of growth. Now Prime Minister Abe imposes a consumption tax, or the United States plummets into a downturn (reducing its demand for Japanese exports), reducing Japan's growth rate. The economy moves up and to the left toward Point B as growth slows and the deficit ratio rises.

Slower growth reduces tax revenue even as it scares households and firms, which reduce spending in an effort to build up savings. The slower growth also reduces imports so the current account "improves" somewhat. From the sectoral balance perspective, the government's balance moves further into deficit (to, say, a 7% fiscal deficit), the current account surplus rises (say from 4% to 5%) and the private sector's surplus grows to 12% (the sum of the other two balances) as households and firms increase saving.

That is the ugly way to increase a fiscal deficit. It is the Japanese way. It is like perpetual bleeding of the patient in the hope that further blood loss will cure her ills.

What is the MMT alternative? Measured and targeted stimulus designed to restore confidence of firms and households. Ramp up the social security safety net to assure the Japanese people that they will be taken care of in their old age. Recreate a commitment to secure jobs and decent pay. Either promote births or encourage immigration to replace the declining workforce. Undertake a Green New Deal (GND) to transition to a carbon-free future.[13]

In that case, we move along the curve from Point A toward Point C. The fiscal deficit increases in the "good" way, while growth improves. So we end up with the same fiscal deficit but higher growth.

Note, however, that the boost to the deficit will only be temporary. Households and firms will begin to spend and their surplus will fall. The current account surplus will fall, too, as imports rise to partially satisfy consumer demand. Tax revenues will increase—not because tax rates rise but because income increases. The fiscal deficit will fall as the domestic private surpluses decline. Precisely how much the deficit will fall depends on the movement of the private surplus and current account surplus—with the deficit falling to equality with their sum.

In terms of the graph above, the Wray Curve shifts out to the right as the economy expands. A new point A will be consistent with a higher rate of growth for a given deficit ratio. (We end up to the right of point A but below point C in the graph above.) There is nothing "natural" about the deficit ratio at Point A—as it depends on the other two sectoral balances.

For the United States, Point A is consistent with a higher growth rate but probably a similar government deficit ratio to that of Japan. Our current account balance is of course negative—which implies a higher fiscal deficit. However, our private sector's surplus is smaller than Japan's for any given growth rate—which implies a lower fiscal deficit. The two essentially offset one another to leave the US deficit ratio at about 5%, like Japan's in the expansionary growth case, but with higher growth than Japan—above 2% compared to Japan's 1%.

Note that we are not proposing a sort of Reverse Laffer Curve. Recall that the Laffer Curve says that tax cuts more than "pay for themselves"—trickle-down growth boosts revenue sufficiently to close a fiscal deficit. I am not arguing that the stimulative increase of government spending will increase tax revenue so much that the deficit ratio returns to its original level (or less). Where it actually ends up depends on movements of the two other sectoral balances.

Not that the size of the deficit—by itself—is important. What is important is whether government budget policy helps in the pursuit of the public and private interests. The government deficit will always adjust to be "just the right size" to balance the other two sectoral balances. But that equality can be consistent with any growth rate—including a rate that is too low (deflationary) or too high (inflationary). Also recall that the sectoral balance equality holds with any fiscal deficit ratio. So while it is likely that a successful stimulus will shift the Wray Curve out to the right,

---

[13] Note: I am presuming that Japan is unhappy with very low growth, and that the country faces many unmet domestic needs. I am not an advocate of "growth for growth's sake"—especially in light of the growing recognition that humanity may well have only a decade or so left on planet earth unless we very quickly change our ways. However, "changing our ways" will require major investments in a Japanese Green New Deal—so even with zero growth, there is a role for ramped up fiscal policy.

we cannot predict exactly where the new fiscal deficit ratio will settle as the growth rate rises.

What is most important about this graph is the recognition that there are (at least) two different growth rates consistent with a given deficit ratio. We can achieve a particular growth rate either in the "ugly" way or in the "good" way—while generating the same deficit ratio. Japan continually operates its economy to produce "ugly" deficits—precisely because it fears fiscal expansion. US deficits are generally a bit less ugly—they grow rapidly in a downturn and stimulate the economy toward recovery that then reduces the deficit. The problem in Japan is that the government always gives in to its fears about deficits—so it imposes a consumption tax as recovery begins, which slows the economy and boosts the deficit. The result is low growth and a high deficit.

c. External constraints

As mentioned above, MMT argues that fiscal and monetary policy space is generally increased when a currency issues its own currency with no promise to convert it to foreign currency or gold. However, many of MMT's critics have argued that smaller countries are better off pegging their exchange rates—to provide stability that helps them to issue debt and lower interest rates. This is claimed to increase policy space—the opposite conclusion of that reached by MMT. It is even argued that floating exchange rates will not enhance sovereignty because without a promise to redeem domestic currency for foreign currency at a fixed rate, even domestic firms and households will not accept the government's currency.

Further, a floating rate is said to create a balance of payments constraint: if the country tries to expand its domestic economy, this will increase the demand for imports, resulting in a trade deficit. That will put downward pressure on the exchange rate, which makes foreign goods more expensive. Unless that depresses demand for imports sufficiently, the likely result is more trade deficits and more currency depreciation—raising the domestic currency costs of imports. This fuels what is called "pass-through inflation", more currency depreciation and more inflation in a vicious cycle. Hence, it is supposed to be better to peg the exchange rate. That reduces the danger of inflation.

In this section we will examine these challenges. To Fix or To Float, that is the question.

MMT argues that a sovereign government that issues its own "nonconvertible" currency cannot become insolvent in its own currency. It cannot be forced into involuntary default on its obligations denominated in its own currency. It can afford to buy anything for sale that is priced in its own currency. It might be able to buy things for sale in foreign currency by offering up its own currency in exchange—but that is not certain. So long as it enforces a tax payable in its own currency, it ensures there is a demand for the domestic currency—there is no need to promise to convert it to foreign currency.

If instead, it promises to convert its currency at a fixed price to something else (gold, foreign currency) then it might not be able to keep that promise. Insolvency and involuntary default become possible. MMT argues that insolvency and default risks are usually more constraining and dangerous than "pass-through" inflation feared by supporters of fixed exchange rate regimes.

Generally speaking, the nonconvertible, floating exchange rate currency system provides more policy space. Government can use fiscal and monetary policy to pursue the domestic agenda. Fixing the currency reduces policy space because the government must consider its promise to convert. That can conflict with the domestic policy agenda. For example, it is usually the case that the government must pursue policy to ensure a positive flow of foreign currency (or gold) to be accumulated as a reserve to maintain the peg. That usually means domestic unemployment to keep wages and imports down while favoring exports (due to cheap labor).

So far, this is just logic. Pegging your currency adds a constraint: you need to obtain that-to-which-you-peg in order to ensure you can convert at the pegged price. How binding is the constraint? It depends. In the case of China today, its "managed" exchange rate is not very binding. For example, China has committed to fairly rapid growth of domestic wages, and it appears that anytime growth slows, government pumps up demand. By contrast, in the case of Nepal, the peg against the Indian currency is very constraining. If Nepal were to pursue China's policy of raising wages, her trade deficit with India would grow; unless she could somehow increase remittances from her workers abroad, reserves of Indian currency, as well as dollars, would be depleted. Her peg would be threatened and a currency crisis would be likely.

Now, would China or Nepal benefit from floating? I have no doubt that China will eventually be in a position where floating would not only be desired, but would become necessary. China will probably float long before it reaches such a position. China will become too wealthy, too developed, to avoid floating. She will stop net accumulating foreign currency reserves and will probably begin to run current account deficits at some point. She will gradually relax capital controls—which exposes her foreign currency reserves if holders of RMB-denominated assets exchange them for foreign currency—denominated assets. She might never go full-bore Western-style "free market" but she will find it to her advantage to float in order to preserve domestic policy space.

If she did not, she could look forward to a quasi-colonial status, subordinate to the reserve currency issuer (the US dollar today). China will not do that.

MMT emphasizes that in "real" terms, imports are a benefit and exports are a cost. Floating the currency and relaxing capital controls allows a nation to enjoy more "benefits" (imports) and fewer "costs" (exports). The nation can "afford" to enjoy all the output it can produce plus whatever output the rest of the world wants to sell to it. It "pays for" those net imports through expansion of its capital account surplus. On the capital account, this is reflected in rest of world accumulation of financial claims denominated in the importer's currency.

The balances balance.

While many say the United States has a "trade imbalance" because the current account is in deficit, there is no imbalance because the capital account is in surplus. Dollar for dollar. There cannot be an imbalance. Foreigners want the dollar assets, and so they sell their output to the United States. Perhaps it is their national interest to do so; perhaps it is not. This is not a matter for me to judge. It is certainly in someone's interest or they would not do it. Maybe the exporters run policy. Maybe the rich elite do. Or maybe it really is in the national interest.

That foreign demand for US dollars means that many countries operate their economies in a way that ensures they can net export to the United States to earn the dollars. Since balances do balance, their net export positions mean that the United States runs a current account deficit. While many think the United States must borrow dollars to "pay for" its trade deficit, it makes more sense to see the US trade deficit as the source of finance for the net exporter's accumulation of dollars. After all, the dollars came from the United States—foreigners cannot create dollar claims on the United States.

Many worry, however, that the world's demand for dollars will soon be exhausted. If the United States continues to supply unwanted dollars, its exchange rate could collapse, they say. But there is a well-developed and highly liquid market for all the currencies issued by the rich developed countries. To put this as succinctly as possible, if you offer US or Canadian or Australian Dollars, or UK Pounds, or Japanese Yen, or Euroland Euros, you will never find a lack of bidders. The only question is over the price. Heck, I have offered Mexican Pesos, and Colombian Pesos, and Malaysian Ringgit, and Turkish Lira, and South African Rand, and many other currencies many times and never found a lack of bidders at airport kiosks.

It is true that the currencies of the rich developed countries do fluctuate in value—perhaps in response to fluctuations of supply and demand, or perhaps in response to domestic fiscal and monetary policy changes. Who knows why. (Economists have not been able to develop any model that can explain exchange rate movements.) This can have some impact on the domestic economy—especially for nations like Australia that rely heavily on imported goods for which they do not have domestic substitutes. When Australia's dollar falls in value, suddenly those imports become very expensive—which can have negative impacts on domestic growth. But since Australia floats, its government can (and does) offset those impacts by using fiscal policy stimulus. If it instead pegged the currency, it *might* be able to prevent the currency depreciation, but it would surrender domestic policy space as its focus would have to be on accumulating foreign currency to protect the exchange rate.

Admittedly, this may not be true for all developing nations. Frankly, I do not know if Nepal would do better if it floated. I suspect that for many of the world's poorest countries, the exchange rate regime is not the central issue—and they are probably screwed whether they fix or they float.

Critics of MMT love to point to such cases as proof that MMT is somehow wrong. They challenge us to find a solution to the problems faced by poor countries.

If MMT cannot find a simple solution to the complex problems facing developing nations, then they claim that somehow MMT is wrong. It is the most bizarre claim.

All we claim is that with a sovereign, floating currency a government of a developing nation can "afford" to employ all its domestic resources that are willing to work for the domestic currency. Will such a nation be able to import all that it wants? Probably not. Would pegging the exchange rate allow it to import more? Maybe— but then it is very likely that it will have to give up full employment at home. And it will be subject to insolvency and default risk (because it has promised to deliver something it might not be able to deliver).

Is that a trade-off that is in the domestic interest? I doubt it, but I am not sure.

What I observe out in the real world is that pegged exchange rates in developing countries are usually in the interests of the elites—who like their luxury imports and vacations in NYC and Disneyworld. Typically somewhere around half the population is either unemployed or "casually" employed (washing windshields of the luxury imports driven by the nation's elite at stoplights). That seems like a bad trade-off to me.

The big bogeyman usually raised is the inflation pass-through discussed above. Yes, a floating currency opens the possibility of exchange rate depreciation that raises the costs of imports and "passes through" to domestic inflation. That inflation impact is usually vastly overstated (Forbes, 2015).

MMT argues that it is probably better to float the currency and then deal with the pass-through inflation, and it makes sense to force as much of the "pain" of fighting the inflation on the rich as possible. After all, they are the ones importing the BMWs and taking the kids to Disneyworld. Let them "pay for" the inflation pressures by reducing their living standards and importing fewer luxuries for them.

The MMT principles apply to all sovereign countries. Yes, they can have full employment at home. Yes, that could lead to trade deficits. Yes, that could (possibly) lead to currency depreciation. Yes that could lead to inflation pass-through. But they have lots of policy options available if they do not like those results. Import controls and capital controls are examples of policy options. Directed employment, directed investment, and targeted development are also policy options. If need be, they can tax the rich to reduce their incomes to the point that they cannot import luxury goods.

Many of the poorest nations must import food. This is a bigger problem to tackle but the best policy response is to use the available policy space to develop domestic food production.[14] I am not flippant about the many real constraints faced by a poor, developing nation. At an early stage of development, imports are very hard to get. The national currency faces little external demand. The world does not want the

---

[14] Fadhel Kaboub, associate professor of economics at Denison University and president of The Global Institute for Sustainable Prosperity, offers a very good overview of the MMT approach to developing countries, arguing that regaining financial sovereignty is a crucial next step for postcolonial nations hoping to achieve social, economic, and environmental justice.

nation's produce, so it cannot export. But borrowing foreign currency to buy food imports can easily lead to excessive debt service and financial collapse.

Neither floating nor fixing is going to easily resolve these problems. That MMT does not have an easy solution to them does not, in my view, prove that MMT is flawed. My suspicion is that floating the currency and taking advantage of the sovereign's ability to spend domestically is a step in the right direction. Capital controls are probably necessary—even more so if the country does not float. Foreign aid is probably necessary to finance needed imports.

Full employment of domestic resources is even more important for the developing nation than it is for the rich, developed nation. The developing nation cannot afford to leave resources unemployed. And yet what we find is precisely the reverse: unemployment is much higher in the developing world because the government thinks it cannot "afford" to offer jobs. Hence, MMT can offer useful advice even if it cannot offer a magic wand to wish away all the problems faced by developing nations.

IV. Secular stagnation

In this section we look at the problems of secular stagnation—a problem that has recently been highlighted even in the mainstream media. Some have even argued that it is the "new normal" as robots take away our jobs. Problems are compounded because we have supposedly run out of the big ideas that spur technological advance and growth. We use our understanding of the government's money to offer alternative assessments of the problems we face and of policy solutions.

a. Bow down to the bubble: Larry Summers and Paul Krugman embrace the secular stagnation thesis

Larry Summers has made a big splash by (finally) recognizing that the United States has had a series of financial bubbles (Summers, 2013). Duh! Who wudduv thought? The Reagan years were just a bubble, driven by thrift (savings and loans) excesses. The Clinton years were just a bubble, driven by dot-com excesses. And the most recent real estate boom and bust was just a bubble, driven by Wall Street's thieving Investment Banks.

Bubbles-R-US. It is all we have got going on.

But please do not blame Summers for the bubbles, the last two of which he played a huge role in fueling by pushing Wall Street's deregulation movement. Summers argues that it is the stagnationary version of TINA[15]: there is no alternative to

---

[15] Prime Minister Thatcher famously argued that "there is no alternative" to free market capitalism, which went by the anacronym TINA.

bubbles because the United States is caught in secular stagnation. So we have got to free Wall Street to fuel them.

Paul Krugman and many others have picked up the argument of Summers (Krugman, 2013). Here is my paraphrase of the argument (some of which relies on somewhat esoteric neoclassical economic theory so I am simplifying):

Since the days of Reagan, the "natural" rate of interest that equates saving and investment at the full employment level of output has drifted deep into negative territory. What this means is that given saving propensities, consumption demand is depressed. To fill the demand gap we need a lot of investment (or government spending or net exports—more later). But given depressed demand, firms don't really want to invest; indeed to get them to invest as much as households want to save at full employment, we would have to pay them interest on their borrowing (that is, charge negative rates on loans). As we know from Keynes, ex-post saving equals investment, but that is achieved only by having insufficient investment so that many people are unemployed. The unemployed are forced to save less than desired to maintain the equality with low investment.

If we could push the real rate well below zero (ie: firms "pay" a negative rate— equivalent to receiving interest on their borrowing) then we could push up investment, raising employment and income, and hence increase saving so that it would come to equality with investment at full employment.

While we cannot push nominal rates below zero (you can hold cash and get zero so why would you lend at a negative rate), we can raise inflation. More technically, the real interest rate is equal to the nominal rate less expected inflation. So if that Expectations Fairy could get everyone to expect 5% or 10% inflation, the real rate would be far enough below zero, and presto-change-o we'd end stagnation.

But we've got a stubborn Fairy. She won't believe the Fed when it says it is holding monetary policy pedal-to-the-metal until the Fed's Chairman gooses inflation. So the only thing the Fed can do is to cause serial asset price bubbles.

In the 1980s Washington bubbled up prices of jack-a-lope ranches in the Southwest; in the 1990s it was pet-dot-com firms that marketed kitty litter on-line; and in the 2000s it was sliced-and-diced NINJA mortgages that defaulted when the first payment came due. They all crashed spectacularly, of course.

But, you see, that's a good thing. Better to have boomed and then busted than never to have boomed at all.

Bow down to the Bubble.

Thanks, Larry Summers, for all you have done for the economy. In his bravura performance, he even managed to work in his preferences for deregulation—in spite of all the havoc he wrought: if we reregulated, he argued, Wall Street might stop producing asset bubbles, and then we would really be up the creek.

Krugman—as he is wont to do—puts all of this into his liquidity-trapped ISLM model. (See Krugman, 2011 for an exposition.) We are in a permanent liquidity trap, he claims, where normal monetary policy will not work. While fiscal policy would work, we cannot use it. (Full disclosure: Summers and Krugman would be willing to use fiscal stimulus, but that is considered by Washington to be out of bounds. Indeed, Krugman could argue that in a liquidity trap, with a horizontal LM curve, fiscal policy is super-duper effective as you would shift out the IS curve without crowding out investment since the interest rate is stuck. But we cannot go there because deficits are a no-no within the beltway.) Hence, we end up with an interest rate that is too high—even at zero, and with political barriers that prevent use of fiscal policy, so we are doomed to secular stagnation.

There is one way out, according to this line of thinking. If the Fed Chairman can send out a boatload of Fairies to convince "markets" that inflation will rise, then the Fed can control both the nominal rate and expected inflation. It can make the "real" market rate equal to the Wicksellian "real" natural rate that equates saving and investment in the Loanable Funds market. This will then encourage investment but it also encourages financial market speculation (as very low interest rates make it cheap to borrow to finance asset purchases)—which gives us the bubbles.

Better to have bubbles than permanent stagnation.

The Summers and Krugman crowd that roots for bubbles to fuel expansion chooses to ignore the most insidious aspect of Bubbleonia: it is the most successful instrument ever devised for moving income and wealth from the bottom 99% to the top 1%. And there is a nice, tight, vicious circle: by taking from those who are willing to spend and giving to those who are far too rich to spend (much of their income), you depress the "real" economy. The only way to counter that is to get the losers of income and wealth to borrow to fuel consumption. As Rick Wolff has powerfully explained, that is what we have been doing since the early 1970s—as wages of workers stagnated and they borrowed in a desperate attempt to keep up with the rising prices of an American living standard (Wolff, 2014).

Bubble-icious asset price booms not only redistribute to the top, but they also ensure that bubbles are the only way to fuel the economy precisely because all the income and wealth are at the top. Financialization of the economy synergizes these processes, adding layers of finance (i.e., debt) on all "real" economic activities. This is why most of the impact of bubbles is in the financial sphere, with relatively little impact on the "real" economy during the bubble phase. The commercial real estate bubble of the Reagan years did create some construction jobs, but the direct economy-wide impact was fairly small. The dot-com bubble had even less impact—it mostly just capitalized future profits of imaginary firms that would never generate a cent of income. The most recent bubble, housing, had a bigger impact because house-building plus furnishing new McMansions did create jobs and incomes, and rising home values generated widespread capital gains that propped up consumption.

But whatever bubbles up must crash. Commercial real estate; dot-coms; houses. Only the last one had nationwide, indeed global, disastrous impacts because not only did the prices of the newly built homes underlying the asset price bubble collapse, but this also depressed virtually all house prices everywhere in the country. And in the bubble phase, people had hocked their already owned homes to fuel consumption. In the aftermath of the bursting bubble, they lost them. When a household loses its house, it also loses its access to consumption of necessities such as automobiles and college for the kids—since the house is generally the only wealth most Americans have to offer as collateral for the loans they need to survive on stagnant wages.

Just as Clinton's dot-com bubble had boosted federal government tax revenue—which grew at a year-over-year pace above 15%, the real estate bubble also boosted growth of federal government revenue at a pace above 15% per year. In the first case, it actually generated the Clinton budget surpluses; in the second, it caused the budget deficit to decline rapidly. Accelerated growth of federal tax revenue sucked income and wealth out of the private sector. Add on top of that the Fed's rate hike of 2004 and skyrocketing energy prices, so that American consumers found their finances squeezed to the breaking point by 2007.

And so we crashed. The rich made out like bandits both on the way up, and even more so on the way down. As I predicted back in 2005, the real estate bubble and collapse would move all wealth to Bush's ownership class. (See the discussion above on the ownership society.) We should also give President Obama credit, as he oversaw what is probably the biggest transfer of wealth to the one-percenters in the ownership class that the world has ever seen.

No wonder Summers neglects to talk about the downside of the upside of bubbles.

The secular stagnationist theory promoted by Summers and Krugman is seriously deficient in identifying the cause. Again, no wonder. The Washington beltway Keynesians like Summers have played a big role because they have never mounted a defense against the antigovernment Neoliberals. Both Krugman and Summers give lip service to the need for more fiscal stimulus, but their deficit dovishness prevents them from offering a coherent argument. They see deficits as inherently bad, but sometimes you need a bit of bad to avoid something even worse.

Here is the real deal. Stagnation results when government spending grows more slowly than GDP. In other words, if government spending as a share of the economy stops rising, we are up that creek without a paddle. This is the Domar Problem, advanced by Evsey Domar in the early postwar period and updated extensively by two Portland State professors, Harold Vatter and John Walker, over their careers (Vatter and Walker, 1997). While virtually all mainstream economists believe in a long-term Say's Law (supply creates demand, so the ultimate constraint on long-term growth comes from the supply side), the real constraint on long-term growth in a developed capitalist economy is always on the demand side.[16]

I know what I am saying is heretical, even though it is fully backed by all the data. Stagnation is not due to a liquidity trap or to a negative "natural" rate of interest. It is in the nature of the productivity of capitalist investment in plant and equipment. To put it in simple terms, the problem is that investment is just too darned productive. The supply-side effect of investment (capacity creation) is much larger than the demand-side effect (the multiplier effect of higher income on consumption), and the outcome is demand-depressing excess capacity. We call that a demand gap. This is not an aberration. It is normal.

Let me draw on a paper I wrote in 2007, which was one of the last papers I wrote before the crisis hit (Wray, 2007). In this paper I focused on long-term stagnation, following the arguments of Domar and Vatter and Walker. Here is a quick summary that lays out the problem.

In the General Theory, Keynes had addressed the demand-side effects of investment: rising investment generates income that in turn induces consumption spending. In his approach, fluctuations of investment "drive" the economy. Whether the economy was operating at full capacity or with substantial excess capacity could then be attributed to the level of effective demand, itself a function of the quantity of investment. If the economy were operating below full capacity, then the solution would be to raise effective demand—either by encouraging more investment or by increasing one of the other components of demand (government spending or exports).

After WWII, "Keynesian policy" came to be identified with "fine-tuning" of effective demand, accomplished through various investment incentives (tax credits, government-financed research and development, countercyclical management of interest rates) and countercyclical fiscal policy. In practice, policy tended to favor inducements to invest over discretionary use of the federal budget—indeed, "more investment" has been the proposed solution to slow growth, high unemployment, low productivity growth, and other perceived social and economic ills for the entire postwar period.

However, Domar had already recognized the problem with such a policy bias at the very beginning of the postwar period. Not only does investment add to aggregate demand, but it also increases potential aggregate supply by adding plant and

---

[16] Note that there is nothing new in the Summers/Krugman recognition of secular stagnation; David Levy called it a "contained depression" in 1991; Wallace Peterson announced a "silent depression" in 1994; and I demonstrated in 1999 that the problem is chronically constrained demand. At a recent Levy Institute conference in Rio, Paul McCulley laid out what he called a fundamental economic principle: Microeconomics and Macroeconomics are inherently different disciplines. Macro is demand-side; micro is supply-side. For any practical time horizon, demand always drives supply. See http://archive.economonitor.com/lrwray/2013/10/14/minsky-does-rio-notes-from-a-conference/. Paul is right—the constraint is always on the demand side in modern developed capitalist economies that issue their own currency.

equipment that increase capacity. Further, note that while it takes an increase of investment to raise aggregate demand (through the multiplier), a constant level of net investment will continually increase potential aggregate supply because investment adds to capacity.[17]

The "Domar problem" results because there is no guarantee that the additional demand created by an increase of investment will absorb the additional capacity created by investment. Indeed, if net investment is constant, and if this adds to capacity at a constant rate, it is extremely unlikely that aggregate demand will grow fast enough to keep capital fully utilized. This refutes Say's Law, since the enhanced ability to supply output would not be met by sufficient demand. As such, "more investment" would not be a reliable solution to a situation in which demand were already insufficient to allow full utilization of existing capacity.

Vatter and Walker carried this a step further, showing that after WWII, the output-to-capital ratio was at least one-third higher than it had been before the war. What this means is that due to capital-saving technological innovations, it takes less fixed capital per unit of output so that the supply-side effects of investment will persistently outpace the demand-side multiplier effects (for example, as a constant level of net investment adds to capacity at a rising rate). The only way to use the extra capacity generated by net investment is to increase other types of demand. These would consist of household spending (on consumption goods, as well as residential "investment" in new houses), government spending (federal, state, and local levels), and foreign spending (net exports).

Vatter and Walker believed that growth of government spending would normally be required to absorb the capacity created by private investment. Indeed, they frequently insisted that government spending would have to grow at a pace that *exceeds* GDP growth in order to avoid stagnation. If GDP grows at 5% per year, government spending must grow at 7%, for example. That means the government sector becomes an ever-rising share of the economy.

This should not be interpreted as endorsement of Keynesian "pump-priming" to "fine-tune" the economy. Indeed, Alvin Hansen (who is name-checked by Summers, who does not fully realize the implications) had previously demonstrated that pump-priming would fail. If government increases its spending and employment in recession, raising aggregate demand and thus, economic activity, only to withdraw the stimulus when expansion gets underway, this will simply take away the jobs that had been created, restoring a situation of excess capacity.

The larger the government, the harder it becomes to cut back spending because jobs, consumption, income, and even investment all depend on the government spending. According to Vatter and Walker, in a well-run fiscal system, government spending will rise rapidly when investment is rising (to absorb the created capacity),

---

[17] More technically, it is only net investment that adds to productive capacity. If a firm is only replacing worn-out equipment, this will not increase capacity (unless the new capital is more productive than the old capital it is replacing).

and then will still rise rapidly when investment falls (to prevent effective demand from collapsing). They call this a "ratchet"—rather than countercyclical swings of government spending, government as a share of the economy should rise indefinitely. Hence, government should grow faster than the economy. If it does not, not only will this leave society with fewer publicly provided services than desired, but it will also generate stagnation through the Domar problem.

Compare this explanation of the chronic stagnation with the Summers/Krugman argument that it is all due to an unobservable "natural" real interest rate that has fallen below zero, and with their argument that to counter the stagnation we need more bubbles.

In my paper I extended the Domar Problem analysis to take account of the headwinds facing the economy of the 2000s: (a) growth of consumption—financed by borrowing—played a surprisingly large role in fueling growth over the past decade; (b) a chronic, and growing, trade deficit worsened the dynamics of growth by creating a large leakage of income that in turn worsens the excess capacity problem in the United States; and (c) there have been fairly substantial changes to tax policy that funnelled tax breaks to the rich—who mostly save rather than consume. Note that all of these problems remain.

I concluded the paper with warnings about the dangers facing the economy. Federal government purchases have not been growing on trend above the rate of GDP growth since the Kennedy years. In the 1960s this was somewhat offset—first by federal transfers to state and local government and later by growth of transfers to households in the form of "welfare" and old-age pensions. However, welfare spending essentially stagnated after the early 1970s (relative to GDP), and President Clinton ended "welfare as we know it" by pushing tight constraints on individuals and on states until that stopped growth of social transfers.

Further, the supposed "unfunded liabilities" of Social Security and Medicare are used by generational warriors in their attempt to dismantle the safety net for seniors—which poses dangers for long-run aggregate demand. While successes of the "deficit warriors" have so far been limited (to payroll tax hikes under President Reagan, and phased increases to the normal retirement age), they might be more successful in the future. Finally, the federal government has been less supportive of state and local government spending since the mid 1970s. Ironically, this has occurred even as responsibilities have "devolved" to the states—leading to a recurring "fiscal crisis" at the state and local government level.

On the other side of fiscal policy, taxes are overly restrictive on all but the rich. State and local taxes are, on the whole, regressive—actually taking a higher percent of income away as we move down the income scale. Given a presumed inverse relation between the propensity to consume and the level of income, regressive taxes reduce aggregate demand. At the federal level, payroll taxes are regressive, but worse, they penalize employment by taxing both wage earners and wage payers. This raises the cost of domestic employment, favoring employment in nations that do not tax payrolls—which encourages imports into the United States.

Another area of concern I raised back in 2007 was the trend rate of growth of private sector debt. To be sure, debt has been growing persistently since 1960; however, private sector deficits during the Clinton years had accelerated the rate of growth of debt relative to income—which rose rapidly as a share of GDP after 1999. I warned that the debt ratio was already too high, especially since real wages had been essentially stagnant since the early 1970s and the wage share (wages as a percent of national income) had reached the lowest share of national income since data began to be collected in 1947—just 45% of GDP in the first quarter of 2006, compared with 53.6% in 1970 or 50% as recently as 2001. So, to some extent, growth of debt is necessary to maintain rising—or even constant—living standards in an environment of stagnant or falling real income, except at the very top of the income distribution.

That explains some of the "push" into debt, while the real estate and commodity price bubbles provided the "pull." After the stock market crash (of the early 2000s), investors looked for alternative earning assets, and found them in commodities and real estate. As discussed earlier in this book, pension funds played an important role in fueling the commodities bubble. And the real estate bubble—which was boosted by fraud throughout the mortgage industry—added a significant boost to aggregate demand and generated 30% of employment growth during the recovery. However, by 2007 that bubble had already burst, with home prices falling after 2006.

Still another area of concern I raised is globalization and external pressure on wages and prices. While many analysts emphasize the effects of increased openness on the US trade balance, that is not really the issue at hand. As elementary economics teaches, imports are a benefit and exports are a cost, so net imports represent net benefits. The problem is that elementary analysis presumes full employment. The United States can reap the net benefits of its trade deficit only if it operates at full capacity. Unfortunately, the instinctual response to trade deficits is to reduce domestic demand by imposing fiscal and monetary policy austerity—which only compounds the problems generated by the leakage of demand to imports. This ensures that the potential benefits of a trade deficit will not be enjoyed.

The correct response is to find employment for those displaced by a trade deficit, and to ramp up domestic demand to cover the trade deficit leakage. That, however, is extremely difficult in a politico-economic environment, in which the trade deficit is attributed to American consumers "living beyond their means," by relying on "foreign savings." In truth, as discussed in the previous section, the US current account deficit is the source of the dollar assets accumulated by foreigners. While it may be true that American consumers are overindebted, their debt is in dollars and it makes little difference whether that is owed to domestic wealth holders or to foreigners. What does matter is that foreign competition has been reducing US wages and salaries, and, perhaps, causing American job loss. This drags down US growth because US policy refuses to respond with job creation, as well as protection for decent living standards.

The final longer-term problem I raised has been the growth of "neoconserva-tive" (also called neoliberal) ideology. While this may not be easy to define in pre-cise terms, it represents a turn against the "mixed economy" in which "Big Government" has a positive role to play. Essentially, it is a return to Herbert Hoover—era *laissez faire* in which the ideal is a small government, and in which private initiative is supposed to fuel economic growth. That may have been fine in the 19th century, when the economy was relatively undeveloped and productive capacity was limited. In that era, high private investment added to demand and to supply to an approximately equal degree. However, technological advance and innovation increased the capacity effects of investment to the extent that they easily outstrip demand-side effects.

Hence, while the neoconservative ideology might be appropriate to some stage of the development of capitalism, it is clearly out of place in the modern economy, where the capacity effects of investment are huge. Further, the proponents of small government ignore the social desire and need for increased provision of social ser-vices as the economy grows. The argument that J.K. Galbraith made in 1958 con-cerning the relative dearth of public services is only very much stronger today—with unmet needs for universal healthcare, for universal access to higher ed-ucation to prepare youth for the "knowledge" economy, and for greater public involvement in finally eliminating the remaining inequalities that result from intran-sigent racism, sexism, and cultural biases. Perhaps even more urgent is the need to tackle climate change (see below).

All of these are difficult issues and there is no plausible argument or evidence that they can be resolved through "private initiative." In fact, the neocon ideology has played an important role in reversing progress made since WWII on these and other fronts. Neocon policies reward the privileged and punish the have-nots. The rich get vouchers for well-funded private schools; the poor see funding of their pub-lic schools reduced. The rich get tax relief on capital gains and inheritances; the poor get higher local sales taxes and federal payroll taxes. The Katrina Hurricane victims are evicted from FEMAville trailers while the Halliburtons got no-bid contracts to rebuild New Orleans as a playland for well-heeled business conventioneers. Obvi-ously, this reduction of the role played by government moves the US economy in the wrong direction.

As Hyman Minsky used to argue, capitalism was a failed system in 1930. The growth of "Big Government" was singled out by Minsky and by Vatter and Walker as the necessary medicine to build a viable and robust version of capitalism. Minsky always insisted that there are "57 varieties" of capitalism, with different systems appropriate to different historical epochs. Unfortunately, the modern Hooverites are attempting to return to 1929, that is, to a system that was not even appropriate to the prewar period—and that crashed in the 1930s. The approach taken by Domar, Galbraith, Minsky, and Vatter and Walker, which recognizes the necessity of the "mixed economy," is the alternative that will help us to formulate policy appropriate to today's problems.

Bubblemania is not the answer.

V. Financing the progressive agenda

In this final section, we will return to our discussion of "government's money" to address the issue of "paying for" the progressive agenda discussed throughout this book. Can government really afford to provide Americans with universal access to healthcare, to higher education, to jobs, and to decent retirement while also doing what it takes to save the planet? The broadly defined GND would be a very good start as it addresses many of these issues while also tackling the problem of excess inequality. Some (wild) estimates have put the cost of the GND at what some might call a "staggering" sum of $93 trillion! How can Uncle Sam pay for that?

In the first part of this section we will argue that for a government that issues its own currency, affordability is never the question: anything technically possible is affordable. We will then turn more directly to "financing" the GND.

a. What is technically possible is affordable

As we have discussed, most economists identify *money* as something we use in exchange. Well, if money is a thing, surely we might run out of it? However, as MMT insists, money is not, and has never been, a thing. Money begins as a unit of account in which we denominate debts and credits and—as Keynes said—for the past 4000 years the money of account has been chosen by the state authorities. Our money of account is a state money of account. All those *things* economists declare to be *money* are denominated in the money of account. What we have, then, is a socially created and generally accepted money of account, and debts that are denominated in that money of account. Within a modern nation, most socially sanctioned money-denominated debts are written in the nation's money of account.

The state issues a currency denominated in the same unit of account that will be accepted if there is an enforceable obligation to make payments to its issuer in that same currency. Hence, "taxes drive money" in the sense that the state can impose tax liabilities and issue the means of paying those liabilities in the form of its own liabilities. As we have discussed, the sovereign currency issuer cannot run out of its own currency. The modern central bank cannot run out of its liabilities—called reserves. And the modern bank cannot run out of its own liabilities—deposits. In short, money is not a scarce resource—it is created by those institutions that issue liabilities that are in demand.

The great institutionalist economist J. Fagg Foster put it this way: "*Whatever is technically feasible is financially possible*". To the perpetual question 'Where is the money coming from?' the answer is now clear. It comes from the only two institutions we permit to create money funds: the treasury of the sovereign government and commercial banks. And the rate at which we permit either to create funds is pretty much a matter of public policy". He argues that as there is no limit to the ability to create funding, "the only question is should they be made available." Finance is not a scarce resource—the only questions are: how much do we want? and where should it be directed?

The real issues concern technical know-how and resource availability. If we know how to do something, and if we have the resources available to do it, then we can financially afford it. It is important to recognize that the major developed countries have already developed the procedures required to allow them to spend up to budgeted amounts. We do not need to make any changes to the way government spends in order to allow it to spend more.

So as we tackle the Green New Deal (GND), we need to assess our technological capabilities to see if they are up to snuff. And then we have to identify the resources as well as the capabilities we will need to implement the various programs. We do not need to worry about "paying for" it.

Of course we face political constraints. We face organized resistance by those who think they will lose—Wall Street opposes universal healthcare provided by a single payer system because the private health insurance system will be eliminated; big coal opposes the move to green energy; low-wage employers fear that a universal Job Guarantee at a living wage will put them out of business as their workers flee poverty-level wages and inhumane working conditions.

So I am not claiming that simply having the finance, the know-how, and the resources makes it easy to implement the GND. Getting the GND is going to be difficult. It is the biggest challenge humans have ever faced. But "financial affordability" is not the barrier.

b. Paying for the Green New Deal

Advocates of the GND strive to change the way that we approach a variety of problems facing society: climate change and destruction of our natural environment, rising inequality, and an economy that leaves too many with inadequate access to food, shelter, healthcare, and affordable education. They see these problems as linked, and so insist on tackling them with an array of programs that have hitherto been seen as disconnected: a carbon-neutral energy policy and reversing climate change; universal single-payer healthcare; student debt relief and free public college; prison reform; ending "forever wars"; increasing care for the young, sick, and old; reducing poverty and inequality; and the job guarantee.

The advocates of MMT have similarly sought to change the way that public finance is viewed: the sovereign government's finances are not like the budgeting by households and firms. Viewed from the MMT perspective, the government uses the monetary system to mobilize real resources and to move some of them to pursuit of the public purpose. Affordability is never an important question for a sovereign government—the relevant question concerns resource availability and suitability. There is thus a natural alliance between MMT and the GND. If we can identify technologically feasible projects that would achieve the GND's goals, and if we can identify the resources to devote to these projects, then we can arrange for the financing of the programs.

Whatever the financial costs, we already have a financial system that can handle them. What is less certain is that we can mobilize the resources that will be required.

This will require a combination of putting excess capacity to work and shifting already employed resources away from existing production to GND projects.

We must approach the GND as what President Carter called the Moral Equivalent of War. He used that term in his fight to reduce inflation; in retrospect, it was a bunch of hyperbole—the inflation of the late 1970s was caused by a spike of oil prices in conjunction with rising food and shelter costs. Inflation was destined to disappear as a real challenge within just a few years. On the other hand, climate change really does threaten the planet. The other challenges we now face threaten the continued existence of civil society. The challenge this time really amount to an existential threat to the very existence of human life on earth.

To be sure, some naysayers reject science; others claim we just cannot afford to mount the effort required to reverse humanity's steady march to oblivion. We will just have to settle for small, incremental change and hope for luck or divine intervention to supplement our meager efforts. Or look to colonization—of Mars?—as a way to preserve a select few representatives of the civilization of homo sapiens in a human zoo waiting for discovery by more advanced life forms that managed to avoid self-annihilation.

Some project the cost at $93 trillion and say it is just too expensive. That is just plain stupid. How can we possibly weigh the costs of failure against the financial costs of the greatest effort we could mount to give us some chance of survival?

If we think about America's biggest challenge over the past century, it is reasonable to point to the combination of the Great Depression and the rise of global fascism in the 1930s. To counter those, we created the New Deal and ramped up military strength. The economic cost of lost employment and output during the 1930s was huge—GDP fell by 50% and official unemployment reached 25%. The benefits of New Deal programs that helped to get the economy back on track almost certainly exceeded the spending on those programs—but we have to admit that we cannot accurately tally up the net benefits gained because we cannot know how the economy would have recovered in the New Deal's absence. In any event, most would agree that it was prudent to tackle the crisis rather than wait any longer—even if we cannot be sure of the net ex-post benefits of action over inaction.

What about WWII? During the war, we moved 50% of the nation's output to government control—largely put to use in the military. The federal deficit grew to 25% of the economy. Government debt grew to 100% of GDP by the end of the war. We proved that government could find the finance. In spite of claims that deficits push up interest rates, the government kept them extremely low throughout the war. In spite of claims that big deficits inevitably cause inflation if not hyperinflation, WWII was the first major US war in which inflation remained relatively low. And remember, the government commanded half of output, and millions of US workers were transferred into uniform so that the economy operated far beyond its normal full employment rate.

Was it worth it? You will not find many who would try to make the argument that the financial expenses incurred were just too much—too much to save democracy and the kinds of freedoms that Americans cherish. What about a crushing debt burden after the war—did the government not have to pay back all that debt? Of course not. The debt was never paid back. Instead, it was held in private portfolios as a very safe asset that helped confidence return. Many had feared that as the war spending wound down we would go right back into a depression. Instead, the United States (and the world taken as a whole) enjoyed an unprecedented "golden age" of capitalism—with the highest sustained average growth rates ever achieved in both the United States and around the world. The plant and equipment created during the war was converted to civilian use (well, not all of it, as the Cold War maintained demand for military use).

Half measures will not do this time, either. It might take all our available resources—and then some—to win this battle. The experts say we have most of the technology we need. We have unused resources to put to use. We can shift others from destructive uses to be engaged in constructive endeavors. We can mobilize the population for greater effort with the promise of greater equality and a shared and sustainable prosperity. We can make a good effort. We might win.

In research with Yeva Nersisyan for the Levy Economics Institute we laid out a fairly comprehensive GND and tallied up the net resource demands (Nersisyan and Wray, 2019). For those who want the details, please go to our working paper as I will only provide a quick summary of the proposal and as well of our projection of resource needs. Our GND would include "greening" projects to eliminate all fossil fuel use, provide single-payer Medicare-for-all healthcare for all Americans, create a universal Job Guarantee program, and impose new taxes on the rich to reduce inequality (not to "pay for" the GND!). In addition we proposed to end the "forever wars" and added some other miscellaneous GND projects such as free universal childcare. We proposed to phase in the program over a period of 10 years.

Some of the JG workers would be employed in GND projects. Some workers would be shifted out of destructive use (coal mining and fracking) into constructive use (solar panels and insulation). There would be large resource savings by phasing out for-profit private health insurance and forever wars. Still, we projected a total net increase of demand on the nation's resources equal to about 1.3% of GDP. We believe this is fully within current capacity—ramping up GDP by 1.3% of GDP should not generate inflation.

As we phase in the various components of the GND we will need resources—labor, capital, natural resources. Some of them are currently unemployed or idle—putting those to use is essentially a free lunch. Employing unemployed resources also does not raise much danger of inflation. However, we will almost certainly need to shift some resources out of current use. In some cases that will help us to achieve our goals: shifting labor out of earth-destroying coal mining is of course desired in its own right. Those resources freed up as we eliminate fossil fuels, as we shut down private health insurance, and as we end the forever wars will be available for use in GND efforts. Since we are substituting one use for another, this also should not be inflationary. However, in many cases those resources we are trying to shift may not have the requisite skills, training, education, and experience. We will have to devote more resources to adequately prepare them for alternative work. That could place additional pressures on resource use (say, resources used in job training).

And, finally, we may need to cut back on some resource uses that are not necessarily uses we wish to eliminate. In other words, there may be some competition between current productive use of resources and new production for the GND. This is where it might be necessary to take special measures to prevent inflation.

In other words, resource pressures could arise that would necessitate some inflation-fighting measures. For reasons discussed below, we thought that the best way to fight inflation should it arise is through postponed consumption. We would ask workers and others to take a small cut in take-home pay now with the promise of more income later. This could be provided by boosting Social Security payments above current law—to provide more retirement income and also to increase income of survivors (paid to spouses and children if a covered worker dies before retirement). So, we would consume a bit less during the phase-in of the GND because of a surcharge on payroll taxes, but would receive better Social Security benefits later.

The following table shows our calculation of net resource demands.

Summary of net GND resource costs (percent of GDP)	
• Greening Projects	5%
• Medicare for All	−3.7%
• Job Guarantee	1%
• Tax the Rich	0%
• End Forever Wars	−1%
• Payroll Tax Surcharge	−2%
• Miscellaneous GND Projects[a]	0%
Net Increase Resource Costs (with payroll tax surcharge)	**−0.7%**
Net Increase Resource Costs (without payroll tax surcharge)	**1.3%**

Notes: *Source of resources is negative; use of resources is positive.*
[a] *Includes student debt relief and free college, public infrastructure, and universal childcare (some of which is included in the JG resource requirement).*

What is interesting is that in terms of resource use, the GND is quite small potatoes compared to the demands placed on the economy during WWII. And, as discussed above, we managed the war without much inflation. How did we do that? We can look back to our WWII experience to see what kinds of measures work.

For inspiration, we can also look to Keynes's 1940 book—*How To Pay for the War*—written to provide advice to the British government as it entered the war. Keynes rightly believed that war planning is not a financial challenge, but a real resource problem. The issue was not how the British would pay for the war, but rather whether the country could produce enough output for the war effort while leaving enough production to satisfy civilian consumption. To estimate the amount left for consumption we need to determine the maximum current output we can produce domestically, how much we can net import, and how much we need for the "war".

My argument is that this is precisely how we prepare for the GND. "Paying for" the GND is not a problem—the only question is: do we have the resources and technological know-how to rise to the challenge? While in normal times we operate with significant underutilization of capacity, during war, Keynes argued, we move from the "age of plenty" to the "age of scarcity" since what is available for consumption is relatively fixed (Keynes, 1940). At the same time, more output produced for military use means more income, which, if spent on consumption, would push up prices. Hence, some of the purchasing power must be withdrawn to prevent inflation. Thus, Keynes rightly viewed taxes as a tool for withdrawing demand, not paying for government spending.

He thought taxes could be used to withdraw half of the added demand. The other half would have to come through savings, voluntary or "forced". Voluntary savings (for example, purchasing War Bonds) would only work if everyone saved enough, which cannot be guaranteed. If households do not save enough, they bid up prices while consuming the same amount of resources, but paying more. The business "profiteers" would get a windfall income, some saved and the rest taxed away (so businesses would effectively act as tax collectors for the Treasury—the extra consumer demand facing a relatively fixed supply of consumption goods would generate extra tax revenues on profits).

Thus voluntary saving plus taxes would still withdraw demand, but on the backs of workers and to the benefit of profiteers. If workers demanded and got higher wages, the process would simply repeat itself with wages constantly playing catch-up to price increases as workers consumed the same amount of real resources. In other words, we would get caught in a vicious inflation cycle.

Keynes's preferred solution was deferred consumption. Instead of taxing away workers' income, which would prevent them from enjoying the fruits of their labor forever (and possibly reduce support for the war effort), he proposed to defer their consumption by depositing a portion of their wages in "blocked" interest-earning deposits. This solution would avoid inflation, while at the same time more evenly distribute financial wealth toward workers. Furthermore, this would solve the problem of the slump that would likely follow the war, as workers could increase consumption after the war at a measured pace, spending out of their deferred income.

Keynes recognized that it is not easy for a "free community" to organize for war. It would be necessary to adapt the distributive system of a free community to the limitations of war, when the size of the "cake" would be fixed. You can think of this problem as the opposite to the secular stagnation problem. Keynes argued one could neither expect the rich to make all of the necessary sacrifice nor put too much of the burden on those of low means. Simply taking income away from the rich would not free up a sufficient quantity of resources to move toward the war effort—their propensity to consume is relatively low and they have the ways and means to avoid or evade taxes. But taking too much income away from those with too little would cause excessive suffering—especially in light of the possibility they would face rising prices on necessities.

To avoid a wage-price spiral, labor would have to agree to moderate wage demands. This would be easier to obtain if a promise were made that workers would not be permanently deprived of the benefits of working harder now. In other words, the choice facing workers is to forego increased consumption altogether, or to defer it. In return for working more now, they would be paid more later—accumulating financial wealth in the meantime.

He recommended three principles to guide war planning:

1. use deferred compensation to reward workers;
2. tax higher incomes while exempting the poor; and
3. maintain adequate minimum standards for those with lower incomes such that they would be better off, not worse off, even during the war.

The deferred compensation would be released in installments, timed with the slump that he expected would follow the war. The system would be "self-liquidating both in terms of real resources and of finance", he said—as resources were withdrawn from the military they could turn to civilian production, with the deferred compensation providing the income needed to buy that output.

While Keynes argued that "some measure of rationing and price control should play a part", he argued that these should be secondary to taxes and deferred compensation. Rationing impinges on consumer choice and inevitably has differential impacts across individuals. Price controls can create shortages. In any case, he argued that an effective program of deferred income will make rationing and price controls easier to implement.

What Keynes wanted to avoid was the UK experience of WWI when the cost of living rose an average of 20%—25% annually over the course of the war, and wage hikes tended to match price hikes, but with about a 1 year lag. This allowed sufficient but permanent loss of consumption by workers to shift resources to the war. By contrast, both the United States and the United Kingdom managed to contain inflation pressures much more successfully in WWII—the United Kingdom hit double digit inflation only in 1940 and 1941, and had remarkably low inflation during the remainder of the war; the United States barely reached above 10% only in 1942 and in other years inflation ranged from 1.7% to 8%.

Both of them adopted a variety of anti-inflation policies that approximated Keynes's policy. Given the circumstances, the policies were remarkably effective. As mentioned above in the United States, government spending rose to nearly half of GDP—with the budget deficit rising to 25% of GDP and the national debt climbing to 100% of GDP. In light of that massive mobilization, it is amazing how low inflation was.

As the GND is phased in, the growth rate of the economy will accelerate and the government's share of GDP will grow from the current 25% or so toward perhaps 35% of GDP. At the same time, there will be reduction of private spending on healthcare so we end up with maybe an overall boost of GDP of less than 2%.

If desired, we can reduce the stimulus through deferred consumption—perhaps through a surcharge on payrolls that will be returned through more generous worker benefits after the GND "war" cools down—as we proposed in our report. I am an optimist. I believe the GND boost will put us on a sustained higher growth path, without inflation, that will generate the additional resources required. The GND will end the secular stagnation Larry Summers worries about and will create a new Golden Age of US capitalism—one that is more inclusive and without the environmental destruction caused in the first Golden Age.

If we compare the GND to the WWII buildup, all of this seems quite manageable. And the inflation effect will be much lower—in part because we are not producing stuff to blow things up and in part because we face strong deflationary pressures from the east—a couple of billion workers in China, India, and some other developing nations have joined the global production force to keep inflation down.

Some of this shift of resources toward the GND will be reversed quickly once the new infrastructure is in place and we have greened our economy. We will then release the deferred compensation and we might end up with a government that is permanently bigger but not by that much—say a third of the economy instead of a quarter. Again, that is no big deal. The first New Deal and WWII grew the federal government from 3% of the economy to 50% of the economy, and finally came to rest at about a quarter of the economy in the postwar period. The prospect of a government at 33% of the economy should not be scary.

We long ago became a postagricultural society. Since WWII we have transitioned to a postindustrial society. It makes sense that we are going to have a bigger government since most provisioning already is, and will increasingly be, coming from the service sector—an area where public service often *Trumps* private service—in education, care services—aged and young, healthcare, the arts, and many forms of environmentally friendly recreation. More parks, less shopping. More walkable cities and less automobile traffic.

In another important contribution—*Economic Possibilities for our Grandchildren*—written in 1930, Keynes speculated about our future—a time when "for the first time since his creation man will be faced with his real, his permanent problem—how to use his freedom from pressing economic cares, how to occupy the leisure, which science and compound interest will have won for him, to live wisely and agreeably and well."

By Keynes's timeline, this should have been reached by 2030. Many proponents have timed our GND to be completely phased in by 2030. We have 10 years to make Keynes's vision become reality. The alternative is annihilation.

Some (both heterodox and orthodox alike) argue we just cannot "afford" survival. It is cheaper to just keep doing what we have been doing and hope for a different result. That is not only the definition of insanity attributed to Einstein, but it is—as Keynes would say—unnecessarily defeatist.

As Winston Churchill said, "You can always count on the Americans to do the right thing after they have tried everything else."

The challenge is big; the alternative is unacceptable. And we do not have time to try everything else. Let us do it right this time.

References

American Society of Civil Engineers, 2016. Infrastructure Report Card. https://www.infrastructurereportcard.org/wp-content/uploads/2016/10/ASCE-Failure-to-Act-2016-FINAL.pdf and Investment Report Card 2017. https://www.infrastructurereportcard.org/solutions/investment/.

Atwood, M., 2008. Payback: Debt and the Shadow Side of Wealth. House of Anansi Press.

Bell, S., Wray, L.R., 2004. The "War on Poverty" After 40 Years: A Minskyan Assessment. Economics Working Paper Archive wp_404. Levy Economics Institute.

Economic Report of the President, 2012. https://www.govinfo.gov/app/details/ERP-2012/summary.

Focus Economics, 2019. Japan Economic Outlook. https://www.focus-economics.com/countries/japan.

Forbes, K., 2015. Much Ado About Something Important: How Do Exchange Rate Movements Affect Inflation. Bank of England, speech. https://www.bankofengland.co.uk/speech/2015/much-ado-about-something-important-how-do-exchange-rate-movements-affect-inflation.

Friedman, M., 1991. Say 'no' to intolerance. Liberty Magazine 4 (6), 17–20.

Galbraith, J.K., 1958. The Affluent Society. Houghton Mifflin Harcourt.

Keynes, J.M., 1930. A Treatise on Money. Macmillan Publishers.

Keynes, J.M., 1940. How to Pay for the War: A Radical Plan for the Chancellor of the Exchequer. Macmillan and Co., Ltd.

Krugman, P., 2011. https://krugman.blogs.nytimes.com/2011/10/09/is-lmentary/?_r=0.

Krugman, P., 2013. https://krugman.blogs.nytimes.com/2013/11/16/secular-stagnation-coalmines-bubbles-and-larry-summers/?_r=0.

Nersisyan, Y., Wray, L.R., 2019. How to Pay for the Green New Deal. WP 931. The Levy Economics Institute.

Nikkei Asian Review, 2019. Growing Modern Monetary Theory Debate Rattles Japan Officials. https://asia.nikkei.com/Economy/Growing-Modern-Monetary-Theory-debate-rattles-Japan-officials.

Reuters, 2019. Japan Policymakers Shun 'Modern Monetary Theory' as Dangerous. https://www.reuters.com/article/japan-economy-fiscal/japan-policymakers-shun-modern-monetary-theory-as-dangerous-idINKCN1RG03L.

Summers, L., 2013. https://equitablegrowth.org/this-mornings-must-watch-larry-summers-on-the-danger-of-a-japan-like-generation-of-secular-stagnation-here-in-the-north-atlantic/. Here is his speech: https://www.youtube.com/watch?v=KYpVzBbQIX0.

Taibbi, M., 2010. https://www.rollingstone.com/politics/politics-news/the-great-american-bubble-machine-195229/.

Vatter, H., Walker, J.F., 1997. The Rise of Big Government in the United States. M.E. Sharpe, Armonk, NY.

Wolff, R.D., 2014. https://truthout.org/articles/the-wages-of-global-capitalism/.

Wray, L.R., 1998. Understanding Modern Money: The Key to Full Employment and Price Stability. Edward Elgar, Northampton, MA.

Wray, L.R., 2007. Demand Constraints and Big Government. WP 448. Levy Economics Institute.

Further reading

Kaboub, F., 2018. https://urpe.wordpress.com/2018/07/09/the-new-postcolonial-economics-with-fadhel-kaboub/.

Kaboub, F., 2019. https://www.bloomberg.com/news/audio/2019-04-05/this-is-how-mmt-applies-to-emerging-markets-podcast.

Keynes, J.M., 1930. Economic Possibilities for Our Grandchildren. Essays in Persuasion. Harcourt Brace, 1932, New York, pp. 358—373.

Index

Printed in the United States
By Bookmasters